Nov. 10, 2002
Banning, Ca.

To; Jim -
    A great marine. Thank you
for your interest in "Dar's Story"
I hope that you enjoy it —

DAR'S STORY
Memoirs of a Secret Service Agent

Darwin D. Horn
USSS

DARWIN HORN

Cover photo: Ike in Des Moines, Iowa, 1956
Arvid Dahlquist, front left, Darwin Horn, front right, Floyd Boring, rear left, Stu Stout, rear right

Editorial services by Carin Chapin, Oak Park, California

Cover and book design by Heidi Lundgren, Westlake Village, California

Published in the United States of America by Darwin Horn

Printed by Haagen Printing, Santa Barbara, California, U.S.A.

First Printing January 2002

Dedication

This book should be dedicated

to the many Secret Service agents

who have been a part of the

135-year history of the Secret Service.

It has been a privilege to be

a small part of the history

of one of the world's

great law enforcement agencies,

as well as the premier agency of the world,

in the field of protection.

Foreword

What a privilege it has been to be the daughter and son of a great man! We've always felt so proud of our father as he went about the work of protecting and assisting world leaders and their families. Everyday we were aware of my fathers' commitment to give his life for any one of them. It often seemed ironic to us that a great man of integrity was willing to die for ones of lesser stature.

Being the child of a Secret Service Agent brings unique challenges. Whenever the question came up, "What does your father do?" In my youth, I was unable to tell people the true answer. I always had to get around answering this question directly, with "he's a screen door salesman." With an insipid answer like this, very few people probed for more information and I was off of the hook!

Neighbors were always baffled because he would drive home in a different car nearly every night. New friends would be astonished when they visited our home and saw us burn twenty-dollar bills in our fireplace. I knew that our lifestyle didn't always add up with the screen door salesman story.

It was always so exciting to watch the evening news and see my father on the job. For thirty years he was present at many historical moments, quietly and powerfully witnessing interactions between world leaders. There he was with the President, the King, the Secretary of State, the presidential candidate, or the spouse and children of any one of them.

For many holidays he was far away with dignitary families. He always gave my mother credit for his success in his work saying, "the secret to being a successful agent is to marry the right woman," and that he did! My mother was able to keep our lives orderly, happy and free from anxiety.

I remember one late night in early June. The phone rang–not something unusual in our home, and I listened as my father quietly answered it. A few muffled instructions were given. Something horrible had just happened. Bobby Kennedy had just been assassinated and my dad was to be on the road for most of that next year.

Though certainly not typical, this year was representative of the life he led. What struck us both was his ability to effectively balance his professional and family responsibilities. True, he was out taking care of other people and their families but we never felt shortchanged.

Growing up as the children of Darwin and Shirley Ann Horn was truly a privilege. They embodied and taught us great lessons of:

* ★ Duty
* ★ Contribution to Society
* ★ Integrity
* ★ Respect for all people (counterfeiters to kings)
* ★ Gratitude (there were always expressions of gratitude from him to us)
* ★ Goodness
* ★ Loyalty
* ★ Teamwork
* ★ Punctuality

We feel grateful that our father has taken these memories and written them down for us, our children and for all the children that will be!

Diane (Horn) Gilman,
Darwin Horn, Jr.

DAR'S STORY
Memoirs of a Secret Service Agent

DARWIN HORN

Introduction

The writing of this book has been a most enjoyable experience. After many years of denying that I would ever write one, I finally tried. Too bad that I didn't start earlier. One of the reasons why I thought that I would never write a book was that there were so many Secret Service agents who had done much more than I had as an agent. I waited for many years for some of them to put their careers in book form as I have done. Several of them have tried, but I don't think that any of them have done what I have done, which is to take my daily reports from the Secret Service and turn them into a diary of sorts. For the thirty years that I was an agent, I had to make out a daily report showing what I had done the previous workday. When I got the inclination to start writing, I retrieved all of those daily reports, put them in order and read each one as I went along writing. When I would get to what I thought was an interesting experience, I stopped reading and started writing. I have endeavored to keep it as simple and as close to the truth as possible.

The first part of the book represents my life prior to entering the Secret Service. The second part of the book represents the thirty years in which I was in the Secret Service. The last part of the book represents the nineteen years that I have spent after my retirement date.

Most certainly my very good friend, Dan Bowling, is owed a debt of gratitude, for without him, this book would not have been. After several years of him suggesting the idea, finally one day he brought a package of spiral notebooks to one of our lunches. He tossed them on the table and demanded that I fill them up. Thanks Dan, you get the first book printed! My thanks also go to my daughter, Diane, and her husband, Barry Gilman, for introducing me to the great world of computers. Without that assistance, I would still be typing.

Time has a way of causing memory to fluctuate—I can vouch for that occurring! I know that some of the incidents portrayed here will not be remembered by others as having occurred in the manner in which I depict. I can only say that if there are errors, they are my responsibility.

In the writing of this book, there have been a number of factors that have become evident—the massive amounts of overtime worked, much of it non-compensatory; the many weekends or partial weekends worked; the many times of working past midnight and then reporting for work at

1

the normal time in the morning; the many protective assignments in which all agents were involved, not only in the United States, but throughout the world; the many arrests made not only in the counterfeiting field, but for criminals who had become involved in the forging of government checks and bonds.

I would be remiss if I didn't mention the great part that wives play in the life of the agents. They are the ones who keep the family going and on an even keel. One axiom in the Secret Service is that you have to marry the right person. If you do not, your life, and hers, will be very difficult.

So here it is, a book that was almost never written. It's about the life of one lucky person. I hope that you enjoy it.

Table of Contents

1925-1936

CHAPTER 1

St. Louis, Missouri
August 1925 - November 1936

I was born August 20, 1925, in St. Louis, Missouri. My parents were Ernest Edward Horn and Myrtle Theresa Wright Horn. My dad was born in St. Louis on December 29, 1897, and my mother was born on a riverboat in the town of San Soo, Arkansas, on May 28, 1902. San Soo no longer exists and it is not known how large a community it was or when it ceased to exist. There is some thought that San Soo could have become the community of Susanville, which is also non-existent at this time.

I was the third child born following Ernest "Ernie" Edward Horn Jr, and Arline Agnes. Later, on August 26, 1937, we were joined by a sister, Nancy Ann, who was born in Los Angeles, California. Ernest was born December 15, 1921, in St. Louis, and Arline was born on February 1, 1924, also in St. Louis. The first years of my life were spent in St. Louis. The first memory that I have was that we lived at 6900 Virginia Avenue, across the street from Blow School, where Ernest and Arline attended kindergarten. That would have been 1926 and 1929 respectively.

In 1930, Dad terminated his employment with the city of St. Louis as a streetcar troubleshooter and opened a tire and battery shop at 7901 Vermont Avenue. With that change, we also moved to a home at 7823 Virginia Avenue, a short distance from my dad's shop and directly behind Uncle Fred's (Krauss) house and business located at 7824 Ivory Avenue.

Ernest and Arline transferred to Lyon School, which was located at Vermont and Koeln avenues, about five blocks from our home. In September 1930, I joined them at Lyon School, attending the afternoon kindergarten session in Miss Le Gay's room. What a sorry experience that was! I cried for the first two weeks and was probably the shyest student they had ever seen. I recall that I never did get the chance to go up to the sand box to participate in group-play. Not that I couldn't have—it's just that I was too afraid.

Some of my earliest classmates were Armand Spielman, Theresa Lady, Billy Lewis, Oliver Guion, John Thompson, Irene Huett, Jean Born, and Melvin Kretchman.

Arline must have been in the first or second grade at that time, and I recall my best friend, Earl Becher, was in her room. Earl lived across the street from my dad's shop and his father had a bar in the front of his residence. During the summer, Red Becher, Earl's dad, had an open pit barbecue stand adjacent to their home. During the hot summer night, the fragrance of the barbecue permeated the entire neighborhood. Suffice to say that we couldn't afford to buy any of Red Becher's barbecue, but on several occasions, Earl invited Ernie and me to finish up some of the pork ribs his dad didn't sell the previous night. Hot or cold, those were the best ribs I have ever eaten. It had to be the homemade sauce that Red made. In later years, Earl confided that he and his sister Ruth never bothered to copy down Red's recipe and they were extremely sorry that they didn't.

Ernie, Earl and I were inseparable. During the summer, our ball games began right after breakfast, and we'd only take a short break for lunch and then continue on right up until dinnertime. The Bellefontine Street car went right past our house, made a quick left turn at the corner and then stopped for about fifteen minutes, as it was the end of the line. Needless to say, we had to stop our ball games frequently to let the streetcars pass.

Summers were magnificent times there. Even though the Great Depression was upon us, we didn't really know how poor we were. However, Dad's shop never did well and he gave it up after about three years and went to work at the chemical works down by the River Des Peres, working there for about two years.

Ernie, Earl and I spent our time fishing for crawfish at Gravois Creek, climbing on boxcars at the "box factory" and watching "Ripper" the blacksmith shoe horses. If you had been good, Ripper would make you a ring out of a horseshoe nail. When that happened, you were the cat's meow of the neighborhood.

In 1932, Ernie and I began collecting stamps. There certainly wasn't any money available to purchase them, so we had to do the next best thing. We began to haunt some of the businesses in the area, particularly Uncle Fred's store. He didn't seem to mind Ernie and me going through his trash taking out any stamps that were available. That worked pretty well for the U.S. stamps but not so well with foreign stamps.

Some of the stores in the area had stamps for sale for one cent a package. Sometimes we would take a penny, and instead of buying candy, we would buy a set of foreign stamps. We could get maybe two or three stamps for that penny, but it was a start. I remember looking at those stamps and wondering about the foreign nation from which they had come and trying to visualize where in the world that nation was located. I suppose the interest that Ernie and I had for stamps certainly helped us both in our geography classes at Lyon School. Stamp collecting has stayed with both Ernie and me throughout our lives, and both of us now have gigantic collections. It has been a very rewarding experience.

During a part of the five years that we lived at 7823 Virginia Avenue, Ernie and I sold papers at the Box Factory, selling "The Times," "The Star" and "The Post" for one cent, two cents, and three cents respectively. We didn't make much money from those papers, but it did start us out in the paper business. And no matter where we lived over the next several years, Ernie and I sold papers.

In 1934, my dad made arrangements for Ernie and me to join the Knot Hole Gang at Sportsman Park. This was the home field of the St. Louis Cardinals and the St. Louis Browns. The Cardinals were our favorite team and several times each year we were allowed to take fifteen cents and go see them play. It was five cents for carfare up, a nickel for a Popsicle during the game, and five cents for carfare home. On several occasions however, we decided to spend the second five cents at the ballpark and then run home. Figuring that the trip home by foot must have been a good eight miles, Ernie and I would walk a block then run a block and ultimately, we would find our way home.

Everyone in St. Louis followed the Cardinals especially since the Browns were not a very good team. It would have been very difficult to find a person in St. Louis then who supported the Browns over the Cardinals. How could you not support a team that had the likes of Dizzy and Paul Dean, Joe Medwick, Frankie Frisch, Pepper Martin, and Rogers Hornsby.

The highlight of our trips to the ballpark was waiting around until after the players had showered to see them as they left the clubhouse and got into their cars. They all had brand new cars, and many of them had the brand new station wagon type that had made its appearance at about that time. Talk about hero worship—that was it at the highest level.

During 1935, our family moved to 7149 Idaho Avenue, seven blocks north of where we previously lived and much closer to Lyon School. Our new home was located in an area adjacent to a vast meadow above the railroad tracks, close to a great snow sled hill and a pond that was close for tadpoles. Only about two blocks from school, this was a most enjoyable place to live. We immediately became friends with Henry and Jimmy Schardan who lived two doors south of us. Henry, Jim, Ernie, and I played baseball, football, soccer and any other sport that was in season. What a great area this was for kids.

Although our home was very small, we had a large yard big enough for chickens and an extensive vegetable garden, and it had a great tree for climbing. We were also very close to Carondlet Park, which was about two blocks away, shorter if you went there by the railroad tracks that ran through a portion of the park.

Being close to the tracks and in the midst of the great depression, it wasn't unusual for hobos who followed the track to come up to our back door asking for a little something to eat. Even though food was scarce, my mom never refused a request. I remember listening to one man who told me of his recent trip to California and all wonderful things he saw there. Going to California was a dream that many families in St. Louis, including ours, had. Many of us had numerous members of our family who had already gone there. We had Aunt May and Uncle Bill Kattner in San Diego, Uncle Vic and Aunt Winnie Horn in Van Nuys, Uncle Herman Horn in Gardena, and Uncle Lou Krauss in the San Fernando Valley.

The winter of 1935-1936 was one of the worse winters in the history of St. Louis. My dad swore that this would be our last winter in St. Louis. Shortly after that, he received a bonus for serving in World War I and said we would use that money to move west. Mom and Dad also used part of the bonus money to buy a 1930 Model A Ford, a black Tudor. I believe they paid about $150 for that car.

Dad kept his promise! We sold some of our furniture, gave away what we couldn't sell, packed a few of our necessities, and on November 4, 1936, we took off for California. Even though it was late in the year, we generally had good weather. We spent nights in Jefferson City, Missouri; Baxter Springs, Kansas; Oklahoma City, Oklahoma; Amarillo, Texas; Hollywood, New Mexico; Deming, New Mexico; Phoenix, Arizona; and finally Los Angeles, California.

We stayed with my dad's brother, Victor Horn, who lived in Van Nuys.

1936-1937

CHAPTER 2

Venice, California
November 1936 - September 1937

W̶e lived with Uncle Vic for about two weeks at his home at 5635 Woodman Avenue, and then found a small house at 2305 1/2 Ocean Avenue in Venice. We were about fifty yards from the canals, about a half mile from the beach, and about a half mile from downtown Venice. What an exciting place to live! Shortly thereafter, On August 26, my mom gave birth to Nancy Ann.

Arline and Ernie went to Venice High School, and I enrolled at Nightingale School, which was located on Pacific Avenue and Washington, about a half block from the beach. From my classroom, I remember looking out the window and seeing an oil well operating. I was in the sixth grade and was placed in Mrs. Myrtle Domer's room. To this day, I consider her to be the best teacher I've ever had. Very quickly, I met Lou Corso and Fraser Giles, two of my best friends of all time. I was in Mrs. Domer's room from November 1936 to June 1937, and it was the most enjoyable school time that I have ever experienced. Others in that class were Buddy Cox, who taught me how to swim, Billy Ray, Alex Goodfellow, Carol Cook, Rosemary Talley, Arthur Lapp, Byrl Kelly, Frances Forbes, Donovan Martin, Richard Smith, and Richard Brown.

Ernie and I quickly began selling papers again. We made decent money selling the "Venice Vanguard," the "Los Angeles Examiner," and the "Los Angeles Times." Living in Venice was exciting for us three children. All summer, we rafted on the canals, swam at the plunge and at the beach, and spent time on the pier. What a change from the life we had in St. Louis.

September rolled around and we moved to 211 W. Beach Street in Inglewood.

1937-1943

CHAPTER 3

Inglewood, California
September 1937 - July 1943

Very quickly, Ernie enrolled as a junior at Inglewood High School and Arline and I enrolled at Crozier Junior High School in the eighth and seventh grades respectively. That year turned out to be one of my worst school years. It was close to being a disaster. Instead of playing football and baseball, I was deeply involved in reading, and although I read some good books, it didn't help me socially very much.

The following year, I was placed in Mrs. Bolton's class with my good friend, Fraser Giles, and we had a superb year. Mrs. Bolton was a fine teacher. We were also fortunate to have numerous great athletes in our group, so we were always playing football, baseball, softball and other sports. Some of those classmates continue to be good friends today. They are Fraser Giles, Robert Stach, Forrest Raybon, Earl Lucas, Thelma Hoffacker, and Rita Durkee. Some, like Paul Manahan, Ross Porter, and LeRoy Reynolds have passed on.

We graduated from Crozier Junior High School in June 1939. Even though the economic conditions in the U.S. were improving, the world conditions were worsening. By the time that we enrolled at Inglewood High School in September 1939, World War II had begun. Those were frightening days. With the war, however, the economy showed great improvement. Prior to that, it was somewhat bleak and again Ernie and I sold papers, and we made a most adequate amount—an amount that our family depended upon in order to eat and to pay the rent. Ernie sold "The Examiner" and "Times" on Saturday at the Sontag Drug Store at Manchester and Market Streets. I started out on Saturdays at the Bank of America at Market and Queen Streets. Then I graduated to the corner by Spaulding's Drug store at Commercial and Queen, and at night, I would scoot over and sell across the street at the old Inglewood Theater. Later on, I sold at Neal's Ranch Market down on La Brea, south of Arbor Vitae. When Neal's Ranch Market burned down in the first part of 1940, I took over the main corner at Market and Queen, in front of the Owl Drug Store.

In 1938, my dad found employment at Swift and Company in Vernon. It was his first steady job since we had arrived in California in November 1936 and he ended up working there until about 1962, at which time he retired.

My four years at Inglewood High were somewhat inauspicious. I was about a "C" student—never flunked any courses, but didn't get very many As either. I realize now that I didn't know how to study and didn't spend much time trying either.

My athletic career was much the same—nothing outstanding. I played two years of junior varsity baseball and two years of varsity. I also played two years of junior varsity football and one year of varsity. In my senior year, I was chosen as the second string All Bay League fullback but wasn't quite sure that I deserved it. Some of the athletes with whom I participated at Inglewood and who are still some of my best friends are Jack Kirkland, John Gates, Joe Daher, Ed Hyduke, Verl Lillywhite, Newell Oestriech, George Eppelman, Rich McHale, Don Cadoo, Dick Carter, Irving Gustavson, and Frank Eldridge. We always had a number of great coaches at Inglewood. Some of them were John Morrow, Arthur Badenoch, Bob Winslow, Martin Ernaga, Walt Selenger, Bob Burley, and Dick Arnett. Each of these had some impact on my life and remain a part of me today.

One of the most interesting and important experiences that I had during my high school time occurred during the summer of 1941. A friend of mine, Bill Satley, and I hitchhiked all the way back to St. Louis, both of us wanting to return to our birthplaces and visit old friends and family members. We left Inglewood early in the morning on June 21, traveling by bus initially to get us out of town. Eight days and thirty-two rides later, we rolled into St. Louis pretty proud of our accomplishment.

Along the way, we managed only to spend five dollars each, living on very little food and a whole lot of Pepsi. We slept on signboard catwalks or in old cars along the road. We walked a great deal, got sun scorched and rained upon, but we made it! I stayed with my Aunt Agnes and Uncle Fred Krauss who operated an appliance store at 7824 Ivory Avenue in St. Louis. They seemed very glad to see me and I helped Uncle Fred in the store and on deliveries. I had a great summer!

When it came time to return home, I was fully expecting to hitchhike, but since I had left in June, my folks had rented a larger home at 944 Holly Street in Inglewood and had taken in a boarder—a co-worker of Ernie's named Dean Gibbs who owned a 1938 Chevrolet. So Dean, Ernie, and Arline came back to St. Louis, picked up Aunt Agnes and me, and drove us back to Inglewood in fifty-two hours.

Things were going along pretty well until Sunday, December 7, 1941, when the Japanese bombed Pearl Harbor. Ernie left the next month for the U.S. Navy. Dean Gibbs got married and then left for the Army Air Corps. Some of the fellows at Inglewood High School also enlisted immediately, and off they went to war. I felt that it was important for me to acquire a high school diploma, so I stayed. Wartime is always very difficult in many ways but for me, those years were also very exciting and fun. I continued to play baseball and football, and in 1943, we had one of the finest baseball teams Inglewood High School has ever had. I graduated in June 1943, and I was chosen as one of the top sixteen graduates in our class.

During the summer of 1942, I worked the graveyard shift for Universal Carloading Company at the train yards at Olympic and Alameda streets in Los Angeles. We unloaded train cars all night and then loaded the trucks all morning so that the merchandise could be delivered to the proper places. There was a lot of war material being shipped at that time, particularly to Cal Ship in Wilmington, California. Though I earned a good deal of money that summer, I lost many hours of sleep and was unable to maintain a physical fitness schedule, so when it came time to report for football practice in September, I was really out of shape. Consequently, I did not do as well as I should have. I also continued to work at Universal on Friday and Sunday nights, which didn't help me get to school on Monday mornings, not having been able to sleep at all before I went to school. Sometimes I think it was a mistake working there, particularly when it affected my football career at Inglewood so drastically.

Ultimately, Universal changed their hours to a daytime job, so when I graduated, I worked there for a month before I joined the Navy in July of 1943.

1943-1946

CHAPTER 4

U.S. Navy
July 1943 - March 1946

Upon joining the navy, I was immediately sent to the San Diego Naval Training Station and was placed in company 43-284 with my good friend from Inglewood, Joe Gonzales. Boot camp was fun and exciting for a couple of seventeen-year-olds. They ran us ragged and worked us morning to night. They fed us quite well though and saw to it that we generally had enough sleep. Our chief was a man named Joe Kelly who had played basketball at the University of Southern California. As most of the coaches at Inglewood were graduates of USC, Joe Kelly knew them all.

After three weeks of boot camp, we were promised liberty from noon to Midnight on a Saturday. Joe and I were so homesick that we planned on hitchhiking home and making it back by midnight. As it happened, we were not released until about 2:30 p.m. Still thinking that we could make it up and back, we took off for Inglewood. We made it up in great time and felt that if we left Inglewood by 7 p.m., we shouldn't have any problem making it back on time. What we didn't realize was that there would be a million other GIs on the road back to San Diego and rides would be at a premium. We walked a lot of miles that night and when midnight came, we were still in South Laguna Beach. We finally arrived at the Naval Station at 5 a.m., five hours late. When we checked in late, they took our dog tags and our company number—that's when we knew we were in trouble. Later that day, we were called up before the captain, who told us that when our company graduated, we would have to report to Company 306 for three additional weeks of boot camp, plus we would not be eligible for any school. It also meant that Joe and I would go out on the first sea draft after Company 306 graduated. Did we feel bad!

Sure enough when 43-284 graduated, there was much excitement of being assigned to schools throughout the country—except for Joe and me. We were told instead to report to 43-306. What a back-breaker. They put Joe and me at the rear of their marching columns and we both felt like fifth wheels. That went on for about a week. One day, I had a very bad toothache and told the chief. He wrote out a note and told me to catch the bus to the dental clinic. On the way up, I noticed that there was a football team practicing cater-corner to the two gyms. I would have liked to have stopped and watched, but I couldn't as I had an appointment with the dentist.

At the clinic, there was not much of a discussion—a shot of Novocaine, a yanking of a molar, and I was finished. The dentist told me to take the afternoon off and to tell my chief that I was exempt from duty the rest of the day. As I returned to base, I saw the football team was still practicing. I watched them play for a while, noticing that their formation was one that I had played for two years at Inglewood High School. I recall thinking to my self as I watched that I could do what those football players were doing.

After a while, I went up to the coach, introduced myself, and told him that I would like to play. He asked me what experience I had, and I told him that I had played at Inglewood High School for three years. After determining that there was still one uniform left, he went ahead and told me I could play. But there was one little problem—I was still in boot camp. He said that it would not be a problem: I should tell my chief that everyday at 2 p.m., I was to report to Lt. Bo Molenda, the head football coach. I went over to the dressing room, checked out all of my gear, got a locker and went back to 43-306 to tell the chief. Talk about changing a life pattern—the chief was glad to get rid of me, as I wouldn't be fouling up his marching patterns any longer.

When 43-306 graduated in September, I was sent to Ships Company, but poor Joe Gonzales made the first sea draft and landed on the USS Monterey Bay, a ship that was coming into San Diego with a short crew from the East Coast. It was going to fill its complement with "boots" from our station. A quick note of interest here was that the Monterey Bay had a young lieutenant aboard by the name of Gerald Ford, who would later become the 38th president. I felt bad about parting with Joe Gonzales. He was a good friend, and I was partly responsible for his plight. Joe served well on the Monterey Bay, but he was severely burned when one of the typhoons hit it in the Western Pacific later on. I didn't see much of Joe after that, and shortly after his discharge, he was killed in a car accident in Inglewood.

Making that football team was a huge goal. I was the youngest player on the team and the only player still in boot camp. Most of the players were officers and chiefs with a sprinkling of some who were attending navy schools on the base. That team had some great players, two of whom became life long friends. Wally Huefner and John Santchi both lived and worked in the South Bay area. Wally was a fireman in Long Beach and John was a longtime coach and teacher at San Pedro High School. Our team had an excellent year. We lost only two games to the Fourth Air Force and ended up the seventh team in the nation. We were able to beat such teams as USC, UCLA, Redlands University, and Fort Ord.

A little background on some of the coaches and players might be of interest here. Bo Molenda, the head coach, had played at the University of Michigan in the mid 1920s. I don't think he graduated, but he played for many years with the Green Bay Packers and the New York Giants. Robert Ripley in his *Believe It Or Not* showcased Bo as the American athlete who had been on the most championship teams. I lost track of him until somewhere around 1980 when Wally Huefner suggested that we try to find him. It didn't take us very long to find that Bo had retired and was living in Banning, California, with his wife. Wally called him, and for a number of years, we visited him and when he could, his wife and he would come into Long Beach and stay with Wally and his wife, Joan. What a privilege to have been associated with Bo Molenda.

A number of other players from the USNTS team played football after the war. Buddy Jungmichel signed as a pro with the Miami Seahawks. Bill Cadenhead, our great left half, returned to the University of Alabama. Even though Cadenhead was one of the finest offensive players I have ever known, because Alabama was loaded with talent, they had him playing defensive half. Bill went into the insurance business after graduating and now resides and works in Florence, Alabama. Bill was one of the nicest guys I have ever known. Mike Dimitro signed up with UCLA and played for several years there. Garner Barnett returned to Arizona State at Tempe and we played against each other for several years. He was a fine halfback and was an integral member of some of those great Arizona State teams. Steve O'Meara, a right halfback, returned to San Jose State and I had the misfortune of playing against him in 1948, when Pepperdine suffered the greatest loss in the history of football. I'm sure there were others from that team who returned to football after World War II, but I am not aware of them. After the war, Bo Molenda signed up as an assistant coach with the Green Bay Packers and was also involved in baseball umpiring, going up as high as AAA ball. I wished that I had known that Bo Molenda was coaching at Green Bay because I would have signed later on with them instead of the Pittsburgh Steelers.

Rumor had it that if you made the team and wanted to attend a navy school, the choice was yours. So when it came time to choose a school, one of the assistant coaches, who had graduated from USC, asked me if I wanted to enter the navy program at USC and play football for the Trojans. I advised him that I would prefer to go to a diesel engine school, which I wanted to do for several reasons. First, I knew nothing about diesel engines. Second, if I went to a four-year college, the war might be over by the time I got out, and I sincerely wanted to do something for the war effort. So on December 18, 1943, I was transferred to the University of Illinois Diesel School at Champaign-Urbana, Illinois. I arrived there on December 23, and was it cold!

At one point during my schooling, I used a weekend pass and traveled by Greyhound— as it was too difficult to hitchhike through all the Midwest snow—to visit Uncle Fred and Aunt Agnes in St. Louis.

After graduating, I was transferred to Treasure Island, and then on to Small Craft Training Center on Terminal Island. After training was complete, we set sail for Pearl Harbor aboard the USS Serene. I was the only water tender aboard the Serene, and believe me, I didn't know a great deal about it. So upon arrival in Pearl Harbor, we received a second class water tender named Carl Dengler, from Detroit, Michigan.

We operated out of Pearl Harbor. We took a slow convoy to Eniwetok. We did some training off Maui, took a convoy back to San Francisco in November and then returned to Pearl Harbor. We did more training around Maui, and then on January 22, 1945, we left Pearl Harbor en route to Eniwetok, Tinian and Iwo Jima, arriving there on February 16, 1945.

We swept the western side of Iwo but found no mines there. We shelled various areas of the island. Apparently, we were bracketed by two torpedoes from one of the subs that was stationed on the southwest corner of Iwo. One of our problems at Iwo was that the island was not very wide and we could see little water geysers occurring in close proximity to our ship. We couldn't tell if the geysers were American shells coming clear across the island, or if the Japanese were trying to hit us.

We arrived at Iwo three days ahead of the marines, and when we weren't sweeping mines, we were being used as anti-submarine and anti-aircraft patrol. I can't recall what day it was, but late one afternoon, we went over to the ship area on the east side of Iwo. As we were anchoring, three Japanese planes flew directly in front of us, toward three destroyers that were next to us and dropped three bombs, all landing between the destroyers. No one got hurt on that run, thank goodness.

That must have been sometime after the raising of the flag on Suribachi. I didn't see it go up, but the word got out very quickly that the flag was up! No matter where you were in the area, you couldn't miss seeing the flag on top of the mountain. That was a very emotional moment in the lives of many American GIs who were at Iwo Jima. And it was at Iwo that the Japanese began to throw themselves off the cliffs on the northeast side of the island, and some of those bodies washed up past us while we were anchored.

We stayed at Iwo for eleven days. Most of the island was under U.S. control by that time, but fighting continued in some areas as stragglers were reluctant to give up. We left Iwo on February 27, and went down to Saipan for several days, and then on to Ulithi arriving there on March 9, and departing ten days later for Okinawa.

While at Ulithi, we had several beach parties with all the beer you could drink—that, and with the intense heat, some of the guys were feeling no pain. This was also a time for provisioning and for any maintenance needed aboard the ship. We departed Ulithi on March 19, en route to Okinawa, arriving there on March 25, six days prior to the invasion. We swept a lot of mines off Okinawa, Kerama Rhetto and Ie Shima. The latter island was where Ernie Pyle was killed—that occurred about the same time that we were sweeping. We also fired at some people who were walking up one of the many paths that led from the water up to the main part of the island. When the Serene wasn't sweeping for mines, we were assigned anti-submarine and anti-aircraft duty as well as being a marker vessel on the first day of the invasion.

On April 6, we escorted the Hobbs Victory from Kerama Rhetto to Okinawa. It was loaded with high-octane aircraft fuel. As it was becoming dark, a Japanese plane came in from the west very low on the water, and despite the firing of two escorts and the Hobbs Victory, the plane crashed into the bridge of the Hobbs Victory. It very quickly became inundated, and the crew began to abandon ship. We could see the men jumping from several parts of the ship. We were able to pick up nine survivors, one of whom died that night aboard the Serene. We had a burial at sea the following morning, and I was chosen as a pallbearer for the ceremony.

Years later, Ed Wilkowski, one of the motor mechanics, checked the file of that sailor who was killed, found out where he lived and the names of some of his relatives, and visited them in Minnesota. Wilkowski was able to give them information that they hadn't received, and he was able to help them with closure. Ed was also one of the pallbearers at that burial, as I recall.

Kamikazes were a particular problem for the smaller ships like the Serene who were an integral part of the defensive rings around Okinawa. We shot at quite a few of them, but never got credit for shooting any down. It was our good fortune to be a smaller ship because on several occasions, the kamikazes dived on the larger ships rather than on us. Although, one of the ships in our squadron did take a kamikaze hit in the after port side that killed all of the men in the after engine room.

On April 1, the first day of the invasion, we were cruising off of Okinawa when a very small Japanese boat came out. We fired on it, as did a destroyer that was close to us. We eventually sunk it with our anti-submarine K-gun explosives. That day we also picked up our first Japanese pilot who hadn't been dead too long. Another fellow and I hauled him aboard where the deceased was searched in relation to any important information that he might have had on him. We subsequently had a burial at sea for that fallen enemy. Several days later, we picked up a second Japanese pilot and did the same procedure with him.

We stayed around Okinawa until May 4, and then we took off for Ulithi, for repairs and provisions arriving on May 9 and staying until May 20. Then back to Okinawa, which was a lot quieter by then. We operated out of Okinawa, making several trips to the Formosa area for mine sweeping activities.

On July 8, with a convoy of LSTs, we departed for Leyte-Samar in the Philippines, arriving there on July 13. This layover was to prepare us for the invasion of Japan, scheduled for November 1 but reset for October 1.

We were at Tacloben, Leyte in the first part of August, during which time the atomic bombs were dropped on Hiroshima and Nagasaki. The night of August 10, 1945, my good friend, Stan Moore, and I were up by the bridge on the port side talking. All of a sudden, we saw a million tracers going up. Very quickly, we heard that the Japanese desired to terminate the war. What a celebration! Someone broke out the beer and a great time was had by all.

We left Leyte on August 23, stopped at Okinawa, and then departed for Sasebo, Japan. We arrived there well before the armistice was signed and were met by a Japanese ship that turned over the mine charts of Japan. We immediately left for the Ross Island area of Korea and swept there for about five days before returning to Nagasaki for several days.

We then returned to Sasebo, operating there for about a month. From October 4 to December 11, we swept mine fields at Iki Shima, and the Tushima Straights. Some of those mine fields were shallow, and we had to follow a sub-chaser specifically configured for minesweeping. It had a very shallow draft and we were able to follow it and sweep the field in some safety. Our last sweep was canceled, so on December 11, we departed Sasebo en route to Eniwetok and Pearl Harbor, arriving there on December 28. Honolulu was heaven! We had all the malts and hamburgers we wanted. We left there on January 3, 1946, and headed to San Diego, arriving there on January 15, and staying for two weeks. My Aunt May and Uncle Bill Kattner, who lived in San Diego, were awaiting my arrival on the dock. It was great to see them. We stayed there for two weeks, during which time most of the older men were transferred to other stations for discharge. Being that I was one of the younger ones aboard the Serene and having no dependents, I stayed aboard, and on January 26, we departed for Panama, arriving there on February 5, then off to Galveston, Texas on February 10. I stayed aboard for five days and was then given leave and transferred to the San Pedro Base for discharge. The great day of discharge was March 24. Stan Moore came down and took me home.

I spent about thirty-two months total in the navy and had some great experiences to show for it. My ratings were as follows: apprentice seaman, seaman second class, fireman second class, fireman first class, and motor machinist mate third class. Our crew still reunites each year at a designated city, allowing the friendships that we developed during our naval careers to thrive today. Some of the great shipmates I had were Stanley Moore, Don Penland, Frank Fries, Elbert Twichell, Walter D. La Roche, John McNeil, Roland Foeckler, Tom Gorman, and Bill Bailey.

We were blessed with having a wonderful group of intelligent officers led by Captain James E. Calloway, Executive Officer Jim Petitt, First Lieutenant Leonard Green, Larry Cuba, Ed Whittenberger, Ralph Callahan, George Kempson, and Don Rambert. A number of these officers have joined us on some of our annual reunions. I recall speaking with Captain Calloway at our reunion in Cocoa, Florida, saying how proud he was to be the captain of a crew that liked each other so much.

That concludes my naval career except for when the Korean War broke out in June 1950. I thought that in some way I might be called back to Service, so I went down to the navy recruiting office in Los Angeles, took and passed an exam for a commission, and was commissioned as an ensign. Then I waited and waited. I was probably the most inactive ensign in the Inactive Reserve for all time. No one came around, no one called. So I rode out that war in the Inactive Reserve.

1946

CHAPTER 5

Los Angeles City College
Los Angeles, California
April 1946 - August 1946

April 1, 1946—one week after I was discharged, Monte Lefton and I signed up for an accelerated course of study for GIs at Los Angeles City College (LACC). It was mid-semester in most schools and rather than waiting until the end of the semester to start, we felt that it would be most advantageous to jump right in. We both earned good grades, and when it came time for summer school, I elected to go and Monte took a respite.

During the spring semester, I was able to break into the LACC baseball team, even though they had already been playing for several months. We had a fair team, and a number of the players went on to four-year schools and did very well. Our coach was Joe Fleming of UCLA football fame. He was a fine coach, but got severely ill and passed away not too long afterwards.

Monte Lefton and I had talked a great deal about where we wanted to go after LACC. We both wanted to play football and really felt that we would end up at USC, where many of our teammates from Inglewood were going. We did go down to USC on several occasions, but no one seemed to want to talk to us. The second time we went down to sign up for classes, I had some difficulty in getting a class that I wanted. It was a frustrating experience and I told Monte that I was leaving and wouldn't attend USC. He agreed and we left. On our way out of USC, we talked about where else we might try to go to school. We agreed that Whittier College would be okay and that Loyola Marymount University was a possibility. Then Monte said, "Why don't we go over to Pepperdine and see what they have to offer." We knew Pepperdine was a very young school and that they were planning on having their first football team in September 1946.

Well, we went over and talked to several people, looked for the coach, but instead found his wife who advised us that he wouldn't be back until about 6 p.m. She invited us to come back at that time. Well we did, and we met Coach Warren Gaer, who advised that he only had one suit left and that he would give that suit to me and Monte would get the first suit that was returned. We thought that sounded pretty good, so we both reported for the first day of practice the following day.

1946-1949

CHAPTER 6

Pepperdine College
Los Angeles, California
August 1946 - June 1949

We didn't look like much that first day of practice, but it didn't take us very long to start looking like a team. Monte got his suit shortly thereafter and I'll tell you, we had tons of fun. That group of men jelled very quickly into a very good small college football team. We beat every one that season, except Arizona State at Tempe, who beat us thirteen to twelve. At the end of the season, we had seven wins and one loss, and we were chosen to go to the Will Rogers Bowl Game in Oklahoma City on January 1, 1947, to play Nebraska Wesleyan. Nebraska Wesleyan was undefeated, but had tied three games during the season. We had beaten such teams as Whittier, Redlands University, Pomona, Loyola, Humboldt State, Cal Poly San Luis Obispo, and Cal Tech—not bad for the first year of competition. So when it came time to play Nebraska Wesleyan, we felt ready for such a worthy opponent.

However, our team was used to playing in sunny California, and when we arrived in Oklahoma City, it was only seventeen degrees. We almost froze. It took us the entire first half of the game to thaw out—luckily we managed to hold them to only one touch down against us. It was the first time that entire season that we were behind at half time. Well, we warmed up in the second half, scored thirty-eight points, and held Wesleyan to only one more touchdown. The final score was thirty-eight to thirteen. That was the end of a magnificent football season. It's been said that we were the only team in the history of American football to have been selected for a bowl game in its first year of competition. And because football was somewhat down on the West Coast after the war, the Los Angeles papers made quite a thing about Pepperdine College being the only West Coast team to win a bowl game.

I also played baseball at Pepperdine beginning in the spring of 1947. We were blessed with fine athletes and a great coaching staff. John Scolinos, our baseball coach, turned out to be one of the most successful baseball coaches in America. Not only was he a great coach, but also he was, and still is, a great friend. In 1999, John was named "College Baseball Coach of the Century." I suppose the best part of that baseball season was beating Cal Berkeley and then having Cal win the College World Series later that year—not bad for a small school. Cal competed against Yale in the finals of the College World Series. Yale had a first baseman by the name of George Bush, who would later become the forty-first president of the United States.

I should digress for a moment to bring up one important fact. During Easter break at Los Angeles City College, I went over to the E.F. Coen Building Construction yard at Sixty-Sixth Street and Crenshaw in Los Angeles, in search of a job. I spoke to Mr. Coen, who hired me for that week and for weekends. It later turned out that he would allow me to work at any time I had free, even for an hour or two. I worked for Mr. Coen throughout my college career. It was a very physically demanding job, but it was great fun. I should tell you that as a young man, Mr. Coen was a football and baseball player and it didn't hurt me at all to be involved in the same sports. One year, Mr. Coen even sponsored our softball team. I worked with a young fellow at Coen's named Stuart Graham. Stu weighed about 135 pounds, was about 5'8" and was the hardest working guy I have ever known. We became very good friends, and on our days off, we contracted small jobs from customers who didn't know how to work cement and brick. It was a privilege to work with Stuart Graham.

During March 1947, my good friend from Inglewood High School, Jack Kirkland, told me that he was going to be married and asked if I would serve as his best man. I was deeply honored, as Jack had been one of my best friends of all time. We had played football and baseball at Inglewood, had double dated, and had a great time just hanging around together. Jack and Shirley remained our friends for all time until recently Shirley passed away.

September 1947 came and the second year of football started. We were undefeated that year, going nine and zero, and beating some of the best small college teams around. There were a number of bowl bids, but the team voted them all down because most of the players wanted to work during that time. Four of us were chosen to join the Pacific Coast All Stars to play in Hawaii in the second annual Hula Bowl. Terry Bell, Ted Kiapos, Bo Williams, and I were chosen. We joined the rest of the group who were mostly from the Pacific Coast Conference. Whittier College had two men, Santa Barbara had two men, and Occidental College supplied one man. All of the PCC teams supplied two men except USC. They were going to the Rose Bowl and would not participate with us. We played two games in Honolulu, winning one and losing one, which was tough as we four from Pepperdine were not accustomed to losing football games. We had a great time in Honolulu. Ernie Case, who had played at UCLA and later for the Baltimore Colts, was the person who had started this program. Interestingly, all four of us Pepperdine College players made the offensive team, which actually showed that we from the small school of Pepperdine could compete with football players from the Pacific Coast Conference schools. During our time with the all-star team, we had all of our expenses paid, plus, when we were through, we all were given $100 for additional expenses. What a great vacation we had!

The spring of 1948 came and that meant baseball. I did not have a particularly good year, but the team did well.

The fall of 1948 came and that meant football again. After two years of great success, the word was out that we should play bigger and better teams. So our schedule was changed to include schools like BYU, Arizona State at Tempe, San Jose State, San Diego State, and Portland State—losing to all of them. We ended up beating Fresno State, Arizona State Flagstaff, Cal Tech, and Loyola. It was not a very fun time after the two previous years, but we weathered it.

The spring of 1949 arrived which meant baseball, and again we had a very good team. I met a young pitcher by the name of Bob Schlatter, who had recently transferred from Missouri Valley College. We quickly became good friends, and at the end of the season, Bob and I were invited to work out with the Los Angeles Angels, which was the AAA club in the old Pacific Coast League. We apparently didn't impress them very much because none of them came around with a contract to sign. Years later, one of the regular scouts told me that he would have signed me in a minute but the word was out that I was going into coaching. Would that have changed my life?

Every year in baseball, we would play the Los Angeles Police Department two or three games, and generally, I did well against them. During the last game in 1949, Sgt. Vic Penny, their manager, came over to me and asked me what I was going to do after I graduated. I had hoped that the Angels would have signed me but it was apparent that they weren't. So I told Vic that I didn't know. He said that I should join the LAPD and play ball for him. That sounded pretty interesting so I asked him how I should go about it. He led me through the process, and after all of the examinations, I came out number two out of 3,500 applicants. When we went up for our physical examination, the number one applicant did not pass, so I ended up number one on the list.

Now we should go back several years to April 1947 regarding an incident that had a most significant impact on my life. I was in the registration line, waiting to sign up for the third semester of my first year at Pepperdine. In front of me was this very nice, personable young lady. At Pepperdine, everyone knew everybody, so I knew her name was Shirley Ann McBride. I also knew that she was a very fine student. We chatted and I ended up inviting her to join me for a Coke after we got through. She agreed. Later, over Cokes, I invited her to join me at the beach, but she declined saying she had an astronomy class at 3 p.m. that she couldn't skip. So we decided instead to go to the beach the following day, and after that, we went to the Inglewood Relays at Sentinel Field in Inglewood. We had a very nice time and ended up going to the movies the following evening. Three dates in two days—that had to be some kind of a record for me.

Needless to say we got along very well, and in July 1948, we became engaged, but agreed not to get married until we both had started our basic careers. That was easy for her as she was an education major and teachers were in short supply. She signed a contract with the Lawndale School District to teach double sessions beginning in September 1948. She was on her way. We eventually married on February 14, 1950, in Inglewood, California.

I graduated in June 1949. Some of the honors that I accumulated during my three years at Pepperdine were: Little All American football in 1946 and 1947; Third string Big All American football in 1947; All Coast 1946 and 1947; leading scorer in the nation in 1947; All American Baseball in 1949; Who's Who in American Colleges and Universities; Athlete of the Month Award from Helms in November 1946; member of the Knights Honorary Organization; and president of the Beachcombers Social Club. The Beachcombers Club was the biggest social club on campus and many of those members are still my good friends today. .

Some of my college football colleagues were Dale and Jack Drager, Terry Bell, Elmer Noonan, Bo Williams, Ted Kiapos, Keith Kenworthy, Tom Bedore, Monte Lefton, Norm Stillwell, Jim Hamilton, Bob Quine, Hal McCormick, Harry Nelson, Charles Calvert, Barney Barnhart, Harry Engelke, Keith Dolan, Walt Reeves, Howard Geiger, Bob Downey, Dick Gibson, Bill Evans, Phil Strom, Bill Johnston, Kent Kofford, Sammy Stephens, Ted Cooyas, Bob Bedore, Jack Paulman,

Rich McKowen, Bill Hicks, Ron Whitson, Bob McCluskey, Marty Cook, Gene Harding, Nelson Loomis, Bobbie Hayes, Vic Lorenzo, Dewey Parke, Bill Burns, Bill Clark, George Eppelman, Bill Owen, Vic Riley, Bill Anderson, Roger Auld, John Bilbrey, Don Clark, Chuck Gibbon, Bill Harris, Bruce Murdock, Pat Murphy, Bob Nall, Carl Neuman, Raul Regalado, and last but not least Ed Hyduke.

In baseball, there was Bob Schlatter, Gil Asa, Rudy Victoria, Robert "Flash" Lewis, Chuck Gibbon, John Gates, George Eppelman, Harry Nelson, Ed Plank, Norm Carpenter, John Bilbrey, Jerry Lowther, and Ed Roginson.

At Pepperdine, because we were a small school—1,500 people at that time—most athletes had to double and triple up their sport careers. Many of the names listed here can be listed in both places. Chuck Gibbon, the finest athlete that we had, could be listed under football, baseball, basketball, track, and golf. He was an outstanding athlete and we were fortunate that he chose to go to school at Pepperdine.

Some of the administrators and teachers should be noted here as well. Our president was Dr. Hugh Tiner, and the dean was E.V. Pullias—both excellent administrators as well as friends. Some of the others who should be noted were Oly Tegner, Kenneth Hahn, Tillie Hall, Coach Al Duer, who was also the director of athletics, Coach Robert "Duck" Dowell, Hubert Derrick, J. Eddie Weems, and Dr. Wade Ruby. Some of the students that should be mentioned were Paul Perry, Dene Golden, Mort Cooper, Lloyd Twomey, Ken Rawson, Barbara Long, Barbara Eppelman, and Ken Ross.

1949-1951

Los Angeles Police Department Los Angeles, California September 1949 - July 1951

In September 1949, I reported to the Los Angeles Police Academy, in Elysian Park with about seventy-five other recruits. We were the top recruits of the approximately 150 that the department would take from the list. Something felt very strange to me initially. I finally determined that the feeling emanated from it being September, and for many years, September meant football. I quickly determined though that the Academy was not too different from football. It was demanding, physical and fun. Even though we went everyday from 8 a.m. to 9 p.m., it was pretty exciting. There were four of us from Pepperdine in that class—Robert Drummond, Bill O'Connor, Dave Brandeis, and I. A number of us stayed for a year or so, and then went to the FBI, State Department, or Secret Service. Many of the men who stayed became the hierarchy of the LAPD. Daryl Gates was in that class, and he became the chief of police. A number of the others became captains and commanders. Ray Ruddell and John McAlistar did extremely well. The turnover in the LAPD was somewhat high at that time. We were warned when we were going through the academy that the life of a police officer is difficult and that our class like every other would have its problems. We were still on probation when one of our classmates was arrested for murder. He was ultimately convicted. Several didn't make probation and one was arrested for beating prisoners. He, too, served time.

Some of the personnel at the Police Academy who had a great affect on us new recruits were Captain Frank Walton, Lt. Tom Reddin, Sgt. Floyd Phillips, officers Ted Combs, Bob Phillips, Dick Hill, and Buck Compton. These fine officers took very, very raw recruits and started them out on exciting and successful law enforcement careers.

After thirteen weeks at the Academy, we graduated. Half of us went to the city jail and the other half went to Parking and Intersection Control. I was chosen for the latter and very quickly was assigned to the corner of Fifth and Hill streets. It was a difficult and hot corner—there was no shade and it was a scorching summer.

Directing traffic was a pretty boring experience, so whenever I could, I became involved in the chasing of pick pockets and shop lifters from the drug store that was on the corner. I recall one incident where a man ran the red light, and I knew he had done it on purpose, so I chased him down to Fifth Street and Olive. As I began to write him a ticket, he noticed my class ring and asked me where I had gone to school. I told him that I had graduated from Pepperdine. "Oh," he said. "Do you know Darwin Horn, the football player?" Trying to hide a grin, I said that I knew Dar pretty well and continued to write the citation. I took special pains to write my name as legibly as possible and have often wondered if he ever took the time to see who wrote him that ticket.

When spring came, it was determined that the LAPD could no longer support a baseball team and that instead, the various departments would have inter-departmental competition. I'm not sure that I would have joined the LAPD at all had I known they were going to cancel the team—baseball was the true reason that I had joined the LAPD in the first place.

There were quite a few of my academy friends in PIC and when the call came out for ball players, about three of us went. We ended up having a very good team and, although we didn't take the championship, we had a very good year—something that PIC had not done for a long time. After about seven months in PIC, the Accident Investigation Division needed officers to fill in for vacation times. I was fortunate to be chosen, and even though I was on the midnight shift, I wasn't battling the sun at Fifth and Hill. After about a month however, we were all sent back to PIC—what a back breaker. It wasn't but several weeks later though that I received the word that I would be transferred permanently to AID.

I worked with a number of fine partners in AID. The first one was Byron "Tom" Barnes and we generally worked all over the city as a fill-in car until we could bid on a certain division. Then we ended up in the South Los Angeles area. After Tom Barnes, I worked with Robert Ballou, one of the finest people I have ever known. Coincidentally, back in 1943, when I was playing for the USNTS in San Diego, Bob had been working in the aircraft industry and playing professional football with the San Diego Bombers. We played against each other but didn't know each other at the time. Tom Barnes retired from the LAPD on a medical and moved to Texas. I haven't seen nor heard from him in years, but Bob and I have kept in touch throughout the years. He remains one of my best friends and now resides in Cambria, California.

My time in accident investigation was very interesting. We had the freedom—if we weren't busy on our own accident calls—to assist other units. One night, we assisted in a car chase that was occurring on Century Blvd., and we were able to pull the car over. It turned out to be a former neighbor of mine when I was a youngster living in Inglewood. Was he embarrassed!

During my two-year career with the LAPD, I was called on several occasions for media interviews. I was interviewed on the radio on January 1, 1950, at the Rose Parade and later, I was the LAPD representative for the sale of tickets to the Policeman's Ball on a local TV station. I was also asked to represent the LAPD at a track meet at the Coliseum for the presentation of medals.

As soon as I left the academy, I signed up for classes at Los Angeles State College, which was then on the campus of Los Angeles City College. Then, in June 1950, I enrolled at USC beginning my work on my master's degree.

In February 1951, while speaking with Jack Kenney, my academic counselor at USC, he asked me if I would like to join the U.S. Secret Service. I said that I would, but I had recently heard that they were not hiring. Mr. Kenney, on the contrary, said that they were. He placed a phone call to a Mr. Fred Wasson to set up an interview for me at the Federal Building at Spring and Temple. After the interview, Mr. Wasson turned me over to an agent named Harold Polenz, who guided me through the hiring process. I owe my life and career to Harold Polenz. After passing their exams, they started a background investigation, which moved very slowly.

June rolled around, and the Pittsburgh Steelers had contacted me to see if I'd be interested in playing for them. They were the only single-wing team left in the NFL, and they needed a single-wing fullback. They sent a contract out, offering me $4,500 per year if I could report to their training camp at Cambridge Springs, Pennsylvania, by July 15, 1951. Not sure where I stood with the Secret Service as it had been months since I heard anything, I called Harold Polenz to inquire about my job status, but he couldn't tell me anything. That pretty much made up my mine—I told him that I was going to play football with the Steelers.

1951

CHAPTER 8

Pittsburgh Steelers
Cambridge Springs, Pennsylvania
July 1951 - September 1951

The first part of July, I resigned from the LAPD and went to the Steelers' training camp, which, in hindsight, ended up being too much of an impulsive decision. As it turned out, on September 1, 1951, Agent Snellbacker called and offered me a position in the Secret Service. He said that if I accepted, I would have to be in L.A. by September 16 and would be immediately transferred to Phoenix. Without hesitation, I told him I would depart the next morning. I signed release waivers and left training camp to pursue what I believed would be a more rewarding career. And I was correct!

1951

CHAPTER 9

United States Secret Service
Los Angeles, California
September 1951 - October 1951

I reported for duty as a U.S. Secret Service agent on September 17, 1951. Agent Polenz took me down to the commissioner's office and I was sworn in as an agent. I was introduced to such fine agents as Vic Carl, Lee Gopadze, Howard Sweeney, Pat Boggs, Frank Leyva, Milt Scheuerman, and John Larson. What a great group of agents they were—hard working, smart, they could do it all! Each one of them took the time to invite me out to assist them on investigations so that I could learn the ropes.

On September 28, I received my first case. It was an investigation of a U.S. Treasurer's check payable to Helena Williams. I will always remember that name. I was unable to solve it and closed it out as unsolved—not a great way to start a thirty-year career, but there would be other cases to solve. The first month in the service was not a very productive month for me. I showed no arrests, closed no cases on my own, but did assist with thirteen. I learned a great deal from the various agents with whom I worked.

On October 12, 1951, Shirley Ann and I moved from 613 1/2 W. 80th St., Los Angeles to Phoenix, Arizona.

1951-1952

CHAPTER 10

Phoenix, Arizona
October 1951 - March 1952

Mr. George Walker was the agent in charge of the Phoenix office. He welcomed me with open arms, as he had been the only agent in the state of Arizona for some time, and there was beginning to be too much work for one agent. What I didn't know about check investigations from the experience I had in Los Angeles, Mr. Walker taught me, and he was a fine teacher. He and I worked the whole state of Arizona and it wasn't long until I was out working my own cases. Mr. Walker had one secretary, Keith Marshall, who helped me immeasurably. He was aware of many types of investigations and kept me from making errors in reporting.

Mr. Walker didn't waste any time in breaking me in. There was work to be done in Tucson, and on October 29, I took off for Tucson with a load of cases to solve. This trip was the first of many trips that I took during my sixth-month assignment in Phoenix. The next road trip began on November 16 and took me into the Navajo Reservation at Window Rock, Arizona.

My first of many arrests for forgery came on December 11. I also began making speeches, my first being on March 7, 1952. I had been in the Secret Service for less than six months, and here I was in front of a group of people sounding like I had years of experience. Mr. Walker was due to make that speech, but he didn't like public speaking very much, so he pawned it off on me. Being that it was my first speech for the Secret Service, I was nervous, but I remember one of the people in the audience coming up to me afterward and saying very proudly that he had never before met a U.S. Secret Service Agent in person. That was very flattering. I was not a complete novice at public speaking at that time, as I had made a number of speeches and media appearances for Pepperdine College and the Los Angeles Police Department. Later, as my career developed, I went on to deliver many speeches for the Secret Service.

On March 31, 1952, after about five great months of working in the Phoenix office with Mr. Walker, I was transferred back to Los Angeles. Shirley Ann and I were delighted to return to L.A. to our families and many friends. Prior to leaving Phoenix, Mr. and Mrs. Walker took Shirley Ann and me out to dinner. Mr. Walker was one of the kindest, best supervisors I had in the Secret Service. We worked so very well together, and prior to leaving, he told me he didn't know how he would get along without me.

Phoenix was always a hotbed of illegal gold activity. Mr. Walker had many cases involving illegal gold, but in all of his time there, he never had a gold case wherein gold was actually obtained. (Before leaving Los Angeles in October, I had helped on a gold case there. My part was most insignificant, but it was enough to whet my appetite.) On January 31, 1952, Mr. Walker received a telephone call from a local jeweler advising him that a guy named Rex Martin had just left his business after attempting to get him to purchase gold—gold that was to be supplied through the Yaqui Indians of Northern Mexico. This had been the story since 1934, when the Gold Reserve Act went into effect.

Mr. Walker sat down with me and went over what information he had and gave me some suggestions as to what to do. So with three months experience as an agent, I was sent out alone to deal in a very complex case. I met the informant at his jewelry store in Phoenix and he surrendered to me a button of gold that had been supplied to him by the suspect, Rex Martin. The story that Martin told the jeweler was that he had access to tons of ore in Mexico, and that he was willing to take any prospective buyers down to Mexico and could cut and process the ore with the buyers.

When I returned to the office with the gold, things happened quickly. Mr. Walker contacted the IRS Intelligence Service and requested that they supply an agent to work with me. They sent Special Agent Jack Williams who turned out to be a great partner. We went over what we knew, and it was proposed that we meet with the suspect at one of the local hotels. Mr. Walker made arrangements, and we called the jeweler, who in turn called the suspect, who agreed to meet us, the "big money men" at the hotel. We had time to put a microphone in our room with a recorder next door, so when the suspect came in, the entire conversation was recorded.

On February 6, SA Williams and I met the suspect at the jewelry store. We agreed to accompany him down to Nogales, Mexico, to buy a vast quantity if we were satisfied. On Friday, February 8, 1952, we met with him at the Marcos de Ninza Hotel in Nogales, Mexico, where he checked in. Jack and I returned to Nogales, Arizona, just across the border. By the time we got to our hotel across the border, we were met by Mr. Walker, Ben Brewer, Jack Williams' supervisor, representatives of U.S. Customs, and U.S. Immigration agents, who were all stationed in Nogales and knew all about Yaqui Indian gold stories. They had heard them for years and knew that most of them were con games where the Americans would be lured into Mexico to be beaten, robbed, and sometimes killed. Most of these escapades were led and directed by a Mexican named Pico de Oro, (tooth of gold) who relished in the acquisition of American dollars as well as American scalps.

We were told by Immigration that we could not take any weapons across the border. If we did and the Mexican Police found us with them, we would be arrested and put into a Mexican jail and they couldn't protect us. Mr. Walker asked us if we still wanted to go saying that If we didn't, other arrangements could probably be made. But Jack and I still wanted to go, and as we had a 7 p.m. meeting in Mexico with Martin, we were anxious to get started.

We were dropped off at the border, and Jack and I walked to Martin's hotel, went to his room and went over what was going to occur. At about 7:30 p.m., there was a knock on the door. Martin answered it and I saw two arms thrusting a package through the door. On opening the package, we found some gold ore, a vial of acid, a washing pan, and a scale. Martin took us to the bathroom and began to process the ore. This took about forty-five minutes, and when Martin was through, there were some gold particles on the bottom of the pan. We weighed them in at nineteen grains—not a lot of gold, but enough to consummate a crime that began in the U.S. Martin allowed us to keep the gold, and we told him that we would buy all the gold he could deliver to us on the U.S. side. He agreed to meet us the next day at our hotel, at which time we would complete the deal.

The next morning, Martin came to meet us in our hotel lobby. Once we knew he had the gold, we identified ourselves as agents and informed him that he was under arrest. Our covering agents swooped in and took Martin off to the sheriffs' office, where he was interrogated. He asked Jack and I if we would go back to his room and bring all of his stuff over to him. We agreed.

When we reached the lobby of his hotel, the desk clerk said that there had been a ton of phone calls to the room that morning. I told him to let the next one go through, and then Jack and I went up and started collecting Martin's stuff. We were also able to obtain the scales, some acid, and the washing pan. Then the phone rang. I answered it with a "yeah," and the voice said, "What happened, where've you been?" I said, "Come on up." He said, "Be there in three minutes." We assumed that this would be Pico de Oro coming to hurt the rich Americans. We were in a difficult position with no weapons—especially if he wasn't coming alone. So we had to come up with a good plan fast! We decided that Jack would go out by the elevator and when the man got out, he would follow him as closely as possible to our room. Then I would open the door and hit him as hard as I could, and Jack was to hit him from the rear.

Well, when I heard the knock on the door, I said, "Who's there?" The voice behind it said "Nacho." I quickly opened the door and knocked him hard on the chin. Jack nailed him from the back, and he went crashing to the floor, out cold. Poor Nacho! When I had a chance, I took my knuckle and pushed his upper lip back. I was expecting to see the mouth full of gold teeth (Pico de Oro), but to my surprise, there wasn't one gold tooth in his mouth. When he came to, all he could mutter was "Please don't kill me." We asked him his name and where he lived. He said he was Ignatio Coronado, that he lived in Phoenix, and that he was a friend of Rex Martin. Nacho agreed to accompany us across the border, back to the U.S. We piled Martin's luggage on Nacho and marched him back across the border to the sheriff's office where he was interrogated and later released.

Martin was found guilty and sentenced to three years. In the process, his precious 1951 Packard Limousine was impounded as it was used to further a crime. Talk about a man's empire crumbling—Martin was married, had a family, a good job, and was deeply involved in his church and neighborhood. All of this went down the tubes when he fell into the trap of attempting to get rich quick. I remember Mr. Walker saying all the way back to Phoenix, "I can't believe that we finally got gold in a gold case."

1952-1954

CHAPTER 11

Los Angeles, California
March 1952 - April 1954

When I reported to the Los Angeles Field Office on March 31, most of the agents that were there when I was hired were still there, except for Agent in Charge Fred Wasson, who had retired. Guy Spaman was acting special agent in charge, and in June, he officially became the SAIC. An agent, Paul Henne, had also joined the office and he was a very welcome addition. Paul had worked in the Washington Field Office for a number of years and spent much of his time on the vice presidential detail.

Shirley Ann and I stayed with her mother at 820 W. 107th Street in Los Angeles for several days until we were able to rent a small duplex apartment at 213 1/2 W. 111th Place in Los Angeles. We stayed there until September, and then moved to 12801 S. Catalina, Gardena—a house that was owned by Bill McBride, Shirley's brother. Our son, Dar Jr., was born on August 8, 1952, just prior to moving to the Catalina street residence. Shirley Ann returned to teaching in the Los Angeles City School District in September and Shirley's sister, Virginia, took care of Dar during the day. Shirley Ann taught at the 186th Street School, close to Western Avenue and quite close to where Virginia, and her husband, Roy, lived.

Work in the LAFO was much different than in Phoenix. There was much work to be done, and much of the time it was a matter of putting out fires as they erupted. During the first few weeks, I recall helping out the other agents when a second agent was needed. I particularly recall working with Victor Carli, who at the time was the assistant agent in charge. He was a great agent, and in later years, when I had Vic's position, I would endeavor to emulate his practices regarding personnel. Vic always worked the biggest counterfeit cases, so when you worked with him you inevitably worked in the counterfeit realm—what a privilege.

Very quickly I received my own cases. I generally worked in the South Los Angeles area, but on occasions I worked in all districts of the metropolitan Los Angeles area. I enjoyed working in the Inglewood area, seeing people whom I had known in school there. Some of them were on the Inglewood Police and Fire Departments. I even went to Inglewood High on several occasions to speak to teachers and administrators that I knew from when I went to school there.

On September 8, 1952, I began a four-week Treasury Enforcement School, where I met Mike Mandalay. Mike had taken my place in Phoenix with Mr. Walker. He had also played football at UCLA at about the same time that I was at Pepperdine. We became very good friends and continue as friends today. Mike left the Secret Service after several years and opened the Ojai Valley Ford Agency in Ojai, California. Shirley Ann and I must have bought about twelve cars from Mike throughout the years.

On September 14, I was assigned my first physical protection assignment, protecting Margaret Truman with Vic Carli and Leon Gopadze. My specific job was to take care of her luggage—you have to start somewhere.

On September 18, I departed for Sacramento to testify in a case against a defendant whom I had arrested in Phoenix. I traveled by train, arriving in Sacramento the following morning where I was met by Steve Byrne, the agent in charge. It was very apparent what a wonderful person Steve Byrne was, and on numerous occasions thereafter, I indicated a desire to go to Sacramento in order to work for Mr. Byrne. Unfortunately, it never occurred.

Most agents remember vividly their first assigned counterfeiting case. At that time, our counterfeiting investigations were top priority, and it was generally the desire of all agents to work primarily in that field. I was no exception. In October 1952, a confidential informant told us that he had heard of a man named Frank Jones, who was interested in making counterfeit notes. The informant provided us with a license plate number of the car used by Jones, as well as a very good physical description of him. Interestingly, Jones was a black man, and at that time, we had never had a counterfeit case where a black person was involved.

Mr. Spaman came over to my desk with all of the paper work on the Jones case, and knowing that I had never been the case agent for a counterfeit case before, said, "Here, solve this one." I was delighted! The first thing I did was to interview the informant in order to obtain any additional information he might have. Then I ran the license number through the DMV, but it came back registered to a woman in West Los Angeles. The LAPD had no record on the registered owner, or on Frank Jones. So out we went to the bank where the registered owner had received the loan for the purchase of her car. We found that a man by the name of Fred Taylor—not Frank Jones—had co-signed on the loan.

Efforts to locate the vehicle at the registered address were unsuccessful, even though we staked it out at various times through out the day and night. But we did score big time at the LAPD when we found a record of a Fred Taylor at the registered address, and this Fred Taylor had recently been released from San Quentin. We obtained mugs and when we showed them to the informant, he positively identified Fred Taylor as the man known as Frank Jones. The investigation took a different direction at this point. We increased surveillance and finally spotted the car being driven by a man who fit Fred Taylor's description. We followed him to various places in Los Angeles, hoping that if he were involved in counterfeiting, we might catch him in the act of passing a note. No such luck—he was simply out socializing.

Much of counterfeit investigations turn out to be a lot waiting and seeing if new counterfeit notes turn up. With the Fred Taylor case, time elapsed and no new notes hit L.A. So other measures had to be taken—we decided to hit his residence. On the evening of January 29, 1953, SAIC Spaman, ASAIC Carli, SA Polenz and I went to his residence. I was chosen to knock on the door, introduce myself and advise him that the Secret Service suspected him of making counterfeit notes. The direct approach theory is that no matter with whom you speak, no one is going to admit to anything. So when he denies it, you merely ask him if he would mind if we would look around, since he isn't guilty of anything. If he does protest, he is advised that a search warrant could be easily obtained, and very few people desire to be the subject of a search warrant.

After pulling the direct approach with Taylor, he quickly advised us that he was staying in the rear apartment and that it would be OK to look around. Taylor signed a "waiver to search," and Spaman, Carli, and Polenz quickly joined me. The apartment was tiny and the four of us kept bumping into each other. I casually picked up a telephone book and fanned it up side down. Sure enough, out dropped four negatives for $20 notes—it was a violation even just to have them in your possession. I recall Taylor saying that he thought he had gotten rid of everything. We later found plates secreted in his walls as well. Even though he never made a counterfeit note, the mere possession of the items was a violation of the counterfeit statutes. Taylor went back to prison for another six years. Needless to say my first counterfeiting assignment was a success.

My second physical protection assignment was on Sunday, July 19, 1953, in conjunction with the visit of Vice President Nixon, when he attended the Boy Scout Jamboree in Orange County, close to Newport Beach. This was the first of many assignments with Mr. Nixon.

On December 2, 1953, we received information from a confidential source that an unidentified person would be at a certain business establishment in Los Angeles on a certain date and time, and had indicated that he was interested in making counterfeit currency. About six of us went to cover the "meet," and when the suspect showed up, Agent Leyva recognized the person in question as a former counterfeiter known as Clifford Vincent. We followed him to his car, but lost him in rush hour traffic in downtown Los Angeles. Several days later, another informant advised us that Vincent would be meeting at another place and time. Again, about three teams of agents went out for surveillance, found Vincent, tailed him for a short while, but lost him in traffic. We would be sorry for that loss because shortly thereafter, numerous new counterfeit $20 bills began surfacing. We knew they had to be notes made by Vincent, but we had no physical evidence as of yet.

We knew we had to find Vincent quickly as Christmas was rapidly approaching and we didn't want L.A. flooded with counterfeit notes. A check with the probation office revealed some sources that were quickly checked out, but to no avail. Most mornings we had about six teams of agents scouring neighborhoods in the Monterey Park, Alhambra and Rosemead areas—arbitrarily setting Rosemead Blvd. as our eastern limit—searching for Vincent and his 1949 black Buick sedan. We knew that whoever found that car would be an instant hero. With all of our work adding up to nothing concrete, we were now caught up in trying to trace down, as quickly as possible, any of the new notes that were appearing in L.A. But again, we proved unsuccessful.

Vincent was from a little town outside of Fresno named of Hanford. Members of the Hanford Police Department knew of Vincent. SAIC Guy Spaman had called the chief of police of Hanford and advised him that we wanted to know if and when Vincent showed up there, especially since Christmas was coming, perhaps he might go home to visit his family.

On Christmas Eve, as Shirley Ann and I were putting up our tree and assembling a very intricate police car toy for Dar Jr., the phone rang. It was Mr. Spaman reporting that Vincent had been seen at his family home in the infamous Buick. He asked me if I could grab Agent Sweeney and take off for Hanford immediately. Very quickly, I met up with Howard Sweeney at his home in Leimert Park, and we left for Hanford in the hopes of possibly catching Vincent in the act of passing notes. We arrived in Hanford about 5 a.m., and lo and behold, there was the 1949 black Buick sedan parked in front of the family home. We sat in our car for several hours before Vincent finally came out, got into his car and departed. Surveillance is difficult enough, but in a very small town, it's almost impossible. We did as well as we could and each time Vincent entered a store or service station, we were right behind him, checking to see if he had passed any counterfeit notes. We found none—indeed, it would have been foolish for him to pass notes in a small community where he was well known.

Sweeney and I had not slept for a day and half and we were physically beat as we followed Vincent back to his family home that evening. From our vantage point, we watched him drain his radiator and go inside. We figured he was in for the night, so we felt safe to find a motel, get some sleep and come back very early the next morning. On our way to find a motel, we met Agents Pat Boggs and Frank Leyva, who had come up from L.A. to help us. They agreed to our plan, so we all found a motel and went straight to sleep. Early the next morning, we got up and went over to Vincent's home only to find the 1949 Buick gone. Were we embarrassed! A quick look around town revealed no 1949 Buick. Sweeney called the boss and told him about our failure. We all headed back to L.A. a very sad and disconsolate group of agents.

That was the last we saw of Vincent until the night of January 20, when after a day of carousing and passing notes, Vincent rear-ended another vehicle badly enough for the police to be called. When the deputies concluded that Vincent had been drinking, they searched his vehicle and found a bundle of what appeared to be counterfeit notes in his glove compartment. That's when we were called out to confirm that the notes were indeed counterfeit. This was another example how so often the local law enforcement groups in the L.A. area helped us out of difficult circumstances. Vincent admitted his involvement in counterfeiting, telling where he had printed the notes and where he had buried the plates and negatives, even going as far as writing out a map. Mr. Spaman, Agent Polenz, and I went up to the Los Angeles National Forest near La Canada, and following the hand drawn map, we were able to locate the cache of evidence. It truly was like finding an old pirate's treasure. I don't recall what kind of a sentence Vincent received, but I know we never heard from him again in the counterfeiting game.

While this case was going on, I received a memo from my chief, advising that I was to be transferred to the Washington Field Office as of April 1, 1954. This was unexpected news. Shirley Ann was teaching in the L.A. City School District, and she determined that if we could extend that reporting date one month, she could attain her tenure in the district. I requested a later reporting date, and they quickly accommodated me, authorizing a new reporting date of May 3. In preparing for my transfer, I cleaned up my cases as well as possible, closed as many as I could, transferred those that could not be closed to other agents, and reassigned all of my judicial cases.

On Friday April 23, Shirley Ann, little Dar and I took off for Washington, D.C., in our 1953 four-door green Nash. I drove clear through the night, took a side trip up to the Grand Canyon and ended up in Holbrook, Arizona the following day. It took us about four and a half days to get to St. Louis, where we stayed for a day before heading on to Washington, D.C., arriving there on May 1. We stayed several days with Agent Milt Scheuerman his wife, Carol, and his family in Hyattsville, Maryland. We ultimately found an apartment at 4631 28th Road South in Arlington, Virginia.

1954

CHAPTER 12

Washington Field Office
Washington, D.C.
May 1954 - August 1954

The Washington Field Office was like no other field office in the Secret Service. We were constantly being called out for special assignments, for assignments with the president and vice president and whatever else came up. I recall a number of very fine agents with whom I worked: Drew O'Malley, Charles Taylor, Jim Griffiths, and ASAIC Tom Kelley. As the office was really under the gun being located in the basement of the Treasury building, where the chief and the secretary of the Treasury worked, it took a special type of SAIC to manage it, and James Beary had been that man for a very long time.

Planning a day's work was next to impossible, and yet they assigned cases to agents to be worked whenever possible. There was always a shortage of cars, and more than likely there would be no cars available for usage. Plus, whenever anything unusual occurred at any of the White House gates, agents from the WFO had to respond. Whenever the president moved, you could bet that you would be assigned "route patrol" or a standing post, and there was a lot of night and weekend work. But in spite of it all, Jim Beary never seemed to be worried about the hullabaloo. For me, however, it was a different story. During the four months I was in that office, my morale sank to the lowest level it would ever be in my thirty years in the Secret Service. After making many arrests while assigned to the LAFO, I ended up with a grand total of three arrests at the WFO—not a great record to say the least. But looking back, I can thank Tom Kelley, Drew O'Malley, and Charlie Taylor for introducing me to the realm of protective research, which involved the interviewing of people who came to Washington endeavoring to speak to, or even wanting to cause harm to, the president. This was a very different type of case, and it took a lot of know-how in order to handle them. Drew and Charlie were tops at this.

In looking back at some of the assignments that we had in support of the White House detail, we worked at Constitution Hall, the Canadian Embassy, the Sheraton Hotel, Washington National Airport, the Capitol, the Statler Hotel, the Shorearm Hotel, Eisenhower's Church, Griffith Stadium for ball games, Arlington National Cemetery, Chestertown, Maryland, the Congressional Hotel, the Armory, the East Gate of the White House, and the Mayflower Hotel. These locations are those where presidents go most and assignments became perfunctory. On a number of occasions, I was assigned to the president's route patrol—traveling the president's route prior to him and trying to determine if there would be any problems. If there was an accident or a construction site, we had to radio in what the problem was and receive a different route, but that didn't occur very frequently.

I took leave from work in August 1954 to be there for the birth of our daughter, Diane, who was born on August 8—the very day of Dar's second birthday. I'm still not sure whether that was an advantage or not. Due to my work schedule, we generally were able to have only one birthday party for both of them, but they didn't seem to mind as long as Diane got her angel's food cake and Dar got his devil's food cake.

In Arlington, we lived in a large apartment complex called Claremont. Our entrance led to two apartments downstairs and two upstairs. When we first moved in, those apartments were occupied by Dick and Shirley Flood, Donald Lopez and his family, and Robert Jones and his family. The Floods moved to Argentine to work in an automobile plant. Donald Lopez, a USAF major, was transferred, and the Jones moved to Tallahassee, Florida, where Robert Jones became a law professor at the university there. All three of them moved pretty quickly after we moved in, but while we were there, they were wonderful neighbors. Later, Don and Sarah Herman moved in across from us. They turned out to be some of the finest neighbors that we have ever had. Though eventually they divorced, we have kept in contact with them through Sarah. All of the families had small children, and none had been married very long, so we were all in the same boat. Our social lives were very close—we played a lot of bridge together as bridge was the "in" card game at that time.

1954-1957

CHAPTER 13

The White House Detail
August 1954 -July 1957

I returned to work after my leave on Friday, August 27. As of that date, I was assigned permanently to the White House detail which at that time was operating out of Denver, Colorado. My first trip with Ike of any importance was a trip that took us to Missoula, Montana; Pendleton, Oregon; Walla Walla, Washington; and Los Angeles, California. When we got to L.A., I was able to see all of my agent friends from the L.A. office. Mr. Spaman had made arrangements to lend me a car after my assignment was over, and I was able to see my good friend, Stan Moore, and his mother, who met me at my parents home. After the assignment in Los Angeles was completed, we returned to Denver. Then on October 16, we returned to Washington, D.C. I had been gone a month and a half, and I barely recognized baby Diane, who had grown a great deal.

On October 23, I took my first of many trips to Gettysburg, Pennsylvania with the president who was involved in the purchasing of a very old farm located on a portion of the Gettysburg Battlefield. This was where the Confederate troops met and formed up for Picket's Charge during the last days of the Gettysburg Battle.

Though 1954 was an off year politically, Ike did some politicking for several GOP lawmakers. On October 29, we departed Washington, making stops in Cleveland, Detroit, Louisville, and Wilmington, Delaware. At each stop, Ike made a campaign speech. It was a long, tiring trip and we were grateful that Ike didn't do too much of that. November 10 and 11 saw us in Abilene, Kansas, where Ike celebrated the groundbreaking for his new presidential library. November 24, we took off for Augusta, Georgia, where Ike played golf on the Master's course for five days. That was the first trip to Augusta for me, but there were many more over the next three years. There were also be many trips to Camp David, which was the old Shangri La of President Roosevelt. Ike had renamed it in the name of his grandson, David Eisenhower.

December 23, we left for Augusta and stayed there for Christmas and New Years, returning to Washington on January 2, 1955. February 10, 1955, we took off for Thomasville, Georgia, and the home of Secretary of Treasury Humphrey. Ike spent five days bird hunting, and we agents spent those days on horseback, patrolling the outer area of the farm. Some fun! On May 1, Shirley Ann, the two children, and I took off for a trip to Canada and New England, visiting Niagara Falls,

Toronto, and the St. Lawrence River. We were able to go through each of the New England States, and even though it was a fast trip, we thoroughly enjoyed it.

It was shortly thereafter that Shirley's brother, Robert, and his wife, Myrtle, came to stay with us. They were our first official visitors to Arlington, but definitely not our last. We loved entertaining visitors as it gave us an opportunity to escort them around Washington. Soon, we had so many people who came to visit us that we put together an agenda to follow, depending upon the amount of days available. Most of the people who came were able to come with me to the White House at night to see the Oval Office, as well as other parts of the West Executive Office Building.

On June 5, we took off for New York. It was the 40th anniversary of Ike's graduation from West Point. While there, I got the opportunity to speak with General Omar Bradley, who has always been one of my World War II heroes. I also was able to speak with their fine football coach, Red Blaik, who told me I had the look of a person who had played a little football. I told him that I had and that I had one year of eligibility remaining. He asked me what it would take to get me signed up. I asked how much he would pay, but he just laughed.

On July 8, about ten of us were sent off to Switzerland for the meeting of the Big Four in Geneva (U.S., England, France and Russia). Talk about a coincidence: I was guarding the front gate of Ike's villa when Oly Tegner and some of his students from Pepperdine who were overseas studying in Lausanne, came driving up to the gate. What a great thing it was to see him!

One very interesting experience that I had during the time I spent in Geneva occurred one evening while I was on duty. President Eisenhower had invited Marshal Georgi Zhukov, of the Russian Army, for a conference at his villa. Zhukov and Eisenhower were comrades in arms from World War II and their conversation was spiced with their experiences when they had been allies fighting a common foe. But, when Mr. Eisenhower proclaimed that America was in favor of instituting a program of open skies wherein planes from each country could fly over other countries to see what was going on, the tone changed quickly—the Russians were strongly against such a policy. Marshal Zhukov was concerned that America was building air bases that were encircling the Soviet Union. Mr. Eisenhower confirmed that they were defensive measures only, and that America was not in the habit of starting wars. It was such a privilege to have heard these two famous generals discussing the great historical events in which they had been involved. My time in Geneva lasted a total of two weeks and it was such wonderful experience, especially because it was my first foreign assignment.

In August, we took off in our 1953 Nash, headed to California for a family vacation. We had a great trip taking the extreme southern route. Back home in L.A., we had a ball with many of our old friends and relatives.

My vacation ended on September 15, at which time I hopped a plane to Denver, where the president was staying at the Doud House. Shirley Ann and the kids stayed in L.A. continuing to visit friends and family. On the 19th, we spent the day in Fraser, Colorado, where Ike loved to fly fish and paint. On September 24, as I reported for my midnight shift, the lights were on in the Doud House. The word was that something was the matter with Mrs. Doud. But about 3 a.m., Agent Leonard Weiss and I were in the back yard talking when Mrs. Eisenhower called down to us that the president's doctor was coming in the back way through the alley. That was when we knew it wasn't Mrs. Doud at all, but rather Mr. Eisenhower who was ill.

Shortly thereafter, the doctor arrived. Several hours later, an ambulance was brought through the alley, and Mr. Eisenhower was carried downstairs and placed in the ambulance. He was taken directly to Fitzimmons Army Hospital, where it was determined that he had had a heart attack. We took turns working the hospital and the Doud House. During this period of time, I was able to read Ike's book, *Crusade in Europe*. He had given Mrs. Doud an autographed copy, and I was very privileged to have been able to read her copy.

On October 22, I flew back to L.A. to pick up my family. I was off until November 10, so we had a nice leisurely trip, going on an entirely different route than what we had ever taken. We stopped in Des Moines, Iowa, to see my old Pepperdine College football coach, Warren Gaer, who was then coaching at his Alma Mater, Drake University. After Des Moines, we headed to Chicago and got caught in a very heavy snowstorm. It was so bad that the highway direction signs had iced up and it was impossible to read them. We finally made our way out and ended up in Akron, Ohio, where we spent a bit of time with Paul and Eunice Dirks. Paul had accepted a position as an assistant minister in an Akron church. Eunice had gone to Pepperdine with us, had taught with Shirley Ann, and was Shirley Ann's maid of honor at our wedding.

Ike returned to the White House on November 11, and after several days there, we took off for Gettysburg, Pennsylvania and the farm, staying there until December 10. As this was a recuperating stay, Ike took no trips during that time. From December 20 to 27, we were at the White House. This gave the agents the opportunity to be at home for Christmas. What a privilege!

On December 28, we took off for Key West, Florida. When we left Washington, the temperature was in the teens, but when we arrived at the air base, close to Key West, it was in the 80s—a welcome change. Off time at Key West was magnificent. We played volleyball, fished, swam, and one day, the press people even challenged the agents to a softball game. It was pretty exciting— even the president showed up. We beat them badly, and I was able to hit a home run with the bases loaded to cinch the victory. One of the members of the press who was present was Bill Henry of the "Los Angeles Times." Bill and I had known each other from my Pepperdine days. He ended up writing a great column about the Secret Service, Pepperdine, and me. That was nice of him, but I'm pretty sure the only reason the story got printed was that there wasn't much else to report on in Key West at that time. They had to write about something—even Life magazine had a big spread about the game, complete with pictures.

On January 1, 1956, I was promoted from grade nine to grade ten, raising my salary from $5,710. per year to $5,915.

On April 9, 1956, we went to Augusta, Georgia for six days. Ike always went to Augusta immediately after the Masters Tournament. He invited the winner to remain there, playing with him for a week of intense golf. I believe that the winner of the Masters that year was Cary Middlecoff.

On June 16, our family took off on a two-week vacation. We spent the first week in Florida, and the headed for St. Louis to spend some time with Aunt Agnes and Cousin Freddy Krauss and his family. On our way to Key West, we stopped in Charleston, South Carolina, to see Virgil and Betty Snyder. They had been our neighbors in Arlington, and Virgil, who was still in the navy, was transferred to Small Craft in Charleston. We then continued to Cocoa, Florida—Merritt Island to be exact—where I located one of my favorite U.S. Navy buddies, Walter D. La Roche, who owned an orange grove on the island. We had dinner with Walter and his wife, Betty, and the next morning, we were off for Key West, Florida. We stayed there long enough for dinner and some famous Key Lime Pie. Then we backtracked up the keys to Islamirada, where we stayed for a few days. We had a nice pool for swimming and a dock facility for ocean swimming. I took Dar fishing for the first time and he caught two fish in less than a minute. Ever after that, he thought all fishing should be that easy. At one point on the trip, we thought Dar had the measles, but a trip to the doctor's office revealed that, in fact, he was just covered in mosquito bites.

After a few days at Islamirada, we left for St. Louis. The weather was so hot and humid along the way that we weren't sure it was even a good idea to continue on to St. Louis. When we finally arrived there, we were sure that we should have stayed in Florida. However, it was nice to see Aunt Aggie and Freddy, and they treated us royally. After a few days in St. Louis, we left for Washington and I headed back to work at the White House.

After spending about two years on White House detail, I was ready for a change. On July 15, I wrote a memo to my chief requesting a transfer to Phoenix, Sacramento, or Los Angeles in that order. My request, however, would go unanswered for almost a year.

On July 20, I flew to Panama for an Inter-American Conference. But since I was assigned the midnight shift, I wasn't able to observe much of the official activities, as I had been able to in Geneva the previous year.

On August 14, 1956, Agent Roy Kellerman and I were sent to Monterey, California, where we were to do the advance arrangements for the president. Prior to coming to Monterey, Ike would be at the Cow Palace in San Francisco, where the Republican Party was holding their National Convention. Of course, Ike and Nixon were chosen to run again, and after that function, everyone came down to Monterey on the train. This was to be a golf vacation for Ike. He stayed there for about five days, before returning to Washington. While in Monterey, my folks and Arline's family came up to visit me. We all had dinner together on the pier. It was very nice to see my family again. I was also able to visit with Bob Clark and his family. Bob was a fine basketball player at Pepperdine and was teaching and coaching in Monterey. The morning that Ike left Monterey, I was able to get Bob and his wife, Barbara, aboard the Columbine, which was Ike's airplane. That was a special perk available to us as Secret Service agents.

On October 9, I was sent to Portland, Oregon, with Arvid Dahlquist and Dale Grubb to advance the president's visit there. After about a week in Portland, we took off for Los Angeles, where we stayed for about two days before returning to Washington. These trips were all political trips, as Ike was running for re-election. Election Day was slated for November 6, but I was working nights so I wasn't able to get involved in any of the election festivities.

To finish the year of 1956, I should tell you of an incident that occurred in December. Everyone in America knew of Ike's delight in playing golf. He loved the game and did quite well at it. He would play every chance he had, spring, summer, fall and winter—no matter where he was. It was no secret that Ike's appearance at any golf course was worth a million dollars in advertisement and notoriety for that course. Ike's home course was Burning Tree Golf Course in Maryland, and whenever he was at the White House, he would play that course. Well, in December, most of the trees and bushes had lost their leaves and the course, generally verdant, was in the throes of winter. It's no secret that when Ike played golf, there would be several agents on the side of him about one stroke ahead, and one man about one and a half strokes ahead of him to make sure all was safe.

On this particular day, my position was the lead agent about one and half strokes ahead. After several holes, it was apparent that we were the only ones on the course, as it was extremely cold. But as I was walking in the middle of the fairway, I noticed some movement in the brush on the right hand side. I thought it might be an animal as it was not too unusual for deer and rabbits to frequent this course. I moved over to the area to verify my hunch. As I approached the tree where I had seen the movement, I saw some additional movement and quickly determined that it was not an animal at all, but a man. I cautiously approached the tree where the man was standing and I said in my most authoritarian voice, "Come out from behind that tree." At this time, all I could see was an elbow—a right arm elbow. Knowing that most men are right handed, I figured that to do any harm, that right elbow had to move. And if that right hand held a weapon, the person would have to move that arm in order to shoot.

When I first ordered the man to come out from behind the tree, I kept a very sharp eye on that elbow, and all throughout this episode, I was thankful that that elbow didn't move. I was able to jump over a fallen log and through some underbrush, and I drew my gun and again ordered the man to come out from behind the tree. And again, the elbow didn't move. Time now was imminent because the president and his party were rapidly approaching my area in their golf carts. I had to do something—now! I very quickly moved around to the front of the tree, on the opposite side of where I had been, and suddenly came face to face with the man. I pointed my gun at him and asked him what the hell he was doing there? He turned around and answered by pointing to his ears and saying "ehhhh?" I suddenly realized that he was about seventy-five year old and very hard of hearing!

I put my gun away, and again asked the old fellow, in a very loud voice, what was he doing there? He told me that he had been looking for golf balls. I told him that this was a private course and asked him to leave immediately. I watched him very closely as he took several steps away, very dejectedly. Then, he stopped, turned around and asked in a most cantankerous voice, "What the hell are you doing here, Sonny?" That experience ended in somewhat of a comical manner, but it certainly could have ended up in a very disastrous way.

On January 13, 1957, Ike took one last trip prior to his second inauguration. We left the White House and flew directly to San Angelo, Texas. The following day, we flew to Woodward, Oklahoma; Clovis, New Mexico; and ended up in Tucson, Arizona. The next day, we flew to Pueblo, Colorado, where our plane had a terrible mishap—our plane crashed through the apron of the taxi area. Before they could get another plane down to us, the plane was down to the superstructure. Several hours later, we flew to Wichita, Kansas, and then on to Washington.

On February 2, 1957, we flew down to Augusta, Georgia, for several days of golf. One night, while we were on the midnight shift, it rained six inches and the wind blew hard, and it was very cold. It was probably the most uncomfortable shift I experienced in my three years on the detail. On March 18, we headed to Bermuda for a meeting with the British. The weather was warm, rainy and windy. We were there for five days and it was a most enjoyable trip.

On April 18, we left for Augusta, Georgia, for Ike's time with the winner of the Masters. Augusta was a fun place to go. There were always golf facilities available for the agents, and we played almost each day.

On May 11, we went to the Farm at Gettysburg, Pennsylvania to work the midnight shift. The weather was magnificent. Around dinner time, Vince Mroz, a supervising agent, and I were standing post at the front door when the door opened and out came the president. He said, "Let's go down by the bass pond," so of course, Vince and I took off with him. As this was before the time that each agent carried his own radio, we couldn't advise anyone that we had left our post and that we were accompanying the president down to the pond. On the way down, we chatted about the weather and how nice it was. When we got to the pond, which was about fifty feet by a hundred feet, we noticed that there were two groundhogs on the other side of the pond running around, up and down the bank, and back into their holes.

When Ike saw them, he said, "OK guys, let's see how good you are." Well, this was certainly unusual. Vince and I looked at each other, pulled our 38s from our holsters, and took aim at the illusive groundhogs. I think that we both started firing about the same time and we each let six rounds go in about a second and a half. But sure enough, neither Vince nor I hit one groundhog. Boy were we embarrassed! But then, groundhogs are very difficult to hit with a pistol.

What we didn't realize was that when the other agents heard the twelve rounds go off, they thought that terrorists for certain were invading the farm. The entire shift came running down the road carrying machine guns, shot guns, rifles, and their own 38s, yelling to us trying to find out what was going on. When they arrived at the pond, Mr. Eisenhower explained how he had asked Vince and me to get him a groundhog and that we had failed miserably. He went on to say that he just might start carrying his old U.S. Army Colt 45 when Vince and I were on duty. Very funny, Mr. President.

On June 3, I received a memo transferring me back to Los Angeles as of August 12. Shirley Ann and I were delighted to be going home to be with relatives and friends.

One of my last assignments on the detail was on June 6. We flew to Mayport, Florida, for a two-day trip on the USS Saratoga, where the navy put on a tremendous show for the president, showing off all of their state-of-the-art equipment, Some of which were drone airplanes that were shot down by their latest smart missiles. I was lucky enough to film the exercise because I was on the midnight shift and had all day off. The last month that I was in D.C., I spent most of the time at the White House, the Gettysburg Farm, and Camp David. My very last shift at the White House was on July 19, where I spent my night wandering through the Gold, Blue and Green rooms, savoring the beauty and history emanating from them. It was sad, but I was certain that in my career I would be able to see these rooms again. And, it was true.

My family and I left Washington on Monday, July 22, in our 1956 dark blue Ford station wagon. We were sad to leave our fine neighbors. I was also quite sad to leave my fellow agents with whom I had served on White House detail: Pat Boggs, Vince Mroz, Arvid Dahlquist, Roy Kellerman, Floyd Boring, Frank Slocum, Dick Roth, and George Weisheit.

The first day of our trip home led us through Virginia, Maryland, Pennsylvania, and Ohio. We ended our first day in Akron, Ohio, where we stayed with Paul and Eunice Dirks. It was nice to see them again, and we enjoyed talking about old times in Los Angeles. Paul had gone to USC and then to a religious school in Dallas, Texas. After he graduated he was assigned to a church in Akron.

The next day, we turned north into Michigan over the Mackinac Straits to Upper Michigan. We traveled through Wisconsin and into Duluth, Minnesota, to visit Shirley Ann's uncle, John McBride, who was a professor at the local university. The next day we traveled through Minnesota, North Dakota, and ended up in Aberdeen, South Dakota. We spent some time with Sarah Herman's parents. Sarah had been our neighbor in Arlington, Virginia—some of the finest neighbors that we have ever had.

From Aberdeen, we traveled west into Wyoming, Montana, and Idaho, and then we dropped down into Utah. In the city of Provo, we stopped to have lunch in the park and to let the children swim in the street side canals. It was very hot and the children had a ball. After Provo, we took off for Las Vegas, where Shirley's sister, Charlotte Penn, lived with her family. A number of Shirley's family came up to meet us, and we had a great time.

When we arrived in Los Angeles, we stayed with Shirley's mother on 107th Street and I requested an additional two weeks vacation in order to look for and purchase a home. SAIC Spaman had advised me that I would be working in the Long Beach/Orange County areas, so we shopped for a home in Orange County, hoping that this would allow me to work out of my home a great deal of the time. We found a home in Anaheim that fit our needs, and we made a down payment. In the meantime, Shirley Ann had seen an article in the "Los Angeles Times" regarding the new subdivision of Rossmoor in the city of Los Alamitos. We decided that we would go to Rossmoor and look at the models. We went through the models and were very impressed. The price was right, we loved the model of our choice, and many other young families were buying in there. We decided immediately that we would buy in Rossmoor and returned to Anaheim in order to retrieve our deposit. That was one of the best decisions we ever made

Our home wasn't going to be ready until the latter part of November, so we stayed with Shirley's mother until then. Little Dar started school at Woodcrest where his cousins, Roy Jr. and Ginger Thurman attended. Roy and Virginia Thurman were also staying at Mom McBride's home and they also ended up buying a home in Rossmoor, somewhat cater-corner to ours with about two feet of overlapping property. Roy made a gate through the wall and it was a very convenient situation.

1957-1977

CHAPTER 14

Los Angeles Field Office
Los Angeles, California
August 1957 - July 1977

I reported for duty to the Los Angeles Field Office on Monday, August 12, 1957. Little did I realize that I would spend the next twenty years there. Initially, I worked a great deal with a young, sharp agent named Lou Mayo. Coincidentally, Lou had also gone to Pepperdine for a short while during 1946-47, but surprisingly I didn't know him then. He lived close to Shirley's mother's home, so much of the time, we rode in to work together. He was a very good partner.

It was also nice to be working again with Agents Vic Carli, Leon Gopadze, Howard Sweeney, Frank Leyva, John Larson, Paul Henne, Jim Hirst, and Bill Bradshaw.

I was quickly assigned all types of cases in Long Beach and Orange County. I met Postal Inspector Kenneth B. Daws and his assistant, Chan Dee, who were assigned to the Long Beach Office of the Postal Inspectors. They were tremendous partners! We made many arrests together, particularly on U.S. Treasurer check cases. We also had the advantage having Ralph Bradford at the Long Beach Police Department. Brad was an examiner of questioned documents and was always available to talk over a case—his favorite expression was "Have you tried this?" He was fun to work with and certainly helped Ken and me in our investigations. Brad and his son, Russell, were excellent photographers as well, so whenever we stumbled upon a counterfeiting plant, we called on them to come down and take photos. Some of their photos even appeared in the "Long Beach Press Telegram."

On December 3, 1957, we moved into our new home in Rossmoor. Were we excited! Dar immediately started school, and Diane stayed home with Shirley Ann. Some of our neighbors were Roy and Virginia Thurman, Donald and Shirley Coscarelli, and later, Bob and Charlotte Kelley, and Bruce and Betty Cordary. Not only were these people great neighbors, but they became life long friends.

1958

CHAPTER 15

Los Angeles Field Office 1958

February 1958 saw Shirley Ann resuming her teaching career, this time in the Long Beach District. She taught there for a year and a half. A part of this time, Dar and Diane went to a private school called Country Day School in Huntington Beach.

On February 23, 1958, I went to Phoenix to assist in the visit of Mrs. Eisenhower, who was staying at the Maine Chance Ranch. I was fortunate to again work for Mr. Walker, who was still SAIC there. I also worked with Pat Boggs, who by that time had taken over the Albuquerque Office. He had been sent to the Phoenix Office in order to help Mr. Walker with the advance arrangements. I was in Phoenix for fifteen days, working the midnight shift as the supervising agent. A very sad note about this trip was that Mr. Walker suffered a stroke after Mrs. Eisenhower departed. He was taken to the Veteran's Hospital, where a short time later he passed away. I lost a very fine friend that day.

Back I went to Los Angeles, returning to the ever mounting check cases. During that period, Agent Frank Slocum and I worked together on many occasions. Frank and I had been on the detail together in D.C. for almost two years. When his time was up there, he called me and asked me how it was working in Los Angeles. I told him what I thought, and it wasn't long thereafter that Frank was transferred to L.A. Of all the agents with whom I worked, Frank was tops. I knew that when we went out on a case, things were going to happen. We worked in Los Angeles together until about 1967, when Frank was transferred to Honolulu as the SAIC. I went to Honolulu on a number of occasions, mostly on protective assignments. We remain the closest of friends, and I always think of Frank as the greatest of the "can do" agents. He continues to live in Hawaii and we call each other every month or so.

The year 1958 went by very quickly. It was great to get back into criminal investigations. At that time, our office was so busy that agents had very little time to sit down and figure out what would be the best tack in solving a case. Sometimes, you were able to do that, but mostly you just put out fires as they erupted. In 1958, I certainly didn't travel as much as I did on the detail. Still, I did take trips to Phoenix, San Diego, Bakersfield, Port Hueneme, and a trip to Blythe and Needles. I also recall that I was working a great variety of cases, as a journeyman agent should, and that I was being called upon to make a number of speeches.

There was one case I should tell you about. It broke on December 9 at Milikan High School in Long Beach. The cafeteria had been receiving a number of counterfeit coins during lunchtime. I was called there to investigate. I interviewed the principal, several assistants, the metal shop teacher, as well as the person in the cafeteria who had accepted the coins. She was sure she could identify the passer, so we obtained a copy of the yearbook. We leafed through it and she was able to say for a fact that a certain person had done the dastardly deed. The metal shop teacher was also able to say that the suspect had been a member of one of his metal shop classes. Some of the other people said that if "Boy A" was involved, "Boy B" would certainly also be involved. It was quickly determined that both boys took metal shop at the same time.

The boys were brought in and shown the coins, and both admitted that they had been involved. They had been making sand molds and needed something to use as patterns. So they used some pocket change they had. The coins weren't the greatest of counterfeit coins but apparently were good enough to pass at the cafeteria when it was busy. One of the boys related that after they had made the coins and filed off the surplus metal, he had taken them to the teacher and showed him what they had made. According to the youngster, the teacher had said "My God, get rid of them." And they did. They bought a couple of hamburgers, several malts, and some French fries.

We were able to talk to the boys about the seriousness of what they had done. The U.S. Attorney in L.A. declined to prosecute them, but the Juvenile Division of the Long Beach Police Department did charge them. That should have been the end of the story, but several months later, I read an article in the Long Beach paper where several youngsters had made a pipe bomb by cutting off match heads and pounding them into a pipe. Unfortunately, the match heads ignited prematurely, blowing the pipe apart, as well as part of the hand of one of the boys—this boy was one of the boys who had been involved in the making of the coins. A very sad ending to the story.

1959

CHAPTER 16

Los Angeles Field Office
1959

The year 1959 turned out to be a good one. Work in the LAFO continued at a hectic pace. We had our share of counterfeiting cases and more than our share of visits by Vice President Nixon. At home, Shirley Ann left the Long Beach School District and began teaching in the Los Alamitos School District. Dar was now in the second grade and Diane was in kindergarten. Shirley Ann taught with several other teachers who became life long friends, Keith and Joan Sharpe, notably. Keith and I started playing softball for the Sugar Shack in Los Alamitos. Keith had a sixteen-foot boat that was really a scow, but what a fishing scow it was. For years, we fished in that boat and probably caught about a million fish. (What did you expect from a fisherman?) Later, we bought a nineteen-foot boat, strictly for fishing. We often invited many of the agents of the LAFO to join us on our fishing expeditions.

The year was a banner year for friends. You will remember my good friend Lou Corso, from Nightingale School in Venice in 1936. I thought Lou had remained in the L.A. area, so I made a concerted effort to locate him. He was living in Torrance and working in Inglewood, and I have to admit that it should have been a lot easier to find him as his name was in the telephone book all the time—some great investigator! Suffice to say that I found his home in Torrance and spoke to his wife, Jane. She was somewhat suspicious, but when I mentioned going to school with Lou in Venice, she agreed to take my card and to have Lou call me. By the time I got back to the office, Lou had called. We quickly rekindled our friendship, which continues today. What a great addition his friendship has been to my life throughout the years. Every January 1, we meet and suffer the agony of defeat or the ecstasy of winning the Rose Bowl game. Both of us are Pacific Ten fans and our New Year starts off very good or very bad, depending upon the score of the game.

Soon after I located Lou, I told Keith Sharpe of Lou's interest in fishing. Keith suggested that we invite him out, and soon Lou became an integral member of the fishing group. Keith and Lou have become very good friends. It's nice when two of your good friends become good friends too.

On June 5, we started preliminary interviews regarding an extensive visit Nixon was planning. Advance arrangements had to be made at Disneyland, Whittier College, Whittier Friends Church, Knott's Berry Farm, Nixon's birth house in Yorba Linda, and the Disneyland Hotel.

Mr. Nixon arrived on June 13 and on the 14th, he inaugurated the Monorail and the Submarine rides at Disneyland. Nixon traveled to so many places on that trip that almost every agent in the office was involved in his protection. We worked day and night, and were very glad when he left on June 15 for San Diego.

On June 22, I worked with Agent Jim Hirst on a case where we had received information that a certain person, name unknown, but driving a certain car with a known license number would be meeting at a specific place looking to manufacture counterfeit notes. We were at the listed meeting place and observed the suspect. A quick check of DMV records revealed the owner of the vehicle and the listed address. We were able to observe the suspect depart the meeting area, but we very quickly lost him in traffic. We decided to head for the suspect's residence. We weren't there two minutes when the suspect arrived. It turned out that he was an artist and had no equipment for the counterfeiting of currency. He had only just been considering the idea of counterfeiting when we were tipped off, so I'll bet he thought that the Secret Service had eyes in the back of their heads to know what he was thinking about.

On July 3, Nixon returned to Los Angeles. This time, we had functions at the Los Angeles Arena, which was newly built, the Coliseum, Hollywood Park Race Track, and at his mother's home in East Whittier. He departed on July 5, after a very strenuous visit.

The year 1959 closed out with a bang as Nixon had been chosen as the Grand Marshal of the Rose Parade in Pasadena. He arrived early on December 31, so we were deeply involved in the pre-parade activities. We attended the football luncheon and then ended the day by going to the float area to see the final work on the floats.

1960

CHAPTER 17

Los Angeles Field Office 1960

Early on January 1, we took Nixon to the Wrigley Home in Pasadena for breakfast. We had to get the motorcade cars clear across Pasadena to the end of the parade route in order to pick him up at the conclusion of the parade. After that, we took him to the Brookside Country Club for lunch, then over to the Rose Bowl for the football game. We had the best seats in the house—first row on the fifty-yard line. At the end of the game, we drove him to the Huntington Sheraton Hotel, where he was staying.

The next day, we took him to the Los Angeles Country Club, where he played a round of golf. After that, we took him to his mother's home in Whittier. He departed the following day, which ended another very busy visit from the vice president. I would be remiss if I didn't mention that on his visits, several LAPD officers from the Bunco-Fugitive Squad always assisted us, including Sergeants John DiBetta and Ken Scarce. Sometimes Detective Carlton Clarke would assist us as well. Later, we worked with detectives from the Robbery Squad, Robby Roberson, and Dick Unland.

It would be appropriate to mention at this time that a young fellow named Bob Haldeman began to show up in our advance arrangement logs. He would later become an integral member of Nixon's White House staff. With all of the staffs with which I worked, Nixon's White House staff was the worst I experienced. It was somewhat satisfying when members of that staff were tried, convicted, and sent to prison. They deserved it.

I should mention here a personal friend of mine, Robert Finch. We had gone to school together from the seventh grade through high school in Inglewood. Bob became Nixon's chief organizer in Los Angeles and ultimately went back to Washington, D.C. as his chief of staff. When Nixon was running for the presidency and was seeking a vice presidential running mate, Bob was offered the job but turned it down. After the election, he did go back to Washington, D.C., and held various high level appointed positions. But Bob didn't get along with Haldeman and Erlichman, and I was glad to hear that he was leaving that group to return to Pasadena and continue his law practice. Bob was never tainted by what had gone on with the Nixon Staff.

Before leaving 1959, I should mention one of the most successful counterfeiting cases I had ever experienced. We started to get hit with a new $20 note in L.A., as well as up the coast as far as San Luis Obispo. On February 5, a man named Franklin Foster drove into Sally's Drive-in at La Brea and Arbor Vitae Avenue in Inglewood. He was in a 1949 Ford and accompanied by several of his children. When he went to pay, the waitress thought the note looked odd and showed it to a supervisor. The supervisor called the Inglewood Police Department. Detectives John Tanneyhill and Roy Schaefer responded and took Foster and his family into custody.

Agent James Leckey and I met the detectives at the Inglewood Police Station. Foster admitted that he had been passing notes that he had received from a man named Haidl. Foster even identified the places he had passed notes and took us to his contact, Haidl, that night in an attempt to make a buy of counterfeit notes. Leckey and I hid in the bushes close to the front door and heard the conversation between Foster and Haidl. Haidl said that he didn't have any notes available that night, but agreed to bring some to Foster's work the following afternoon.

We processed Foster quickly with a low bond in order to get him to Gardena in time for the meet. Haidl was very prompt, and when Foster gave the signal that he had received additional notes from him, four cars full of agents roared into the station and arrested Haidl. But Haidl had brought his six-year-old son along, and when we came screaming in, the son thought we were going to kill his father. We had more difficulty comforting the son than we had arresting the father.

Like Foster, Haidl desired to cooperate, and we put in a call to his contact, a man known as "Huggie." A meeting was set up for the following day at the Wich Stand at Florence and Figueroa. Leckey was assigned the undercover work, and he did a great job at it. He was able to convince Huggie that he was a high roller who could buy notes in large batches. As soon as money exchanged hands, Leckey gave the signal and the guys screamed in to make the bust. Huggie became our third defendant on three levels of this counterfeit hierarchy.

Like the others, Huggie cooperated, identifying the manufacturer and the moneyman behind the entire venture. The rest was easy. Huggie set up a meeting for purchasing notes at a print shop out on Sunset Blvd. When the buy occurred at the print shop, we searched it but came up with no hard proof. One of the defendants advised us that the plates and negatives were in his car at his home. Leckey and I went to that location, found the car on the street, searched it and came up with everything that was used to make the notes.

What a great success story—a five-level case where people from all levels were identified and arrested. When all was said and done, we had arrested five people and seized six vehicles. Everyone in the LAFO worked on it and Agent Leckey did an excellent job. Like so many of our cases, it all started when the Inglewood detectives responded to the call of a possible counterfeit note.

In the early part of 1960, Agent Harry More and I worked together quite often. Harry had followed me to the D.C. detail and had come back to L.A. in 1959. It was Harry who was responsible for me returning to my master's program at USC, which I had left in 1953. Harry remained with the Secret Service for a short time thereafter, and then resigned to accept a teaching position in law enforcement in Pennsylvania. He ultimately went to Washington State University in Pullman and received his doctorate degree from the University of Idaho at Moscow. As a result of Harry's insistence, I received my master's degree from USC in 1967.

1960 was an election year and thus was very busy. On October 21 and 22, we were in San Diego for President Eisenhower's last visit to California as president. He delivered a speech at the Chula Vista Country Club on behalf of Nixon who was running for the presidency.

On October 31, SAIC Spaman, Agent More, and I went up to Fresno where Nixon was going to spend some time in the San Joaquin Valley. Nixon arrived there on November 4 and had a whirlwind visit. More took care of the arrival at the Fresno Airport and brought him to the Manchester Shopping Center where I was. There was a large crowd, and very frankly, we lost control of them. We were extremely shorthanded and I was the only Secret Service agent on duty prior to the arrival. The crowd inundated Nixon's car, and one fellow got his foot caught in the well of the convertible that we were using as a limo. But, the Nixons loved it! It showed that there was a lot of positive feeling about his candidacy. After the shopping center, we took the Nixons to the California Hotel and then to KFRE- TV Station. We returned to the hotel for a few hours and then took him to the airport. Harry and I took off for Los Angeles as soon as we tied up all the loose ends.

The day after we returned to Los Angeles, More and I went out to the Ontario Airport to advance Nixon's arrival there. Then we went to Whittier to set up the polling place where Nixon was to vote that Tuesday. Nixon arrived late Monday night at Ontario Airport. The following morning, he voted and then took off for Tijuana, Mexico, escorted by Agent Sherwood, who was in charge of Nixon's detail and, Sgt. John DiBetta of the LAP.D. After a long and arduous campaign, he wanted a few hours to unwind. Late that afternoon, we returned to the Ambassador Hotel, where there was a great quantity of agents on hand preparing for the possibility of a "president-elect" detail, if Nixon was elected.

The election was very close, but by 11:30 p.m., it was the general belief that Kennedy had won. Nixon and his family went down to the "Victory Room" to show the flag, but I didn't go with them as they had plenty of men. I instead watched it on TV in the command post. It was a very sad experience. As I recall, Nixon waited until the next morning to advise the nation that it was probably true that he had lost the election. Nixon left Los Angeles the following day. I took off for about four days on annual leave, as did quite a few of the other agents. It had been a very difficult, time consuming experience.

Before 1960 closed, there were very important personnel changes that occurred in the LAFO. Our fine assistant agent in charge, Victor D. Carli, retired. Vic had been the number two man in the LAFO for quite some time, and he was always the person to whom the younger agents would go if they had a problem. As a young man in San Francisco, he began his career as a private detective, and then was hired by the old Bureau of Narcotics. He transferred to the Secret Service in the early 1930s and was sent to Los Angeles, where he spent the rest of his career devoted to counterfeit cases. How nice it was for him to choose me on a number of occasions to accompany him on investigations. It's no secret that I patterned my supervisory career after Vic Carli and Mr. Walker of the Phoenix office. After Vic Carli retired, Shirley Ann and I made a point to visit Vic in San Anselmo, where he had retired.

To replace Vic Carli as ASAIC, the Secret Service pulled SAIC Pat Boggs out of the Albuquerque office. I had worked with Pat when I was a very young agent in Los Angeles and then again at the White House detail. Pat had been called back to the detail for a second assignment, this time as the number two man on one of the shifts. Pat was always a person to whom you could go for good advice. He stayed in the LAFO for six years and was then transferred to the Chicago office as the special agent in charge—a well-deserved assignment for Pat Boggs.

1961

CHAPTER 18

Los Angeles Field Office 1961

The year 1961 was rather nondescript. It was nice, however, that some of us "younger" agents were now getting counterfeiting assignments and interviewing informants. Cases that were previously assigned only to the older agents like Carli, Gopadze, Sweeney, Bradshaw, and Hirst were now going to us.

A sign of the times became apparent to me in September when I was asked to go to Bakersfield. The Cold War was heating up; people throughout the U.S. were building bomb shelters in their yards. And I was to go to Bakersfield to make arrangements with the Kern County Sheriff's Office to relocate our office there in case of an atomic attack. That put things into perspective quickly for me!

Covering Long Beach and San Pedro, I was often meeting ships and interviewing ship personnel, mostly in regards to counterfeiting activities. On September 10, Agent Glenn Weaver, several U.S. Customs Agents, and I met at Berth 188 in Wilmington to board a ship named Saracens. We searched the ship as well as possible but didn't find any contraband. Unfortunately, search dogs were not common at that time, but we certainly could have used a couple of dogs on that assignment.

November 15, we began advance arrangements for President Kennedy. We spent the day interviewing people and checking out sites that the president would be visiting. On November 18, SA Milton Wilhite and I went to LAX to obtain the podium that the president used. After that, we went to the Los Angeles Country Club, where the president would be playing a round of golf. We then went to the Palladium, where people turned out to give the president a real Hollywood welcome. In case you are interested, I don't ever recall seeing Marilyn Monroe at any of these functions.

The year ended with SA Ken Thompson and I going to Las Vegas as the police there had arrested a passer of counterfeit notes. We left on December 24, worked all that day, night, and early morning of Christmas. The Las Vegas detectives had done a fine job and for us it was just a matter of picking up the notes and interviewing suspects and witnesses. I got back to Los Angeles on December 26, having entirely missed Christmas with Shirley Ann and the children. Unfortunate as it was, it was not an unusual occurrence in the Secret Service.

1962

CHAPTER 19

Los Angeles Field Office 1962

In contrast, the year 1962 came in like thunder. At one time, L.A. wasn't considered a busy office for counterfeiting, but suddenly that year, we found ourselves inundated with cases, arresting people from Los Angeles, to Long Beach, to Capistrano Beach, to Santa Monica.

One case in particular was the Chris Newcomb, David Harding and Bill Brining case that broke in Long Beach in June. SA Ken Thompson did the preliminary work and then Agents Bill Sheridan, Roger Grunwald, and I staked out a site on Atlantic Avenue, just south of Wardlow, where we suspected that the notes were being printed. During the first night of the stakeout, we observed nothing unusual. We continued surveillance the following morning, pretending to be car salesmen in an adjoining business lot to the suspected site. Finally, Chris Newcomb came out of the building, attempted to depart in his vehicle, but the three of us grabbed him before he went anywhere. The second suspect, Bill Brining, saw the whole thing out his window and quickly let the curtain fall back, covering the window. We cuffed Newcomb and quickly entered the building, where we arrested Brining. In a search of the building, we found the printing press, the photographic equipment, and several very large stacks of counterfeit bills located in the dark room. What we didn't know was that Newcomb had dug a hole underneath his garage floor where he was planning to set up his printing equipment and make additional notes.

A third defendant, David Harding, was not there and it took us several days to locate and arrest him. We were finally able to arrest David Harding, and prior to trial, we were able to arrest Newcomb a second time when he continued to be involved in counterfeiting activities while he was out on bond.

We were indebted to Ralph Bradford and his son, Russell, both of whom worked for the Long Beach Police Department. They helped in the search of the plant as well as the taking of some very professional photos.

We went to trial on all three defendants, but convicted only Chris Newcomb—Brining and Harding were acquitted. It was somewhat difficult to lose two defendants in a counterfeiting case. That doesn't happen very often in the Secret Service. However, several years later, David Harding again came to our attention in a counterfeiting case, and this time, we were able to convict him. Brining led a good life after his experience. I ran into him at the Long Beach Airport in 1965. I spoke with him for a short while, and he introduced me to his son. He told his son said that I was responsible for straightening him out.

In l980, I received a call from Al Joaquin, a Los Angeles agent, who advised me that they had arrested Newcomb again. I think that may have been his fourth arrest for counterfeiting—some counterfeiters never learn. It's true that the manufacturing of counterfeit notes does become a disease for some people. While they are spending their years in prison for making notes, they are planning their next experience in the great world of counterfeiting. This is one of the reasons why the Secret Service developed a program of watching former counterfeiters when they have been released from prison.

Before we leave the year 1962, I believe it would be appropriate to insert a story about one of the most renown of all counterfeiters that the Secret Service has ever known. I put this in the year 1962 because that is the year in which he was released from prison. His name was Marion John Williams, and he was born sometime around 1909. His release date in 1962 resulted from his fifth arrest in the counterfeiting of our currency. The following is Marion John William's story:

In 1924, at the age of nineteen, Marion John was living in Seattle and was without a job. In the need of fast money, he got the bright idea to counterfeit $1 coins. He made coins that were of exquisite quality, but even so, they were quickly identified as counterfeit. He was arrested, found guilty, and sentenced to sixty days in the county jail. Marion John did his time easily, and at the end of the sixty days, he was released.

Back in society and still without a job, Marion John again returned to counterfeiting $1 coins. In 1926, he was arrested a second time. This time, the judge sentenced Marion John to five years in a federal prison. Marion John again did his time very well. He became a model prisoner, and for his good behavior, his sentence was terminated early.

Again unable to cope with the outside world, still in Seattle and unemployed, Marion John began counterfeiting yet again. In 1932, he was arrested for the third time, and this time sentenced to eight years in a federal prison, which was again reduced for good behavior. Now this was about the time that the U.S. was beginning to become involved in World War II and jobs became plentiful—except for Marion John. In 1943, at the height of World War II, Marion John again entered the counterfeit field. This time, he made counterfeit $10 and $20 bills of exquisite quality, as were all of his counterfeits. This time, when he was captured, the judge sentenced him to a ten-year-period in a federal prison, where he served about six years of the ten-year sentence.

In 195l in Seattle, there appeared some new counterfeit $10 and $20 notes. These were quickly identified as the work of Marion John William. He was swiftly apprehended, found guilty, and this time the judge sentenced him to fifteen years—the maximum sentence in counterfeiting. This time, Marion John served eleven years and was released in 1962. It is no secret that the Secret Service likes to keep in touch with former counterfeiters like Marion John Williams. After all, he was one of our best customers. The Seattle office kept a pretty close watch on him, but on one dark and stormy night in 1970, Marion John escaped the surveillance team and was off and running to parts unknown. Unfortunately for me, his car was found several weeks later in Long Beach, which meant he had suddenly become my business.

It wasn't too long after the car was found that there appeared a brand new counterfeit $20 note of exquisite quality. We sent several of the phony bills to the lab in Washington. Quickly, the lab advised us that it was indeed the work of Marion John Williams. So the hunt was on. We distributed circulars, interviewed several people who had accepted the notes, but we always came up with a big fat zero. It appeared as though Marion John was going about his business very wisely. He wasn't passing too many at one time, just about enough to live, to eat, and to pay his rent. When counterfeiters become greedy and pass too many notes in an area in a short time, they are bound to get caught. But Marion John knew this well, and for a year or so, he was very successful.

In 1972, Marion John Williams was living in a small apartment in the rear of a residence in Long Beach. He had befriended a young man who was down on his luck, allowing him to stay with Marion John in his small apartment. One day while Marion John was out passing notes, the young man stayed at home. In looking around the apartment, he found a box of $20 bills. The box was full of notes that Marion John had made but had ruined in some manner, so he wasn't about to try to cash any of them. The young man was not aware of what Marion John had been doing and merely saw a box of $20 bills. He helped himself to a handful, stuffed them into his pocket, and took off for a large mall in Downey. He passed quite a few of them successfully. But in one five- and ten-cent store, the very young clerk looked at the tendered note and thought that it looked odd. She showed the note to her supervisor, who immediately called the Downey Police Department. Several officers came and arrested the passer.

When the officers determined that the note was counterfeit and that the passer had some more of them on him, our office was called. Agents responded, and in interviewing the passer, determined that the passer lived with an old man he called Uncle John. The passer agreed to take the agents to the apartment. Seeing no activity there, they went to the front house, where they found a very old Marion John Williams. Williams was arrested for counterfeiting for the sixth time. In searching the apartment, the agents found his very unusual plates, made of glass, and etched using the sun. Williams was very cooperative and admitted what he had done. He was ultimately sentenced to three years at Terminal Island Prison. He was out in about half that time. There was no other indication that Marion John Williams ever attempted to reenter the counterfeit field after his last release from prison. So ends the story of one of America's master counterfeiters.

Another counterfeiting story I would like to tell you about is one that occurred many years ago in the 1930s. It was known to the Secret Service agents who worked the case as "the case of Mr. 880". There was even a movie made of it. It was a classic case, not because of the quality of the notes like Marion John Williams, but because the notes were so bad. It all started in New York City sometime during 1932. The counterfeiter was a man named Emerich Juettner. Juettner was born about 1875, making him about 57 years old when he entered the counterfeit arena. Born in Eastern Europe, Juettner came to America in the 1920s. Without a job and little opportunity to acquire one, he got the bright idea that he would make counterfeit money. He made $1 bills only, and spent about ten to fifteen of them each week. He passed them mainly in bars, at the subways, and in five- and ten-cent stores, passing only enough to survive. He printed some of his notes on the old style tablet paper, green in color with lines drawn across it for assisting the writer for neatness. On some of the bills, he had even misspelled Washington, D.C., as Wahsington, D.C. That should have been a major tip-off to people who accepted them. Juettner operated in New York City from 1932 to 1948, and during that period of time, I'd estimated that he passed a little more than $5,000 worth.

However, in 1948, Juettner's luck ran out. One day, when he was out passing notes, his apartment caught fire and the fire department responded. During this process, the firemen threw a number of items out the window that they thought might catch fire. When the fire was all out, the firemen left, not bothering to retrieve the items that they had thrown from the apartment. In the meantime, a tremendous winter blizzard hit New York City. It very quickly covered up all of the items that had been thrown from the apartment. Several weeks later, a spring thaw hit the city. Several young boys were playing in the alley one day and stumbled onto one of the plates. A quick investigation revealed it to be a copper plate of a $1 bill, and that's when the Secret Service was called. Agents Sam Collaghan and Tom Burke responded. Their investigation revealed that there had been a fire in one of the apartments, and that items had been thrown from the window. Juettner was located and agreed to a search of his apartment. The agents found over twenty-five counterfeit notes, as well as other plates, negatives, and ink that had been used to print the notes. For all of his counterfeit activity, Juettner received nine months in jail. His notes continued to show up in the banking system for a number of years, and the last one was found on May 7, 1973 at a bank in New Jersey. So ends the saga of Mr. 880

The year 1962 faded into history and we were now facing the new year of 1963. What a tumultuous year it would turn out to be.

1963

CHAPTER 20

Los Angeles Field Office 1963

Counterfeiting remained a high priority and the amount of counterfeiting increased. This meant that our time spent in court and in preparing for the cases also increased. Working with the assistant U.S. Attorneys was always a good team effort. So very many of the fine attorneys in the Los Angeles area began their law careers in the office of the U.S. Attorney. Some of them even became the U.S. Attorney and many of them have graduated to become judges on the municipal, superior and federal levels.

On July 26, Earle Harding, brother of David Harding was arrested when he and another defendant tried to sell Agent Tom Behl negatives of counterfeit $20 notes. During the interrogation, Chris Newcomb was named. Agents Bob Tomsic, Larry Hess, and I went out and arrested Newcomb again. He had to know that someone talked because we were able to find negatives of $20 notes in his home very quickly. Some time later, Earle's brother, David, again became involved in counterfeiting while living in San Diego. Later, on a trip to Los Angeles, he was arrested again.

October 14 saw the beginning of a very large counterfeiting case in the South Bay. A fairly good $20 note began to appear in San Pedro, Wilmington, and Lomita. Quickly, a suspect by the name of Robert Boehm was identified as a passer.

The great Frank Slocum and I partnered up once again. We picked up a number of the notes from banks and businesses, and soon were able to identify a William Pearson as another passer. We found out where he lived, staked him out for a while, and arrested him late on October 21. That's when things began to fall apart for this counterfeiting group. We were able to locate the photography shop in Long Beach where the negatives were made. We then discovered that they had been printed by a pressman named Robert Spencer, who worked for the News Pilot, a local paper in San Pedro. Nyler Davis was one of the passers and distributors of this note. When we got close to him, he put the word out that he wouldn't be taken alive and that he'd take as many down with him as possible. We found out where he was staying, and on October 30, Agent Milton Wilhite and I staked out his house. When he came home, we let him park his car, and when he got out, Wilhite and I got out of our car, drew down on him and told him to climb his car. He knew what we meant and very quickly we cuffed him and had him in custody. It turned out to be an easier arrest than I was expecting considering all his tough talk. I was glad to have Milt Wilhite along that day, as he was a very good marksman.

The following day, we arrested the photographer, a man named Cruz, who had worked at the photography shop in Long Beach. His arrest was interesting because it had resulted from asking the owner of the photography shop, "Who is the photographer here who works nights?" Cruz was very quickly identified as that person.

During this time, several youngsters playing in a culvert on Western Avenue, north of 19th Street in San Pedro, found a box. The box contained notes, negatives, and plates. Some of the notes were given to various friends of the boys. Some were being passed in the local stores in the south part of San Pedro. On one of the plates, there was a perfect imprint of a thumb. Undoubtedly, it belonged to the person who had made the plates. We had a good idea who the printer was by this time, and if we could compare his prints with the print on the plate, we would be in business. We didn't have any luck finding a record of him in any of the local police departments, but we did find that he had a misdemeanor traffic warrant at the Los Angeles Police Department. Detectives from the San Pedro Harbor Division of the Los Angeles Police Department agreed to go and arrest the suspect at the News Pilot. They brought him on a warrant, fingerprinted him, and gave us the print cards. We took them immediately to Ralph Bradford at the Long Beach Police Department, who was an expert in fingerprints. It all worked out according to plan, and Bradford confirmed that we had the right guy. We went back to the LAPD in San Pedro where they released Spencer to us. We took him to the LAFO for interrogation.

Spencer admitted everything, plus identified an area in the San Pedro Marina where he had dumped many of his plates. Again the LAPD became involved because they had a diving group who volunteered to retrieve the plates. They were very successful in finding the plates from the murky waters of the marina. Interestingly, one of the members of that fine diving team was a young officer named Johnny Clapp, with whom I had gone through the LAPD Academy in 1949.

November 23, 1963—the day that President Kennedy was shot in Dallas. The day actually started out as a very normal day for me—little did I know what it would turn into. I picked up Agent Wilhite at his home about 8 a.m., and we went down to Pierpoint Landing, where we disposed of a multitude of coin slugs. We were in the office by 9:15 a.m., did a few perfunctory duties, and left again at 10:30 to go to Cheli Air Force Base in Maywood, to dispose of a printing press that we had seized in a counterfeiting case.

Then it happened: we heard the news flash on the radio advising that President Kennedy had been shot. We scrambled back to the office and some of us immediately started to go through files that we had in relation to people who had shown unusual interests in President Kennedy. But it was soon apparent that none of our subjects could have been involved in the assassination. A short time later, we heard that the president had died. We were stunned. Nothing like this had ever happened during our careers in the Secret Service.

We were expecting the Washington office to begin hammering us with tasks right away, but as it turned out, not a single request came through to our office that sad day. We all went home around 5 p.m. feeling rather helpless. But then, about 6 p.m., the office did receive a call with information regarding the telescopic sight that was used on the assassination rifle. It was a scope made in Japan with the inscription "Hollywood Optics" on it. ASAIC Pat Boggs phoned me immediately, requesting that I find out as much as possible regarding "Hollywood Optics." I met Agent Fred Clarke in Hollywood and together we began our investigation to determine if that scope had, in fact, come through the Los Angeles area.

The first Hollywood Optic store we located had gone out of business, but we quickly learned that there was another one on Hollywood Blvd. in the main part of Hollywood. By the time we arrived there, it must have been about 11 p.m., and Hollywood Optics had long been closed for the day. Peering in through the window, I saw an emergency number listed on a placard just inside the door. So, we called the number, identified ourselves, and told the person a little bit about the investigation. To say the least, he was skeptical of our story, but did agree to come down and meet with us. It had been a crazy day and you couldn't blame a person being a little suspicious. He had arranged for an LAPD officer to escort him to meet us at his place of business.

Upon arrival, he assured us that his Hollywood Optics did not deal in Japanese made telescopic sights that could be used to assassinate a president. He couldn't recall any other Hollywood Optics in the area other than the one that had gone out of business some time before. With midnight approaching and this line of questioning going straight into a dead-end, Agent Clarke and I called it a night.

The following morning, I went to LAPD Robbery Division and met with Lt. Pena and Sgt. Gonzalez, who were both extremely cooperative. We checked the literature that they had and called a number of their informants. Some time later, we were able to identify Ordnance Optics at 11029 Washington Blvd., Culver City, as the probable supplier of the telescopic sight used in Dallas. With the two detectives, we went to Ordnance Optics and interviewed the owner, Martin Retting. He not only had the type of scope used in the assassination, but he also had a gun that was similar to the one that Oswald had used. Mr. Retting showed us paper work that revealed that Oswald's scope had gone through his business. Later that scope was sent to Fields in Chicago, from where it was determined Oswald had bought it. Thanks to LAPD detectives Pena and Gonzalez, this proved to be a very successful day.

The following day, Agents Robert Heyn, Tom Behl, Milton Wilhite, George Sheaks, and I took off to Washington, D.C., to assist in the burial of the president. Agent Charles Taylor, an old friend of mine from the Washington Field Office days, and I were assigned surveillance from an adjoining hillside of the burial site at Arlington National Cemetery. The following day, I was on duty at the Capitol for a formal function, after which I was released from duty and sent back to L.A., ending a very sad and difficult experience.

However, that wasn't the end of our part of the investigation regarding the assassination. On November 29, I went out to Terminal Island Prison in order to interview an informant regarding Jack Ruby, but nothing much materialized from that interview. It's not unusual that after such a dastardly occurrence, people come out of the woodwork with ideas and thoughts. You can't ignore the calls because you never know which one will be true. From that time forward, during almost every speech I ever made for the Secret Service, questions about the Kennedy assassination arose, particularly regarding a conspiracy. Even though there have been many books written about the assassination—many of them expounding theories of conspiracy between Oswald, Ruby, Fidel Castro, the Mafia, and/or the communist party—so far there has been no concrete evidence to associate any of the above with a conspiracy involving Lee Harvey Oswald. You must be aware that some books have been written based on a theory that the authors have simply concocted in order to sell books. There have even been several movies based on conspiracy theories, but nothing tangible has emanated from any of the movies. I'm sure that questions and theories about the Kennedy assassination will continue to linger.

I knew most of the agents who were in Dallas that day from my days on the detail. Roy Kellerman was in charge that day and was riding in the right front seat of the limousine. Bill Greer was driving. Rufus Youngblood was with Vice President Johnson two cars back. Most of the men riding the follow-up car were newer agents who had joined the detail after I left. Some of the agents were affected so dramatically by the experience that they needed professional counseling. A few of them even felt completely responsible for what had occurred. This is pure nonsense: given the circumstances of the shooting, there was little they could have done. I can understand their intense feeling toward what happened to the president, but for them to think they were totally responsible for what happened is not correct.

I had an opportunity to go through the presidential limo with Roy Kellerman while I was in Washington for the burial services. There was an imprint on the inside of the windshield, where a portion of a bullet had struck it. This imprint was directly between where Roy Kellerman and Bill Greer were seated. They were lucky not to have been struck.

To show you how incidents can change your life, listen to this story: Gerry Behn was the agent in charge of the White House detail. Roy Kellerman was his assistant. Stu Knight was the agent in charge of Vice President Johnson's detail. Gerry Behn opted not to go on the Texas trip and had Kellerman go in his place. When Stu Knight heard that Gerry Behn wasn't going, he told his assistant, Rufus Youngblood, that because Behn wasn't going, he wouldn't go either. As it happened, Youngblood became a great hero due to his bravery in Dallas, and he experienced a meteoric rise in his career as a result. This is not to say that Stu Knight would not have acted in a like manner—knowing Stu, I rather think he would have. It didn't hurt Stu Knight's career that badly because he ultimately became the director of the Secret Service. It did, however, have a negative result on Gerry Behn's career. He was transferred to an administrative position in Headquarters, which was very unusual, as he had no experience for that assignment. He had been on the detail for many years, and was very good at what he did. At the time Youngblood was promoted, Gerry Behn became the odd man out, which really wasn't fair to him. Again, politics had reared its ugly head in the Secret Service. Rufus Youngblood became the SAIC of the White House detail, and ultimately, he became the deputy director of the Secret Service.

The assassination also had a great impact on major policies within Secret Service. There was some talk about removing protection of the president from the Secret Service, and giving that responsibility to the Federal Bureau of Investigation. I don't know how true it was, but the rumor was that J. Edgar Hoover declined the offer. There was also a great demand to modernize; a demand for more personnel; and a demand that cooperation between the FBI and us be extended. Apparently, the FBI knew about Oswald, his living in Russia, and of his residence in the Dallas area. You never know what might have occurred if we had known these details about him. Probably, our Intelligence Division agents would have at least interviewed Oswald, as that would have been pretty typical protocol. What they would have done with the information retrieved from that interview is merely conjecture. But, it's interesting to think, "What if?"

The assassination had an impact on most of our careers as well. Larger branch offices, such as ours in L.A. were divided into squads with a designated squad leader. For us, that meant four of us were chosen to be squad leaders: John Larson for check forgery; Leon Gopadze for counterfeiting; Frank Slocum for intelligence; and I took over the Special Investigations Squad. I was thrilled with my new title as it came with a raise in status and pay. Not long after that, we all received another raise in grade to a GS 14. In less than a year or so, we jumped two very significant grades.

The year 1963 was almost over, but it wouldn't finish quietly. On December 31, Agents Behl, Cameron, Clarke, Hess, Heyn, Larson, Sheaks, Slocum, Wilhite, and I left for Dallas. President Johnson had indicated that he might want to go to the Cotton Bowl football game on January 1, but hadn't made up his mind one way or the other yet. The only way to take care of the situation was to send as many agents as possible to Dallas, put them on stand by, and wait for Johnson to make up his mind. Johnson was known for doing that, as he felt it added a little more security if his plans weren't totally divulged. But it made it very difficult for us, and much time and money were wasted. As it happened, Johnson did not go to the Cotton Bowl game. We spent several days in Dallas doing very little. Some of the guys went to the assassination site, but I didn't. I'm still not ready to go there. We left Dallas on January 1, arriving in Los Angeles after 8 p.m. There went our holidays—again.

1964

CHAPTER 21

Los Angeles Field Office
1964

During the latter part of January, our office received a radiogram from a Greek ship that was en route to Los Angeles from Yokohama, Japan. The radiogram referred to a code indicated that the ship had a counterfeiting violation. Because I handled the port area of Los Angeles, the radiogram was given to me to resolve. I called my good friend Jack Enochs, a special agent of the U.S. Customs Service. I told him what I had and asked him if he would like to accompany me. He was able to determine that the Greek ship, the Vrontados Pioneer, was due in San Pedro on February 1, at about 11 a.m. Enochs made arrangements for a Coast Guard cutter to take us out to the ship as it approached the three-mile limit. When the ship came into view, the Coast Guard stopped it and announced that it would be boarded immediately. Enochs and I were the boarding party. We had to scramble up a Jacob's ladder in our suits and street shoes, and carrying our briefcases. I don't think that we looked much like a boarding party.

As we scrambled over the gunwale, the captain met us. Jack and I introduced ourselves, and I asked him what his counterfeiting problem was. He looked at us in a queer manner and said that he didn't have a counterfeiting problem. He said that he had copied the code from a section from a U.S. Commerce Law Book from the 1930s, and in that book, Title 18, Section 471 was mutiny—not counterfeiting. He said that on the way to Los Angeles, the ship had engine trouble, immobilizing it for several days in the middle of the ocean. They had run out of food, and the Chinese crew had endeavored to kill him with an ax. He locked himself in the wheelhouse and had been there for a number of days. We checked the Commerce Law Book and found his citation code to be correct. I went and yelled down to the captain of the Coast Guard cutter, informing him of the real story. The Coast Guard captain yelled back for us to tell the captain to follow his wake into the harbor. Then the Coast Guard crew cranked up several cannons and pointed them directly at the Greek ship. To say the least, Enochs and I were a little uncomfortable aboard a Greek ship with a mutinous crew and cannons aimed directly at us.

As the ship headed toward the harbor, we inspected the crew's mess, the meat locker, and the bakery. It was one of the dirtiest ships Enochs and I had ever seen. The mess smelled like there was something dead in it. The meat locker had one side of beef that was completely green, and the bakery had one very stale loaf of bread in it. This ship actually had run out of food. Upon arriving in the harbor and tying up, Immigration and Customs officials met us and immediately put a quarantine on the ship.

For years, Jack and I told everyone who would listen how he and I quelled a mutiny on the high seas! Jack and I remained great friends throughout our careers. Later, when the Drug Enforcement Agency was created, Jack transferred over there, as they needed experienced agents from Customs to get them going. Then in 1984, Jack and I both worked for the U.S. State Department in their background investigation group.

On February 21, President and Mrs. Johnson came to Los Angeles where the president was receiving an honorary degree from UCLA. I dressed in cap and gown and marched in with the faculty, sitting directly in back of the president.

In April, I attended handwriting school in Washington, D.C. For years, we had all worked check cases, and most of us became quite adept at determining who wrote what. At this school, however, they took us to another level. I had already attended Ralph Bradford's handwriting school at the Long Beach Police Department. For years, Brad had done most of our Secret Service handwriting work and he was very good. He was always available and accommodating. It was great to just sit and talk to him about any problems we were having—he listened intently and then very wisely asked if we had tried this or that. He was uncanny. Brad and I became very good friends. When Brad retired, his son, Russell, took over and he now is in private practice in San Pedro. Like his dad before him, Russ was always great to work with.

During a trial in Las Vegas, I was testifying as to my experience in handwriting. I told the court how long I had been working check cases and how many schools of handwriting I had attended. It was determined fairly easily by the judge, defense, and prosecution that I was indeed an expert. Most examiners of questioned documents go through a much more difficult experience before they are acclaimed an expert. My experience now allows me to testify at anytime as an expert. But handwriting is a very peculiar field—you can be fooled very easily, so I have stayed out of it as far as private practice goes.

One experience should be of interest here. The Intelligence Unit in Washington, D.C. received a very harsh, threatening letter addressed to President Kennedy prior to his assassination. Washington sent it out to us, as it was postmarked from Costa Mesa, but there was no name or address on it. The case was assigned to me. I showed it to Shirley Ann, who had great experience in the field of education. She perused it and determined that the language and handwriting skills indicated about a 7th grade level.

The next day, I went to Costa Mesa and started with the intermediate schools, going through all of the student cards that had a decent amount of handwriting on them. The school administrators were magnificent and cooperated with enthusiasm. I struck out at the first school, but at the second school, we hit pay dirt. We were able to identify a young girl who had written the letter. I interviewed the girl and her parents after school. Were they embarrassed! The youngster didn't mean any harm to the president and admitted that she was very foolish in what she had done. Case closed. Thank you, Ralph Bradford.

November 2, the day before the national election: President Johnson was running against Senator Barry Goldwater. Six of us from Los Angeles had been assigned to the Goldwater elect detail in Phoenix. We had to catch a flight to Las Vegas, and then one to Kingman, Arizona, where the Ford Motor Car Company had their proving grounds. We had to pick up all of the cars for the detail, and then drive them to Phoenix, where we met SAIC Vince Mroz, who would have been in charge of the elect detail in the event that Goldwater won the election, but Johnson defeated Goldwater by one of the biggest margins in U.S. election history. The victory was apparent very early in the evening. We quickly disbanded the detail and returned the cars to Ford Motor Company in Kingman and then returned to Los Angeles. I was disappointed about that election in several ways. One was that we would have to deal with Johnson for another four years. But also, it would have been a good detail with Vince Mroz in charge. I had worked for Vince on the White House detail for several years. I have always maintained that he was one of the best agents the Secret Service ever had—a very talented agent who for sure ought to write his own book.

On November 11, Keith Sharpe and I took off on his boat for several days of fishing on the Salton Sea. Normally, we tried to get out at least twice a year for some good corvina fishing. This year though, my Secret Service work was so demanding that this was our only trip for the year. We caught a lot of fish and did a little duck hunting too. It was almost embarrassing the amount of fish that we caught. We also smoked a whole box of cigars—so many, so quickly in fact that I got tired of them and quit smoking altogether. I used to smoke a pipe and cigars—never cigarettes—but I vowed to quit, and I did forever more. I guess I would say that the trip was a huge success because of that. We had to return by Sunday, November 15, as I was scheduled to leave Los Angeles that evening to go to El Paso, Texas, to take over that office for several weeks for my good friend, SAIC George Weisheit. George was going to Washington for a two-week school. El Paso was a very fine office and George ran it very well.

I was chosen as the agent to go to El Paso because they needed an agent who could make a speech at a banking group in Odessa, Texas. I had been doing many of the speeches for the LAFO, so it was natural choice. El Paso was a very comfortable office. There was quite a lot of work and field trips were very extensive as their cities are spread very far apart. The Postal Inspectors Office was also very active in El Paso. With several inspectors, we were able to arrest five suspects in the two weeks that I was there.

Shortly after returning to L.A. in the beginning of December, I took my annual leave that lasted through New Years. Our family joined the Corso family for New Year's Day and the Rose Bowl game—a function that was becoming a tradition.

So 1964 was now history and we were now getting ready for 1965. It was to be a very busy and successful year.

1965

CHAPTER 22

Los Angeles Field Office 1965

On January 16, SA Hess and I departed LAX en route to Washington as a part of the inaugural detail. On Inauguration Day, I was posted at the Capitol and then later at the International Inn, where the president and vice president both came. The following day, we returned to Los Angeles. On our return flight, I ran into Jack Kenney, the person responsible for me joining the Secret Service. He had been my instructor and counselor at USC and had made that first telephone call for me to the Secret Service. He was traveling with Frank Walton who had been the captain at the LAPD Academy when I went through. He was retired from the LAPD at this time and was working for a U.S. governmental agency.

The following counterfeit story is probably one of the best cases in which I was ever involved. Case 2047 began in September 1961, when three new notes made their appearance: a $10 bill passed in San Bernardino; a $20 bill passed in Victorville; and a $50 bill that we received from the Los Alamitos Race Track. All of the notes had been printed on genuine currency paper, but outside of that, the workmanship of the notes wasn't very good. Because of the genuine paper though, the note felt genuine, so it was indeed somewhat of a deceptive note, and it stayed around a long time. The notes were sent to the Secret Service lab in Washington, where they quickly determined that all of the notes were made by the same source. There was very little information, however, obtained regarding the passers.

After that first week, and almost every weekend thereafter, we were hit very consistently on the weekends with the notes being passed in stores very close to freeways. Hence the name of the case became the celebrated "freeway" case. We picked up enough information to determine that the passer was a sloppily dressed white female about thirty-years-old, about 5'4" tall, and weighed about 130 pounds. Some witnesses thought that she might have been accompanied by a child about four or five years old. No vehicle had been observed, initially. Despite the solid description, however, we had absolutely no luck finding her. The notes very quickly spread from San Diego all the way to San Francisco, many of them being passed at stores like Sears and J. C. Penney. During the latter part of January 1963, there were about eight notes passed in Madera. I went to Madera and ran all of the notes out to see if any acceptor of the notes recalled any information about the passer. There wasn't much information available. One of the stores that had accepted several of the notes was Rascos Department Store. Rascos was very cooperative. I gave them information about the notes with a request that they supply it to every one of their stores. They did, and the results were almost earth shattering.

On February 8 at the Rascos Store in Sangar, California, the female passer entered the store and bought several items, giving the young girl clerk a fake $20 bill. This store had received the warning notice that Rascos had sent to each of their stores regarding counterfeit bills. When the clerk saw the bill, she suspected that it was one of the counterfeits and she immediately showed it to the manager, Bill Williams. Williams wasn't quite sure, so he took the bill next door to a bank to see if they could tell him for certain if the bill was counterfeit. The bank employees confirmed that the bill was indeed bad. Williams quickly returned to his store to find that the passer was gone. But, the clerk had wisely followed the passer out and saw her cross the street and enter a drug store on the corner. Williams took off running over to the drug store. When the suspect saw Williams, she escaped through the side door.

Williams, being a reserve police officer on the Sangar Police Department, chased her across a parking lot to another street. The woman ran south for a half block, turned left and ran across the street, continuing east bound, all the time yelling that she was being molested and calling for help. She ran another block and a half and was aiming for a white and brown station wagon parked at the south curb. Just as Williams was about to catch her, a man leaped out of the station wagon and grabbed him. Williams identified himself as a reserve police officer and showed the man his badge. The man allowed him to put the badge away, and then in an obvious attempt to stall, he asked Williams to show it to him again. This took valuable time. Williams finally continued his chase, but he could no longer see the passer. The suspect had run to the corner, turned south and had run through a yard west bound. She stopped long enough to tear up about six of the notes and throw them into a culvert. Then she ran into the alley and waited. The man who had stopped Williams got into his car, went around the block, came up the alley, and picked up the passer. As he approached the street, he had to wait for a police car that was responding to Williams call. The passer scrunched down in the front seat so she couldn't be seen. They got away clean even though an all points bulletin (APB) had been sent throughout the San Joaquin Valley.

Williams was able to describe the two people and the vehicle involved. However, Williams thought that the car was a 1957 Pontiac station wagon, when in fact it was a 1957 Oldsmobile—a detail that would lead us in circles for a year! As that was about our only solid clue at the time, we gave it a good shot. I was able to obtain IBM cards of every 1957 Pontiac station wagon registered in the state of California from the DMV. What a task! There were over 1200 of them. We sent all the cards of the cars registered in the San Francisco and Sacramento areas to those offices, and we kept the rest. Every agent in the LAFO received the cards of the vehicles in their area with a request to check on the cars and the owners to see if they might be our suspects. We all worked very diligently to check them out, one by one.

I contacted the Pontiac Division of General Motors Corporation and supplied them information to assist in arresting the suspects. We contacted all of the major stores in Central and Southern California. We gave them all of the information that we had. We went to every police department and major bank, and we must have spoken to 100,000 people about the 2047 notes. I took a trip up the coast, stopping in every city to speak at police departments, banks and stores.

A number of us spent Friday nights and Saturdays at stores like Sears, J.C. Penney, Thrifty Drug Stores, and any store convenient to the freeways. Our overtime hours were astronomical. As we spread the word to the stores, many of them posted the information right on their registers. So, on several occasions, the passer saw the clerk checking the bill with the poster on the register. When the passer saw this, she would ask where some other type of merchandise was. She would go to that area of the store and slip out the door, leaving the suspected note with the clerk. We definitely were hunting down a smart one. We chased her around California for two more years.

Finally, on Saturday, June 19, 1965, the day before Father's Day, the passer went alone to the Sears Store in Lodi, looking for a gift. Lodi was in the Sacramento district and SAIC Steve Byrne and his men had done their job in advising people in that area about the 2047. It happened that when the passer went to pay for the gift with a counterfeit $20 bill, the clerk realized that it was counterfeit and immediately called for assistance. When the passer heard this, she ran out of the store. The clerk and her supervisor followed her. They lost sight of her, but luckily a Lodi police unit was cruising by. They stopped the officers and told them what they knew, climbed into the car, and they all went in search of the suspect.

They spotted the suspect in her car just about ready to leave the parking lot. The officers leapt out and arrested her. She was taken to the station where Steve Byrne was brought in. The passer was identified as Delia Green. She would give no additional information. Delia Green and her partner had made a pact that if either of them was arrested, the arrested person would give no personal information in order to protect their children. This would enable the remaining person to be free in order to take care of their children. They had four children between them, and they had very strong feelings about them.

When word got out that Delia Green was arrested, there were quite a few people in the San Joaquin Valley who knew that Delia was the common law wife of a man named John L. Franzke. Ultimately Franzke was located in Madera and was arrested by members of the Madera County Sheriff's Office on November 15. Franzke was lodged in the county jail in Hanford, and on November 16, I went there to meet SAIC Byrne, SA Larry Sheafe, and SA Hugh Petit, all of the Sacramento office. We went out to Franzke's residence and searched it, finding several pattern notes, a mountain of artificial flowers, tons of nylon stockings, and a myriad of other inexpensive items that were purchased in order to facilitate the passing of their notes.

Franzke was somewhat cooperative in admitting he made the notes, taking us step by step through his process. He told us of the agreement that he and Delia Green had regarding the children. He professed sorrow in what he had done and said that he would like to make full restitution. But we knew that there was no way to do that—he was going to prison. Headquarters figured that they had passed about $42,000 worth of counterfeits in the four years that they were involved. While we were there, we met the sister of Franzke, who was the owner of the so-called brown and white Pontiac station wagon, which turned out to be an Oldsmobile, of course.

I have often wondered what happened to that family. Their children must be in their forties by now. Delia and John would be in their seventies. It has always seemed to me that they were two people that the world passed by. They were very poor and had a number of children quite quickly. In the need of money, they started their counterfeiting adventure. I believe that they tried to catch up by making counterfeit currency, which is such a huge mistake, but let me tell you, they had plenty of company—so many counterfeiters get involved due to economic problems, attempting to counterfeit as a way to surmount their problems. It rarely succeeds.

I don't recall the sentence that Franzke received, but he must have pled guilty since I never had to go to trial on him. I was somewhat taken aback on November 16 when I received information that Delia Green had been released from custody due to insufficient evidence. The Sacramento office handled the bulk of the prosecution, as the U.S. Attorney's Office in Los Angeles declined to prosecute. I later heard that Delia Green had gone to the Napa area. But I'm quite sure that Franzke spent some time with the big boys in federal prison. But, no matter what occurred in the courtroom, the important factor was that the 2047 case was laid to rest. Some of those notes floated around in the economy for sometime, but eventually the note dried up.

That wraps up the 2047 saga, but there was another adventure awaiting us in the wings as always. But before we get to that, let's go back to July 5, 1965, the hundredth anniversary of the U.S. Secret Service. Shirley Ann and I hosted our entire office, plus some very special friends with whom our office worked, at our home in Rossmoor. Postal Inspector Kenneth Daws and his wife, Blanche, joined us. What a fine turn out we had at that party. SAIC Spaman and his wife came, which was somewhat unusual because they never participated in the social functions of the office. The party turned out to be a huge success.

1965 was a very important year for the Secret Service. We began to recruit new agents and did we hit a number of jackpots! One of my very favorite new recruits was a young man who had come to us from the Oakland Police Department, Jimmie L.C. Miller. He didn't need a great amount of instruction, as he came to us already with a solid knowledge of police work. I was able to work with him on several occasions, but he was destined to be transferred to the White House detail on President Johnson's staff. Jimmie became a super agent and went up the Secret Service ladder quickly. We brought him back to the LAFO in the 1970s when he was assigned as a supervisor of our check squad. Upon his return to our group, I invited him into our fishing group. Jimmie finally left the LAFO and was assigned various supervisory positions throughout the United States. When I was in Paris, he was the SAIC of our Honolulu Office—we loved to proclaim that between us, we ran about 75 percent of the world! Jimmie and his wife, Elaine, remain some of our finest friends.

The next big case that hit Los Angeles was the Denis Loraine counterfeiting case, and it involved about $375,000 worth of counterfeit $100 bills. These bills were made in the U.S., and at the request of Denis Loraine, a man named Robert Terry would take them to Thomas Roe in Lausanne, Switzerland.

Robert Terry arrived in Geneva on July 27, 1965, met up with Roe and then quickly returned to the U.S. We would later learn that the notes were of two types. The first, about $300,000 of fairly deceptive $100 bills, and the second was a lot of about $75,000 worth of imperfectly printed notes. Terry would later advise that he had wrapped the notes in his dirty laundry in the hopes that the Swiss Customs agents would not search his bags thoroughly. When Roe received the notes, he paid Terry $5,000 for serving as his courier. All the while this escapade was going on, there were many Trans-Atlantic and domestic telephone calls being made by the conspirators.

Thomas Roe lived in Lausanne, Switzerland, and at the time, he was having financial difficulties. When he got the counterfeit notes from Terry, he thought he was home free. All he had to do was to turn it into legitimate currency. In a hurry to accumulate good money, Roe visited a number of banks in Geneva and exchanged some of the counterfeit American $100 bills for genuine Swiss currency. He was exchanging as much as $5,000 at the time and doing pretty well until one employee looked at the American notes and saw that they were all the same and undoubtedly counterfeit. He called the police and they went looking for Roe and found him in another Geneva bank. He was quickly arrested and interrogated. Roe admitted his part and quickly identified Terry and Loraine, even providing their telephone numbers and hotels where they would be staying.

The Swiss police notified our office in Paris and our Paris Agent, Paul Rundle, responded. Paul was a super agent. Before this case was over, we would become good friends. When Paul got to Geneva and learned about the case, he called Paris and Washington with the details. Our New York, Miami, and Los Angeles offices became involved. Paul Scanlon in New York, Doggie Marshall in Miami, and Pat Boggs in Los Angeles were to be the three main agents in this case, initially. Pat Boggs received information about Robert Terry, including his telephone number as well as the name of the Sunset Towers Hotel in West Hollywood where he was supposedly staying.

Sometime after midnight on July 31, we spotted Terry, somewhat intoxicated, weaving across Sunset Blvd. Poor Terry—he had Agents Boggs, Slocum, Lefler, Luzania, and I waiting for him. He didn't stand much of a chance. When he got to our side of the street, we arrested him. Terry gave us permission to search his room, but we found nothing of interest. However, his information led us to discover that Denis Loraine was in Las Vegas getting married.

Pat Boggs and I caught a flight to Vegas, where we were met by Agent John Larson, who was already in Las Vegas on a field trip. John had Detectives Hanief and Reid, standing by to work with us. We all proceeded to the Dunes Hotel, where we were met by their security officers. Boggs, Larson, and I went up to suite 1007, where we arrested Loraine and hauled him off to the Clark County Jail. Boggs, Larson and I, along with the two detectives, endeavored to interrogate Loraine, but it didn't prove to be very productive. Boggs and I caught a 2:30 p.m. flight back to Los Angeles leaving John Larson there to make the final arrangements. Pat and I were dead to the world having worked about one and half days without any sleep.

I was appointed case agent, though they could have appointed any of the six or seven agents who worked the case. Being case agent was a very demanding position. The U.S. Attorney's Office in Los Angeles appointed J. Brin Shulman to the case. Shulman and I worked like beavers. He was a young, intelligent attorney who certainly knew what he was doing. We almost lived together until the trial began in the first part of January 1966.

Paul Rundle and the Paris office did a great job as well. Paul made arrangements through the Swiss police to have Thomas Roe brought to Los Angeles for pre-trial examination and then later for the trial. I had made arrangements with the federal prison on Terminal Island to house Roe when he wasn't needed for trial. Somehow, Loraine made bond and was staying at the home of Mickey Hargitay, the former husband of Jane Mansfield. Boggs and I went out there to chat with him, but we didn't get very far.

Starting in December, Shulman and I started interviewing witnesses and informants. Roe arrived in Los Angeles with Paul Rundle about December 26. It was a very inconvenient matter to pick Roe up each morning at Terminal Island Prison and then to deposit him there very late every night. Sometimes I took Roe out for dinner before returning him to Terminal Island. He learned to like Mexican food and we would usually end up at my favorite Mexican restaurant in Wilmington.

We put Paul Rundle up at the Biltmore Hotel, and on one occasion, Paul came out to our home in Rossmoor for dinner. Our children loved Paul. (I believe that it was due to my relationship with Paul that I eventually ended up in Paris as the agent in charge. But that's a story that comes later.) Paul told some great stories about his adventures in Paris. He was the only working agent there outside of the SAIC, so Paul did the bulk of the travel. He was all over Europe, Africa, and the Middle East. Eventually however, Paul got tired of the constant travel and ultimately returned to the U.S.

The Loraine trial started, and co-defendant Robert Terry changed his plea to guilty. Shulman was the only attorney for the government, but each of the five defendants had one or two attorneys. Loraine had two, one of whom was Melvin Belli, from San Francisco, but he proved no match for the wits of Shulman.

The trial resulted in four convictions and one acquittal. Friedland, an attorney from New York acting as his own attorney, was the only one acquitted. Friedland was a broke attorney who couldn't afford to hire another attorney. He probably was involved in some way, but the jury did not see it. I always hated to lose a defendant in a counterfeiting case. Loraine was sentenced to six years, and then deported after his sentence was served—some way to start a marriage!

Before 1965 is put to rest there is one experience I should relate. There was a movement that year for U.S. Treasury Agents to form their own organization calling themselves the U.S. Treasury Agents Association. Raymond Dole of the Alcohol, Tobacco Tax unit was the prime mover of the organization. There had already been chapters formed throughout the U.S., but none had been formed in the western states. Dole contacted the supervisors of all Treasury groups, inviting them to attend an inaugural meeting. ASAIC Pat Boggs asked Frank Slocum and me to represent the Secret Service. We attended the meeting and quickly became involved by being assigned to write the constitution and by-laws for the organization. Frank Slocum was very good at that type of thing, and in several days, we had put together our constitution.

When it came time for the election of officers, it was apparent that Raymond Dole should have had the honor of being the first president. But Raymond found himself in a position where he could not accept the presidency because he was being transferred to their Riverside office. Therefore, our organization was up creek without a president. Dole put out the word before he left that he would have to resign from the organization and that I should be elected president. Thanks a lot, Dole!

There were others who would have enjoyed being chosen much more than I did. But I undertook the responsibility for a year and it turned out to be a pretty good year. The organization had a good following, and after a year, I turned the office over to my good friend, Don Read of IRS Intelligence. If Frank Slocum had still been in the LAFO, I would have liked for him to have had the honor, but in the latter part of 1966, Frank had been promoted to be the SAIC of the Honolulu office. I believe that the organization folded up pretty quickly after Don Read's, year but I'm not sure. I know that other areas kept their chapters going for some time, especially in the Washington area.

1966

CHAPTER 23

Los Angeles Field Office
1966

Beginning on May 14, John Larson and I started the Key Bank Employee Seminar, a workshop we held in our office on Saturday mornings. We invited about twenty-five bank employees to each meeting. Larson lectured on check forgery, and I took the counterfeiting section. Soon we had bankers calling and asking for some more spaces for their employees. It was a pleasant success, and it gave the bank employees an opportunity to learn the very basics about forged checks and bad money. One of the first to attend the seminar was our good friend and neighbor in Rossmoor, Charlotte Kelley. She was a supervisor for the Bank of America in Seal Beach, and was very interested particularly in the counterfeiting field. Larson and I also invited some of the new agents to assist us, and we gave each of them a portion of the presentation so that they could get used to speaking to groups.

Larson and I did the seminar for several years, and then because of other responsibilities and missing our Saturday mornings, we eventually dropped it. I will tell you something though, and this is how I got the idea to have the seminars in the first place: almost each time that you would go into a bank, store, or police department, you never knew how many employees you would end up speaking to. Some banks would go down to a skeleton crew and you would find yourself talking to ten or fifteen people. That got to be common, and it certainly helped to improve your speaking ability before groups. I certainly learned that from the 2047 case.

1966 was very important for our family. In July, Mom McBride passed away. She was truly an epic American story. Widowed with eight children, she worked hard to keep the family together, and she even had enough strength left to allow her husband's father to live with them. Later, she would have Florence McBride, join the family. Florence was an orphan who had come to O'Neill, Nebraska, on the orphan train. The McBride family, having all boys, wanted a girl and adopted Florence. She was a very positive addition to the family. Florence McBride will forever live in the memory of all of the grandchildren. She took all of the children to places like Disneyland and other attractions. She never drove a car but knew the bus schedules backward and forward and that's how she traveled around the Los Angeles area. Mom McBride was one of the best cooks of all time and much of that rubbed off on Shirley Ann. We still prepare dinners from the recipes of Mom McBride.

The summer of 1966 saw Shirley Ann chosen as a principal in the Los Alamitos School District. She started at Rush School, then went to Rossmoor School, and ended up as the principal of the Los Alamitos Elementary School. Shirley Ann was a principal for twenty-one years. When she retired in 1987, she became the director of a childcare center, Kids Korner, which she ran for a number of years.

The third factor of 1966 was that we moved to the Palos Verdes Peninsula, which later became known as Rancho Palos Verdes. We lived at One Martingale Drive for over twenty-one years. This meant about a fifty-mile round trip for Shirley Ann, but there wasn't much change in the distance for me to the office. We probably had one of the finest views on the peninsula. It was a great party house and we had more than a few of those through the years.

We were blessed with some mighty fine neighbors. At first, we had Tex Wofford and his wife, who lived just above us. After several years, they sold to Mike and Marilyn Szilagy, who became some of the finest neighbors that we ever had. Mike and Marilyn had two sons, Mike and Mark, who became like family to us. When I went to Paris, those boys helped Shirley Ann a great deal. Mike and Marilyn have remained some of the finest friends that we have. Since we've moved to Rolling Hills, we very much miss the homemade baked bread that Mike always had in store. We ate more than our fair share, and Mike was always very generous with it. It's been very interesting to watch their two sons grow up and become adults. Mike Jr. is now a doctor. We always knew that he would be one. Mark does a myriad of things and is certainly his own man. He marches to his own drummer and is a very nice young man. Shirley Ann would adopt those two kids in a minute if Mike and Marilyn would allow it.

We also had two fine neighbors in Snowy and Ruth Coates. We didn't really meet them until Snowy and I had retired in 1981. He had been a very successful salesman for General Motors. Just talking to him for five minutes, you'd know Snowy is a natural salesman. Ruth was a very fine teacher in the Torrance School District, and it was my privilege to go to her class one day and speak. You could tell by the demeanor in the class that learning went on there, and that those pupils were some lucky kids to have Ruth for a teacher. Snowy and I are both stamp collectors, so we had something in common to start our friendship. Then we found out that we were both in the navy during World War II and had served in the same general area in the Western Pacific. Snowy has been a very fine friend throughout the years.

Back to Secret Service work: On September 22, Lynda Johnson, the daughter of the president, arrived at LAX. We took her to Beverly Hills, where she remained for several days.

On Sunday, September 25, V.P. Humphrey arrived at Burbank Airport for conferences at Lockheed. The night of September 26, Humphrey spoke at the Century Plaza. The following day, he departed Los Angeles. I can recall the many times that Mr. Humphrey spoke. He invariably spoke much too long, and when we thought he was ending, he was only getting started. He was a very fine man, but he just didn't know how to end a speech, much to our constant discomfort.

In October 1966, two of our most stalwart agents were transferred. Pat Boggs, our ASAIC, went to Chicago as the SAIC. Frank Slocum went to Honolulu as the SAIC. Both of these were great choices by the Secret Service. To replace Boggs, Stu Knight was transferred to Los Angeles from Washington, D.C. He had very large shoes to fill. Knight stayed in Los Angeles for about three years, and then returned to Washington. He ultimately became the director of the Secret Service.

In November, I attended the Administrative-Supervisory School in Washington. The Service had a multitude of schools, and as you climbed the ladder, they would endeavor to teach you, or introduce you to a new position through their various schools.

1967

CHAPTER 24

Los Angeles Field Office
1967

The year 1967 was a new one in my career. On January 14, we met Lynda Johnson at LAX and took her first to a residence in Brentwood, then later to the residence of actor George Hamilton. I believe that Hamilton lived in the old Pickford home in Beverly Hills. Lynda visited Hamilton on several occasions before departing Los Angeles on January 16. Hamilton treated us extremely well—it's entirely possible that we wore out his pool table playing pool. On one of those nights, we ended up escorting them to a restaurant in Malibu overlooking the water. It had to be difficult for Lynda and Hamilton to have a very romantic dinner with four burly agents watching them. The hours with Lynda were very long. Most of the time, we got off anywhere from midnight to 3 a.m., and then had to be back to work at 9 a.m. It was always nice to see protectees depart our district so we could get back to our regular work.

On January 18, I attended a meeting of the Toastmasters group in Rolling Hills and was very impressed with many of the members. For some time, I had been doing many of the speaking assignments for our office. It had become easy for me, but still, I knew that I could do much better. After that first meeting, I wanted to join the group, if they would have me. I attended a second meeting the following week and then on February 1, I was inducted into the organization.

February 1 was a day to remember. Not only was I accepted in Toastmasters, but I received my master's degree in public administration from the University of Southern California. The day also hit a bit of a sour note when I was bitten by the biggest, meanest German Shepherd that I had ever seen. The dog belonged to the owner of a coin store in Van Nuys, who used him for protection. The dog got loose and grabbed my thigh. I knew he had bitten me, but the owner kept insisting that he hadn't because he didn't see where my suit pants had been damaged. We went into a back room and I took my pants down and showed him. I could see immediately that he thought I was going to sue him and he insisted that he take me to his doctor. I agreed and the doctor gave me a tetanus shot and put some medication on the bites. The teeth of that dog were so sharp that they went right through the fabric without tearing it. Interestingly, about six months later, a robber entered that store and shot and killed the owner. Sounds like the dog was on duty at the wrong time. I wonder if there is any way that a dog owner can teach a dog the difference between a good guy and a bad guy.

Back to Toastmasters. I enjoyed my experience a great deal. Of all of the classes, meetings, and seminars I have taken, I learned more from Toastmasters than from any other single activity. I met people like Jerry Hay, Dick Johnston, Tom Johnson, John Landry, David Rose, Marvin Nordby, Jack Krieger, Dave Gilbert, Bob Yates, Art Chapman, and Jerry Slagter. They were all great Toastmasters. It was surprising how we all taught each other. I stayed with that group for four and a half years, bringing in such excellent members as Dick Lefler and Don Read. Dick was a fellow agent and Don was the IRS Inspection agent who took over the presidency of the U.S. Treasury Agents Association from me years before.

The Toastmasters program was a series of thirty-two speeches, which I made in thirty-two months. When you complete that series, you become known as an "Able Toastmaster". I was pleased to be about the only one in that group who had obtained that level.

Because I worked for the U.S. Treasury, I was chosen to be their treasurer. Six months after that, I was chosen to be the education vice president. Six months after that, I was chosen to be the president. I didn't seek the position and never really wanted it. There were others who wanted it, but I felt that I owed the organization a great deal, so I accepted it. It was a great experience and I did learn a lot. One problem presented itself though. By the time I was elected president, it was 1968 and that year was a terrible year for the nation and law enforcement. It was also an election year and I was traveling a great deal. My good friend, Jerry Hay, took over when I couldn't be there, and I think he ended up running the group as often as I did.

Let's stick with 1967 for just a little while longer. After the Kennedy half dollar came out, we had a rash of coin collectors who took the coins and gold plated them, making a very attractive collector's coin. However, according to the Gold Regulations, it was an unlawful usage of gold, making the coins illegal and subject to seizure. The coin dealers were sure angry when we showed up at the coin shows and seized every one of those coins. Some people were so angry that they wanted to physically fight us! Some people were almost arrested because they failed to cooperate.

These gold coins were also being used for jewelry. If the jeweler had attached the coin permanently to some item, it was deemed illegal and subject to seizure. We sure didn't make many friends on that assignment. I remember one numismatist/coin dealer in particular who was a fireman in Los Angeles. He lived in Ontario and was a private pilot on the side. I had dealt with him one day at his store in Ontario and had seized a number of the gold plated Kennedy coins. He was very unhappy and was unwilling to surrender the coins. I gave him a simple choice: either surrender them or get arrested. Some choice! He hesitantly surrendered them, but later we received information that he was still dealing the coins and that he was going to be at the Burbank Coin Show. How dumb can you get?

Four of us from the Special Investigations squad went to the coin show. We sent Agent Gary Miller into the show to find the suspect. Gary found the booth and bought some of the coins. After five minutes, the rest of us entered and Gary waved us over. Sure enough, the same person that I had seized the coins from previously had just sold some more of the coins to Gary Miller. While we were searching his collection, he threatened that we wouldn't get out of the building without a physical fight—bad decision on his part. We cleaned the dealer out of all of his coins and Gary told the guy that we would discuss the case with the U.S. Attorney's Office and that he would be hearing from us. Well, unfortunately, the U.S. Attorney's Office declined to prosecute. However, several months later, I read an article in the paper that the man's plane had crashed and he was killed.

Another great case that we had in the Special Investigations Squad involved a very fine agent, Dick Cameron. There was a coin dealer in Seal Beach who had come into the office and proudly showed us some enlarged one-cent coins. What he didn't know was that it didn't matter how large or small they were, they were still deemed as counterfeit. He surrendered them and was advised about the severity of the counterfeit statutes.

About a month later, I saw an advertisement in a coin magazine where this same man was selling the same coins. Dick Cameron lived in Rossmoor, which was very close to Seal Beach. So, I assigned the case to Dick to work as an undercover assignment. Dick arranged to meet the suspect at the Parasol Restaurant in Rossmoor, ostensibly to buy as many of the coins as possible. Gary Miller and I covered Dick in the restaurant while Dick made a deal with the suspect to buy whatever the suspect had. I believe that the suspect had five of the coins in his possession. Dick bought them and gave us the signal. Gary and I moved in and arrested the poor guy, who ended up going to jail for five pennies. We have always kidded Cameron about his great undercover caper— putting a fellow in jail for a nickel. Dick Cameron was a very fine agent. He went on to do some great things for the Secret Service. He is still a very fine friend of mine.

People would say, "How could you arrest a fellow for enlarged coins?" I would always tell them that the size didn't matter; it was the fact that they were in similitude to our coins. There was a bank in Los Angeles that as an advertisement made some one-dollar coins that replicated silver dollars. They were four feet in diameter, made of aluminum, and must have weighed a hundred pounds or more. When we seized them, the bank people cried. They were so large and heavy that we couldn't carry them into the office, we had to roll them in.

I had some excellent young agents in the Special Investigations Squad. For a while, Bob Tomsic and I were the only ones in it. Then, through the years, I had such fine agents as Garrick Newman, Alan Baker, Gary Miller, Dick Cameron, Larry Sheafe, Glen Winn, Tom Nagle, Bob Caughey, Bob Barker, and a host of others. I was always pleased to watch these agents climb the ladder in the Secret Service.

On April 17, SA Bob Tomsic and I took off for Palm Springs regarding a new counterfeit note that had showed up there. There were three suspects: Charlie and King Pickford, and Charles Hoffmeier. Upon arrival in Palm Springs, we rented a motel room cater-corner to the address of the suspects. With the cooperation of the Palm Springs Police Department, we watched the residence for several days and were able to photograph a number of the suspects as they entered the residence. We also had a good idea where the print shop was located. We followed the suspects on a number of occasions through Palm Springs, hoping that they might try to pass some of the notes. This resulted in several very early and long days without any success.

Then, on April 21, Tomsic and I hadn't even gotten out of bed yet when we heard one of the suspects departing. I threw on some clothes, grabbed the keys, jumped into the car and followed him. I could see his car in the far distance and it appeared that he was en route to the Palm Springs Airport. Hustling, I was able to see the suspect parking his car in the airport parking lot. I got out and followed him into the passenger area and got in back of him in the line. I was able to hear him order a round trip ticket to San Francisco, via Los Angeles. I was in business!

With the assistance of an airline official, I was able to get flight times and numbers, and I called this information into Stu Knight, who in turn got a hold of SA Dale Wunderlich on the radio making sure he was able get to LAX in time to meet the flight. I had been able to give a very good description of the suspect, including what color and type of clothing he was wearing. Dale saw him get off of the plane and tailed him into the men's room, where Dale saw him changing clothes. Dale was able to get the time of departure in Los Angeles and arrival time in San Francisco. The San Francisco agents were advised, and my old friend Doug Duncan and several other agents were able to meet the plane. They observed him rent a car and followed him to a bar where he passed a counterfeit note. Doug Duncan and his group arrested the suspect for passing a counterfeit $20 note. The suspect was identified as Charles Hoffmeier. His counterfeiting career came to an abrupt halt. What a great team effort that was, and what a fine job the San Francisco agents did. Later that day, Tomsic was able to get a search warrant for the print shop, and we found the negatives secreted on the inside the water basin. Later on, we found one of the counterfeit notes at the residence of the suspects.

The case finally came to a close on May 19, when we got word that suspects King Pickford and Gene Hansworth would be meeting and dealing at a small restaurant on Lincoln Blvd. in Venice. We had agents Tomsic, Wilhite, Luzania, Newman, and Zarzana to assist. We went in like gangbusters and made the arrests.

Bob Tomsic could have told this story much better than I because it was his case, but unfortunately Bob passed away several years ago. It was a very successful venture on our part, helped along greatly by the Palm Springs officers, the airline officials, and the San Francisco agents.

1968

CHAPTER 25

Los Angeles Field Office 1968

The year 1968 ended up being one of the worst years for law enforcement in the history of law enforcement. Generally, it had to do with protective activities relative to the war in Viet Nam.

For us, it started on Saturday, February 17, at the El Toro Marine Corps Air Base. President Johnson had come to bid adieu to a group of U.S. Marines departing El Toro en route to Viet Nam. Interestingly, we were able to speak to a number of these marines. The captain in charge was going to Viet Nam for his third tour. Many of the others were going over for their second tour. I have often wondered how many of these brave young men never returned.

We were assigned to the president until midnight and then met the next morning again at El Toro, at which time we were advised to go to the Seven Lakes Golf Course in Palm Desert because President Johnson had planned a day of golf with former president Eisenhower.

June 4 was primary day in California. As the evening wore on, it was evident that Senator Robert Kennedy would be the big winner. And with that announcement, the terrible part of the year of 1968 would begin.

I was not aware that Senator Kennedy would make his victory speech at the Ambassador Hotel in Los Angeles that night. As a matter of fact, June 4 was just a typical day in the LAFO. At about 3 p.m., I picked up Inspector James Burke at LAX. He was coming to Los Angeles to head up a special detail of agents to help us out in the counterfeiting field, as we were being hit hard and needed help. Along with Burke, there were about seven other ace investigators from offices throughout the United States who also reported that day. After picking up Burke and taking him to the office, I caught up on my administrative details and then went home for the day. My Special Investigations Squad was not slated to help in any counterfeiting cases at that time.

The evening of June 4 was a pleasant one in Palos Verdes. Shirley Ann and I watched the election returns on TV and went to bed about 11 p.m. But then, at 12:30 a.m., my phone rang. It was Virginia Thurman, Shirley's sister. She asked if we were watching TV. We had not been, as we had been asleep for some time. She told me that I had better turn it on because "you are not going to believe it."

We turned on the TV and, of course, most of the stations were covering the shooting of Robert Kennedy, which had occurred at the Ambassador Hotel. I had known the Kennedy group had its difficulties with the city of Los Angeles and the Los Angeles Police Department, and I was aware that security was going to be very sparse. The Secret Service had no involvement at all at this point. Shirley Ann and I watched for a while and then returned to bed.

The problem that the city of Los Angeles had with the Kennedys resulted from a Senate inquiry headed by Robert Kennedy. When the mayor of Los Angeles, Sam Yorty, was called to testify about the Watts Riots of 1965, Mayor Yorty was given a very bad time, and as a result, concluded that he didn't need a snot-nosed, young senator (Robert Kennedy) to tell him how to run his city. Ever after that experience, Los Angeles and the Kennedys did not get along very well.

That very night, President Johnson decreed that, henceforth, all major candidates for the presidency and vice presidency would be protected by the Secret Service. At 5 a.m., that decree was made known to me when my ASAIC Stu Knight phoned and told me that I was to go down to the Good Samaritan Hospital to afford protection for Senator Kennedy, his wife, and other members of his family. Initially, it was thought that it would be a joint effort of the LAPD, the FBI, and the Secret Service.

Arriving at Good Samaritan at about 6 a.m., I was met by Inspector Louis Sporrer of the LAPD. Lou and I had been classmates at Inglewood High School and officers of the LAPD together. We were good friends. Lou was one of the finest officers I have ever known. We agreed that his men would serve as security on the perimeter of the hospital and screen people as they entered the hospital. The Secret Service would do the inside security, though I was the only Secret Service agent there at the time. At about 6:30 a.m., they wheeled Senator Kennedy off the elevator at the 5th floor landing and immediately placed him in the intensive care ward.

Soon I had two agents, Dick Cameron and Milton Wilhite, to assist. Cameron took over the main checkpoint at the entrance to the suite. Wilhite was assigned the bedside area and to keep a log off everyone who was entering the intensive care unit. He also had the responsibility of obtaining any intelligence information garnered from the many attending doctors.

When Agent Tom Nagle appeared a short time later, I put him in the foyer of the ward to take care of any emergencies that may arise. Tom and I made sure the doors to the ward were all locked except for the main entrance and we even padlocked the emergency exit. At that point I felt pretty well assured that we could handle any emergency involving people entering the suite.

The LAPD sent over two of their finest sergeants, Robby Roberson and his partner Dick Unland. They were very familiar with our procedures. They were the two officers always assigned to us for protection activities. It was great to have them there.

Mrs. Kennedy and her sister-in-law, Jean Kennedy Smith, were staying in a room adjacent to the foyer, very close to the room where the senator was fighting for his life.

Somewhere around 10 a.m., I received a telephone call that I shall never forget. It was from Kenneth Hahn, the Los Angeles County supervisor and a very good friend of mine from Pepperdine College. He had heard that I was at Good Samaritan Hospital. He asked how things were going and how the senator was doing. The senator's condition had not looked good from the beginning. I gave Kenny an update as to what was going on. He said that if there was anything that we needed that was not forthcoming, that I should call him immediately. He said that Los Angeles was not going to experience what Dallas had experienced on November 22, 1963. That was great support. I knew that Kenny was referring to the removal of the body to Washington, in case the senator expired.

As it turned out, we had no problems other than with several members of the Kennedy staff who made it known that they didn't appreciate police officers or law enforcement personnel. I quickly determined that they used the initials TMBS—too many blue suits—to show their discontent.

The morning and the afternoon dragged by and the news was not encouraging. One of the senator's children called and wanted to speak to Mrs. Kennedy. I went into her room and awakened her. The look on her face made me think that she thought I was going to tell her that her husband had died. Not so. He was still fighting for his life valiantly.

I left Good Samaritan at about midnight and dropped several Kennedy family members off at LAX. I then went home, thinking that my assignment was probably done—boy was I wrong. At 1 a.m. on June 6 the doctors announced that the senator had lost his battle and passed away. I was not aware of that until 5:15 a.m. when ASAIC Knight called and told me of the sad news. He said that a detail was being formed, mostly from the special counterfeiting squad, and I was in charge of it. The detail would accompany the body and Mrs. Kennedy to either Washington or New York City, or both. My good friend, Carl Hardy of the Seattle office, served as my assistant. The following agents made up the detail: George Sheaks of LAFO, Dennis Prouty of Salt Lake City, Paul Sweeney of New York, and Ed Williams of Washington. Also there were Agents Allan Dillon, John Carrell, Steve Miller, and James Plichta, who became involved. It's amazing how the Secret Service can draw personnel like the above and mold them quickly into a very smooth running group. Those agents were super.

I arrived at Good Samaritan Hospital at 6:45 a.m. and quickly began making arrangements for departure. At this time, the senator was undergoing an autopsy. Arrangements had been made for us to have SA Tom Nagle and ATSAIC John Larson in the autopsy room. Larson was a shorthand specialist and always took copious notes.

At 12:30 p.m., the motorcade was formed. The body was placed in the hearse and Mrs. Kennedy rode with her husband's body. As we left Good Samaritan Hospital, headed for West Imperial Complex at LAX where the plane was waiting, I was not ready for what I was about to experience. People were lined up on both sides of the street, throwing flowers and kneeling. It became almost too emotional, even for me.

We brought the motorcade up as close to the plane as possible. The Air Force had flown in a jet and it was heavily loaded. They loaded the casket in the front of the plane. People were being asked to get on the plane as quickly as possible. I was the last one to get on the plane. After I entered, they closed the doors and we took off for La Guardia Airport, in New York City.

We landed at La Guardia at 9 p.m. before what seemed to be a million people. There were several hundred New York City police officers working this arrival. The weather was extremely hot and humid, and it had been a very long and difficult day. One of the staff people got into an argument with a police officer, and in less than a minute, the staff person was about 100 yards out in the peripheral area. Before we had left the Good Samaritan Hospital, Sgt. Dick Unland of the Los Angeles Police Department had a problem with the same staff member. You can understand a person being very emotional about what had occurred.

The senator's body was removed from the plane, placed in a hearse, and taken to St. Patrick's Cathedral, where funeral services were held. After that, we took Mrs. Kennedy to the Plaza Hotel, where the New York Field Office had made security arrangements. Our detail would take over the following morning.

It had to be well after 1 a.m. when we finished and I still had to attend a meeting at the Pan Am Building with Steve Smith, husband of Jean Kennedy Smith, Mrs. John F. Kennedy, and several other staff members. Arrangements were being made regarding times of functions as well as who would be attending the various activities. The form of the grave was discussed with Mrs. J. F. Kennedy. She had important information as a result of having prior experience with the burial of her husband. Steve and Jean Smith were very fine people and Steve served the Kennedys well in the field of finance.

During the afternoon of June 7, Mrs. Ethel Kennedy wanted to go to the lake in Central Park, but there was no way she was going there without being noticed, so we accompanied her. We stayed for about thirty minutes, and many people paid their respects to her husband. At 8 p.m., we went to St. Patrick's Cathedral for a service. Then we took Mrs. Kennedy to the residence of Steve and Jean Smith for a very late dinner. We left there about 10:30 p.m. and headed back at the Plaza Hotel.

During the early morning hours of June 8, Mrs. Kennedy came out of her suite and asked the agents if they could take her to St. Patrick's. Later, we took Ms. Kennedy back to St. Patrick's for the funeral service. The church was full and the crowd outside was tremendous. The New York City Police did a great job. Their experience certainly was evident. The service was over at 11:45 a.m.

Then, it was off to Washington, D.C. The casket was placed in the hearse and we headed for the train station. We rolled the hearse right up to the last car, which was an observation car. Ted Kennedy wanted the casket to be placed at the very end of that car on the outside so that people could see it. The casket turned out to be much too large to fit on the rear. Arrangements had to be made to put the coffin inside the car. The only problem we had was that we couldn't get it up the steps and into the car, as there wasn't enough room to maneuver it. We were stymied until several men from the railroad appeared. It wasn't a problem to them. They merely unscrewed a series of bolts on the side of the car, removed several panels, and the coffin was easily carried into the car. When the coffin was safely in, the two men replaced the panels, put the bolts back on, and we were in business. Workers had to do the same process in reverse when we arrived in Washington. After that experience, I wished I had obtained the names of those fellows. They really saved the day for us.

What a very hot uncomfortable ride we were about to have. The temperature was in the 90s with a like number for humidity. When we started out, the air conditioner worked, but shortly thereafter, it went out. It became unbearable.

After about an hour, as we were approaching Elizabeth Station in New Jersey, a young mother and her son stepped out onto another track in order to see our train better. She didn't realize that a northbound train was approaching. It struck her and her son, killing them both.

At about 3:20 p.m., we were approaching an area where quite a few people were on both sides of the tracks. Several men were on top of a train on the west side of the tracks. When our train approached, in order to get a better view, one of the men arose and grabbed the high-tension power line that propelled the electric train. He was instantly thrown off of the car to the ground. When we passed, his body was still smoldering. I heard later that this man had survived—what a miracle.

To make matters just a little bit worse, some of the staff people determined that the people couldn't see the casket, as it was on the floor of the observation car. They came to me and presented the problem. Whatever they wanted to do would be all right with me, although I couldn't spare any personnel to assist them. Someone from the staff had the idea to get some chairs to place under the casket. They located three chairs and placed one at the head of the casket and the other two at the foot of the casket. It seemed to work well until we arrived at the first curve and the casket slipped off the chairs and bounced heavily on the floor of the car. They replaced the casket on the chairs and then got four members of the staff, as well as friends, to stand by the casket and hold onto the casket whenever we approached a curve. They had no more problems, but they had to do this the entire time until we arrived in Washington, D.C.

To make matters still worse, someone came to me and told me that Cardinal Cushing, the Kennedy's cardinal from Boston, had suffered a heart attack, and that I was needed to assist him. He wasn't that far from our car, so I did go to see if I could help out. I'm sure a doctor would have been more appropriate, but I'm not sure if we had one aboard the train. I told Cardinal Cushing that we would be in Baltimore soon and that we could have an ambulance standing by for him. The Cardinal didn't think that was any great idea and said he wanted to go with the group into Washington. We made arrangements via telephone and radio, and we did have an ambulance waiting for him on our arrival in Washington despite his resistance.

I would be remiss if I didn't mention that we had a chopper accompanying us all the way to Washington. It flew about a mile ahead of us and reported to the agent who was riding in the engine with the engineer. The chopper agent could tell the engine agent that there were so many people standing a mile or so ahead of us so that the engineer could be advised. The train would be slowed down so that the people could get a better view. No wonder it took nine hours to make that trip. The problem we had as a result of the train slowing down so frequently was at five miles per hour, the automatic brakes went into effect and after doing that so often, the automatic brakes went out. As a result of this, the air conditioning unit went out. That made it a very uncomfortable ride.

We finally arrived in Washington at 9:25 p.m. It took us a few minutes to get the casket out of the train car, Cardinal Cushing into an ambulance, and to line up the motorcade. The Washington agents and a multitude of supervisors from headquarters did a magnificent job. Very quickly, I was told there was intelligence obtained that indicated that as we would pass the Justice Building, the motorcade would be the subject of a terrorist hit. The Justice Building had been Senator Kennedy's home when his brother was the president. This was a very serious matter.

The motorcade eventually began and down Pennsylvania Avenue we went. As we approached the Justice Building, I saw Vince Mroz, who was now a deputy assistant director, and was evidently in charge of getting the motorcade safely past the Justice Building. I knew there was no way anything was going to occur with Vince in charge. And so it was. I have never seen so many agents and police officers in one area before, and what a great job they all did.

It took thirty minutes for the motorcade to get to Arlington Cemetery and to the grave site. There was a very emotional thirty-minute service there, and then we departed for Hickory Hill, the residence of Robert and Ethel Kennedy.

There were many people waiting for Mrs. Kennedy to arrive. It was truly an Irish wake. There was no way that our little detail could have stayed there because of our long and exhaustive day. The U.S. Marshal's Service had been requested to supply protection for the midnight shift, and when we heard this, our group happily left for our hotel to get some sleep before having to return to Hickory Hill the following morning. Thereafter, we had U.S. Marshals with us on each shift. They were a fine group to work with and really did a great job.

On Sunday, June 9, Mrs. Kennedy went to the grave site twice. Each time, the security office cleared people out so that she could have some privacy. At 10:20 a.m., we departed for Arlington with Mrs. Kennedy, Bill Barry, Rafer Johnson, and Andy Williams. Bill Barry had been on Senator Kennedy's staff, and Johnson and Williams were very good friends and supporters of him.

That evening, we took Mrs. Kennedy to her church, St. Luke's Catholic Church, in McLean, Virginia. People were extremely kind and considerate, and Mrs. Kennedy showed great strength. After the church service, we returned for the second visit of the day to Arlington National Cemetery. Most people didn't know that Mrs. Kennedy was expecting their eleventh child. She had the following children, with their ages at that time: Kathleen, 16; Joseph, 15; Robert, 14; David 12; Mary Courtney, 11; Michael, 10; Mary Kerry, 8; Christopher, 4; Matthew, 3; and Douglas, 14 months.

Not all of the children were present at all of the functions that week, but there were enough present at most events to cause us some concern from a safety standpoint. I appointed Agent George Sheaks to be in charge of the children and I don't recall that we had any major problems. George was always counting children, hoping that he got the correct number at the end, which wasn't exactly easy—the children were all very active and never stayed in one place for very long.

On June 9, Mrs. Kennedy wanted to go to the Lincoln Memorial, that magnificent memorial that exudes such a great feeling. We didn't stay very long, as it was impossible for her to be there without being recognized.

On Monday, June 10, we established a routine of three shifts around the clock, supported so very well by our friends from the U.S. Marshal's Office. U.S. Marshals can do everything and they have proved this throughout the history of America. Some of the marshals who helped us were: Tom Patterson, Ray Brown, John Rogers, Ray Pope, Walter Allen, Charles Artley, Harry Cottwen, Henry Johnson, Bill Colquit, Louis McKinney, Jack Greaner, and Dan Dotson.

On June 12, Mrs. Kennedy went to the senate office building, where Senator Kennedy's staff was in attendance. It was a very emotional experience, going into his office and seeing the pictures of his children, and a valentine addressed to "Bobby, the best Godfather ever." There were many tears shed during this event, which only showed how truly loved he was by his staff.

I met up with Floyd Boring, my former supervisor on the White House detail who had retired and then went to work for the Kennedy group. Floyd was a fine Secret Service agent and an excellent boss.

After the Senate office building, we went to Kennedy headquarters and met with more members of his staff. Again, more tears and strong feelings were shown. When they set up security at Hickory Hill, SAIC Harry Geiglein of the Washington Field Office and his agents made arrangements for us to have our command post in the basement. It worked out quite well. You can imagine how the children saw it as a nice place to visit. Mrs. Kennedy supplied us with all of the Cokes we could drink and often had other goodies brought down to us. I recall seeing their ten-year old, Michael, coming down to the basement, taking a seat, and reading Newsweek magazine about the assassination of his father. What a heart breaker that was.

The days began to mount, and finally we heard that the Kennedy detail might possibly extend until June 26. This was not a definite date, but it gave us some room to plan. As it turned out, it was not true. On Saturday, June 22, we began our last day at Hickory Hill. The afternoon and midnight shifts were terminated, and we operated there until about 3 p.m., at which time we took Mrs. Kennedy to Washington National Airport. Everyone was cut loose but me, as I was to escort Mrs. Kennedy to Edgartown, on Martha's Vineyard. The chief of police of Edgartown, Jim Arena, met us with some of his officers. They agreed to assist in security at the hotel as well as at the church services at St. Elizabeth's Church the following morning. Chief Arena showed me around town and we took a look at the church to make sure I would know what to expect once the family arrived there.

The following morning, we all attended the church services, then left Edgartown on Ted Kennedy's boat, en route to Hyannis Port. It was a magnificent boat ride with a very calm sea. They stopped the boat in the mid-channel area, and everyone who wanted to went swimming. We arrived in Hyannis Port at about 6 p.m. I was able to take a shower and change clothes, and at 7 p.m., I departed Hyannis Port in a private plane back to Washington. The next morning, I caught a flight to LAX. I went into the office but wasn't worth much, so I left at 4 p.m. to go home. It was wonderful to see my family again—it was always difficult to leave them for so long.

I assumed that the difficult times were over, at least for the rest of the year—boy was I wrong. Governor Reagan had thrown his hat into the national political arena. Because he was a major figure, he received a detail of Secret Service agents. This detail was headed by a very astute agent named John Simpson, who put together one of the best details of all time.

Right when I returned to Los Angeles, I was advised that I had been assigned to this detail. I was to work in Los Angeles, particularly with Mrs. Reagan. Agent Dick Cameron headed Mrs. Reagan's security and traveled with her to Sacramento when she went there. I would coordinate with Cameron and make sure we would be ready for her when she came to town.

On June 27, I did my first advance for her, and on the 28th, I worked for the first time at their residence located in Pacific Palisades. Standing out at the Reagan residence all day in the cool air, I caught some kind of a bug, so that night when we flew into Sacramento as soon as possible, I hibernated. They were able to get me to a doctor the following day where I received a shot of penicillin, but my illness lingered for the next four days.

On July 9, I received a telephone call from Sacramento, advising that Governor Reagan would be attending the Governor's Conference in Cincinnati, from July 22 to 24, and that I should fly to Cincinnati as quickly as possible to be the advance agent for the conference. I was advised that Agent Robert Heyn would be all the detail they could afford to send to help me.

I departed LAX at 12:45 a.m. on July 10—talk about a "red eye" flight, that was it. I arrived in Cincinnati at 9:10 a.m. and was met by Agent Branch Walton, a very young agent who had only several months experience in the Secret Service. He and SAIC Jim Griffiths were the only two agents left in the office. Walton and I went directly to a meeting that was underway. I was introduced to the group as the man with all of the answers. That certainly wasn't true and I'm afraid it got me started me off on the wrong foot with some of the participants. I generally got along very well with local law enforcement agencies because that's where I started my career. However, I did have some problems with the Ohio State Police. They were actually in charge of the security at the conference, except they shouldn't have endeavored to make security arrangements for the many Secret Service details that would be coming to Cincinnati.

Quickly, I was advised by Washington that of the eight details now being handled by the service, seven of them would come to Cincinnati to speak at the conference. Due to a very acute shortage of personnel, I was to coordinate each of the visits, plus, Governor Rockefeller would remain in Cincinnati for several days. What an impossible task this would turn out to be. Griffiths, Walton, and I tried our very best, but it sure was difficult.

My first and biggest problem with the Ohio police was about the usage of limousines. They had obtained a Cadillac limousine for each of the governors who would be attending the conference. That would have been great for me and would have saved me a lot of difficulty. But when I was talking to Lem Johns, who was coordinating details from Washington, and I told him about the Cadillacs, he said that under no circumstance would the Secret Service use any General Motor vehicles for protectees because the White House had a contract with Ford that enabled them to furnish all vehicles used by the Secret Service in protection activities. When I told the head of the police about this arrangement, he wanted to argue. I couldn't argue—all I could say was that it was a decision made in Washington. He was very angry, and this put me in a very delicate position. I had to call Ford at their office in Cleveland, advise them what was needed and they would then transport them down to us in Cincinnati. They did and the vehicles were excellent.

I don't know how I got through until the 24th. We took each arrival and departure and marked them off. Griffiths, Walton, and I really had our hands full. I felt sorry for Jim Griffiths, a very good friend of mine from our Washington days. He had to remain in Cincinnati after I left and I'm afraid I didn't make too many friends for him with the state police. I later learned that the major in charge of the state police telephoned Washington and complained about me. I didn't learn about that until later in the assignment. No one in Washington ever called me to tell me about that problem.

There were a million things to do. Reagan was to speak at the conference, which was being held very close to our hotel. Several days before Reagan arrived, Agent Bob Heyn arrived. I showed him the convention hall and told him that I would bring Reagan to him and that he should take care of him once he arrived at the hall. Bob did a fine job and he certainly helped take some responsibility off of Griffiths, Walton, and me.

All in all, the visit was pure pandemonium, but that's what politicians like—the more people ranting and raving the better. They certainly got that in Cincinnati. I was delighted when Governor Reagan departed on the 24th. It had been a very frustrating experience and I didn't feel as if I had done the greatest job. But I have an adage that I have used with young agents who are getting their wings in making advances. It goes like this, "If your protectee is living at midnight and he is safe and comfortable, whatever you did that day worked." Some agents will disagree with that, but that's how I feel.

I was glad to leave Cincinnati, which I did as quickly as I could after Reagan departed. I took two days off, and on Sunday the 28th, I was on back on duty at the Reagan beach house at Trancas Beach, just north of Malibu. We were there for about four days and then returned to their home in the Palisades.

On Saturday, August 3, we departed for the Republican Convention in Miami, where I was in charge of the command post. It was extremely hot and humid in Miami, but my assignment turned out to be a good one. We all worked long hours in Miami. One day, I worked seventeen hours, and for three days straight, I worked fifteen hours. The convention was exciting. Governor Reagan gave it a mighty try, but the Republican Party chose Mr. Nixon and Mr. Agnew as the standard bearers.

After the convention was over, the Reagans had a very nice farewell party for all of the agents. All in all, it was a very good detail run by John Simpson, Bob Dowling and my very good friend, Doug Duncan. These were all very good and talented agents.

The convention was over in time for me to catch a flight to Chicago, where my old friends from the U.S. Navy were having our annual USS Serene reunion. I was able to make the main banquet on Saturday night and a part of Sunday before going back to L.A.

Back in L.A., I was immediately sent to the Reagan residence in the Palisades to clean out the trailer that we had used for a command post. There were typewriters and forms and other items that we couldn't leave in the trailer when it was hauled away. Endeavoring to do this very quietly, I didn't check in with anyone inside the home. When Mrs. Reagan saw me, she came out, gave me big hug and said, "Darwin, please don't take the trailer." That kind of told the whole story— John Simpson had put together a magnificent detail that jelled so very well with the protectee and his family. They truly became like a family to us. Ever after that, the Reagans and the Secret Service have been on the same cycle. The Reagans were very nice people with whom to work.

One would think that enough is enough for one year. I sure thought so too. I took about four and a half days of annual leave and our family went down to Ensenada, Mexico. We always enjoyed Ensenada. It was a nice quiet time with the family and a chance for Dar and me to do a little fishing.

When we got home, I received a phone call from the office advising that a group of us from the LAFO was being sent to Chicago to help out at the Democratic National Convention. We were in for a shocker. Chicago looked like an armed encampment. There were barbed wire enclosures and National Guard troops lined the streets. Identification cards became a necessity. Pat Boggs was now in charge in Chicago. He had much to do with the planning and execution of the security at the convention. What a tremendous task that was. I was put in charge of one gate area that had about six specific entrances. To get inside the Stockyards Convention Center, you had to have a color-coded identification card that was inserted into the gate—that is, if it was working correctly. Ours didn't work very well and we ended up doing it by eye. On top of that, people were going berserk. It was hot and humid, and when they couldn't get in, all hell would break loose. I had several groups that had to be physically subdued. It was not a very pleasant assignment, but it went pretty well along with the rest of 1968.

The convention concluded on August 29. On the 30th, we took off for home, grateful that we had survived Chicago. But if I thought 1968 had run its course yet, I was wrong again!

On September 9, I had received word that I had been selected to attend the International Association of Chiefs of Police Convention (IACP) in Honolulu. I had been a member of that organization for some time, but this would be the first convention that I attended. I also was scheduled to work an advance for vice presidential nominee Ted Agnew, and then attend the convention. Agnew made a speech at the Honolulu International Center, and then visited Honolulu for a number of appearances at radio and TV stations. He also played a round of golf at the Waialae

Country Club. After Honolulu, he had stops in Maui, Kauai, and Hawaii before leaving the islands on September 23.

As the IACP convention wasn't due to start until October 6, I helped SAIC Frank Slocum in some of his investigations. It was nice to work with Slocum again. (I should say Frank and I did the bulk of the advance for Governor Agnew's visits, for it surely was more than a one-man job.) The convention wrapped up on October 9, and I had made arrangements to return to Los Angeles the following day. But then Washington called, advising me that vice presidential nominee Curtis LeMay was coming through Honolulu en route to Viet Nam. I was asked to join the group of advance men and to proceed to Saigon with the group. In order to travel to Asia, I immediately had to get a series of seven shots at the U.S. Public Health Center. I met up with Agent Paul Rundle, who was in charge of this assignment, when he arrived at the Honolulu Airport later that night. Paul had my visa with him as well as instructions as to what my assignment would be.

The group arrived in Honolulu after midnight and I joined up with them on the flight. We made stops in Wake Island and Guam and then flew directly into Tan Son Nhut Airport in Saigon. I was assigned to do Saigon with my good friend Hank Schwoebel, who was from the Transportation Office of the White House. It was always good to work with Hank Schwoebel.

LeMay made other stops in Nha Trang, Bien Hoa, Da Nang, Long Binh, and the USS Benawah, which was called "Yankee Station, located in the Mekong Delta." I was somewhat disappointed drawing Saigon. I had wanted to go to Da Nang because my sister's boy, Richard Knapp, had been assigned there as a member of the U.S. Army and it would have been nice to see him. But Saigon was the first and last stop made, so I guess I lucked out. LeMay spent less than two days in Saigon, but we were very busy. We had many briefings with the military as well as with Ambassador Bunker.

After leaving Saigon on the 17th, LeMay made a whirlwind tour of Viet Nam and returned to Saigon on October 19, at which time he had a visit with President Thieu of Viet Nam. LeMay concluded his trip, leaving from Tan Son Nhut on the 19th via a Pan Am flight to San Francisco. It was good to have him depart Viet Nam without any security problems that we couldn't surmount.

During the time that I was in Saigon, I worked with Captain Dave Barnett of the U.S. Army and Leo Cramsey, a U.S. State Department regional security officer. I knew Leo from my White House days, as he was the assistant agent in charge of Secretary of State John Foster Dulles' detail. Leo and I would meet a number of times during our careers in some odd places throughout the world. Some enterprising movie producer should find Leo Cramsey and make a movie of his life. It would be a big seller.

I was asked by U.S. Army authorities to spend some time with them in order to evaluate their physical protection program regarding their commanding officer. What a difficult task they had, and I made several recommendations. On the whole, they were doing what they had to do in a very difficult situation.

Most of the agents who had worked Viet Nam met in Saigon after their assignments had been completed, and on Saturday, October 19, we departed Saigon en route to Guam, Honolulu, and Los Angeles.

This ended a most interesting saga of my career, and was I glad to get home. I took three days off and reported back to the office on October 24. At this point, I felt that the escapades of 1968 were just about over. This time, finally, I was right.

It was fun getting back to my Toastmaster's organization. I was the president, but for most of my term, I was traveling. Jerry Hay very adroitly filled in for me, and the organization didn't suffer in my absence. I used a number of my experiences as topics for speeches that I was required to make.

On October 25, we received information that a group of bond thieves was going to cash a large amount of government bonds at a bank in the San Fernando Valley. Working with the LAPD detectives, we set up the bank. I was to play the part of the bondman at the bank. When the people came in with the bonds, we already knew they were stolen. When the bonds were presented, I made some calculations and then gave a signal. About four LAPD detectives and agents swarmed in to make the arrest. One of the arrestees told us that there was another player at the adjacent restaurant and described him. An LAPD detective and I went over, spotted the guy and swooped him out under arrest. We let the LAPD handle them first, and then we got in line for a second shot at them.

On October 29, I left for Las Vegas with a briefcase full of assignments. I only stayed for a few days—I never really cared for Las Vegas as some of the other agents did. I got there as quickly as possible, worked long days to get rid of the work, and got back home. I did enjoy dinner in Vegas however. The food was always good and quite inexpensive. I generally stayed at the Orbit Inn, which was close to downtown and convenient to the police and sheriff's offices. Both of those organizations had some very competent officers, and many of them looked out for our interests when we weren't there. It got to the point that there was so much work in Las Vegas that we opened a resident agency there. Initially, it was only one man but eventually increased to several.

On November 3, I helped work a function at the Beverly Hilton for Senator Edmund Muskie. The following day, we had Muskie and V.P. Humphrey at the ABC Studios in Hollywood. At this time, Mr. Humphrey was the democratic nominee and Mr. Muskie was the vice presidential nominee. Much later that night, we dropped them both off at LAX. The following day was Election Day, and they had to get back to Maine and Minnesota respectively for their voting.

We lucked out in Los Angeles for this election. We didn't have any candidate voting here, and we didn't have any elect details to set up. You will recall that Mr. Nixon, who was running for the presidency, had changed his residence to New York. We were fortunate for once.

It was a pretty close election, and I can recall some of the agents on the Humphrey detail prematurely proclaiming a victory the previous day, but it didn't happen and I was glad. I don't know how many times I stood at a speech site listening to Humphrey speak and hoping that he would conclude soon. He was a speaker who did not know when to stop and I believe that speaking trait cost him some valuable votes.

You have to wonder though—what if Humphrey had won? There wouldn't have been Watergate, as I don't think Humphrey would have allowed his staff to run the show as Nixon's staff did. It's interesting to ponder how dramatically history would have changed.

On November 29, Mr. and Mrs. Nixon arrived at LAX. Mr. Nixon was taken to the Century Plaza Hotel. Agent Bagby and I took Mrs. Nixon to Malibu, and then we all returned to the Century Plaza Hotel to meet up with Mr. Nixon. On the 30th, Agent Dick Lefler and I advanced the Good Shepherd Church in Beverly Hills for the Nixons. After that, we went to the Beverly Hills Hotel for a function. Still later, we went to LAX to prepare for the Nixons departure.

A personal note before we say adios to 1968. I was elected to the Pepperdine College Alumni Board. With all of the other things going on, I really didn't need this added to my plate. But

Shirley Ann and I owe so much to Pepperdine that we can never say no when Pepperdine asks for something. I went on the board thinking I would serve for a three-year term, and then let someone else have a turn. That didn't happen. After two years, I was asked to run for the presidency. Just what I needed! Well, I did, and I was elected. All in all, I spent four years on the board—one year as the president and then an extra year as the president emeritus. It turned out to be a wonderful experience and I left thinking that it truly was a great thing; one that more alumni should undertake. I believe that all alumni should be given the opportunity to serve on their alumni board. Shirley Ann and I have been blessed by our association with Pepperdine and we have endeavored to live by its tenets.

The year 1968 was finally over. What a year it was! There was much travel and many problems. My assignments took me from the streets full of revolution in Chicago, to the streets of Saigon; from the beaches in Miami to the beaches in Malibu; and to the shores of the Ohio River in Cincinnati. Never would I experience another year like that one. But, believe me, just one of those years for each career is enough!

1969

CHAPTER 26

Los Angeles Field Office 1969

On January 16, 1969, quite a few of us from the LAFO were sent to Washington to help out in the inauguration of President Nixon. I drew assignments at the National Gallery for the Distinguished Ladies Ball; the Mayflower Hotel for one of the inaugural balls; Constitution Hall for the inaugural concert; and to the Capitol for the inaugural proceedings.

January 20 was Inauguration Day. We all kept busy leapfrogging ahead of the Nixons and the Agnews, going from one place to another. I didn't get through until 2 a.m. We left that day from the Baltimore Airport at 1 p.m. and landed at LAX at 3 p.m. It had been a very busy and difficult assignment, but extremely interesting.

During 1969, Agent Gary Miller and I worked a counterfeit coin case out in Newbury Park. Several dealers there had advertised 1940 D 25-cent coins for sale. Gary and I knew that quite a few of those coins had been counterfeited and distributed throughout the numismatists and dealers in the Los Angeles area. When we saw the advertisement in the paper, we figured that we should see what they had. I called the dealer and made an appointment for the following day. I told the dealer that if I liked the commodity, I would buy all he had. Gary and I set up the deal—I would go into the place of business, dicker with the two dealers on price, and if I saw any counterfeit coins, I would arrest them. I would then call the other agents in to assist in the arrest. I wasn't carrying a weapon, but I did have a radio in my briefcase to use to call to the other agents in.

Instead of a business, however, the address turned out to be a residence. Gary and several others situated themselves in the immediate area as I went in to negotiate with the two dealers. They were very wary of the situation and it took some talking for them to relax and to begin to show me what they had to sell. It wasn't long before I observed some of the counterfeit coins. At this point, I had seen enough to identify myself as an agent and I advised them that they were under arrest.

Close to one of the dealers was a bar stool covered by a newspaper. After I radioed the other agents in, one of the dealers uncovered the stool. The paper had been covering a weapon. I grabbed it. The one dealer said he was relieved to find that I was an agent, because he had thought I was a criminal out to steal their coins. That was one case where people were going to jail relieved.

Another coin case that we worked on dealt with one of the best informants that the Secret Service ever had. His code name was Lord Jim. Because Lord Jim worked in gold much of the time, I dealt with him more than most of the other agents. Lord Jim was basically a con man, and his job for us was to out-con the other con men, which he did very well. Not only did he work for the Secret Service, but also for U.S. Customs, the LAPD, the FBI, and any other law enforcement agency that had jurisdiction in whatever caper in which he was involved.

One day he called me and advised that he had a coin dealer lined up who wanted to sell him some 1968 coin sets from Canada that contained several coins as well as a $20 gold Canadian coin. The coins were legal to own in Canada, but the U.S. Treasury put the gold coin on the restricted list, indicating that they thought Canada was making them primarily to sell to American tourists who would be coming to Canada for their World Fair. U.S. Treasury officials thought that to allow the gold coin into the U.S. would be against the best interests of the United States.

Lord Jim said he could get some of these sets that had the gold coin. I called Sgt. Robby Roberson of the LAPD Fraud Squad, and when I told him what Lord Jim had, he became very interested. The two of us went out see what we could put together with Lord Jim. Lord Jim agreed to make an appointment with the dealer for the following day. At that time, Lord Jim was supposedly going to introduce the dealer to a couple of "big timers." Boy would he be disappointed when those big timers turned out to be Robby and me.

For the meeting, I was to bring along a flash roll in order to show the dealer that we meant business. We didn't have very much genuine currency in the office for a flash roll, but I figured we could put together a good size roll of counterfeit money and the dealer wouldn't know the difference. Robby and I went out to Lord Jim's home to await the dealer's arrival. For back up, we stashed several officers and agents inside Jim's very large home. The dealer showed up on time, and Jim made the introductions. Robby was the man with the money, and I was the guy who knew about coins. As we got down to business, I noticed that several of the sets did not have the $20 gold coin in them. There were some there, however, which at least put us in business. I asked him where the missing gold coins were. He said that he had them in his home, and if we made a deal, he'd go get them.

So, to get things going, we made an offer on the coins he had there, and Robby handed over about $400 from our flash roll. The dealer gave me the coins, and then to our surprise, he put the money on the coffee table and began to look at it very closely. Attempting to remain calm, I asked him somewhat casually what he was doing. Before he even answered, we knew that he had already noticed several of the bills had the same serial numbers—there went our cover! I quickly told the dealer who we were and that he was under arrest.

He had made a huge error in judgment when he told me the other gold coins were at his residence, as it enabled us to obtain a search warrant. We booked him and then headed out to the man's home, search warrant in hand. His home looked like an armed castle! He had bars all over the windows, and the front door was locked and chained. Robby and I went around the back, which wasn't as heavily protected, but it was locked. We thrust a shovel under the sliding glass door and slid it open. Upon entry, we quickly found his safe, which was of course locked.

While we were searching the residence, the dealer made bond and had arrived at his home, shocked to find that we not only were there, but that we had been able to surpass his security measures. We told him that we had found his safe, and we gave him a choice: he could open it for us, or we would blow it open—some choice! Well, it didn't take him very long to open it for us. Inside, we found just what we were looking for: the Canadian sets with the gold coins. After searching the rest of the house, those coins were all we found that was illegal. Most of the time when coin dealers were arrested, they received a probationary sentence and perhaps a fine. It was rare that any of them spent much time in prison. And this case ended no differently.

On January 31, ASAIC Stu Knight, Agent Kazuo Yakura, and I met several U.S. Customs agents at the United Airlines air freight warehouse at LAX. Customs had received information from an informant that a delivery of gold coins had been brought across the Canadian border into the state of Washington. These coins had been taken to Portland, Oregon, where they were shipped out to Los Angeles. Not only were they smuggled into the United States, but it was thought that a number of them were counterfeit.

The coins arrived in a very large steamer trunk marked "automotive parts." We knew that was of course just a cover, and we waited for the addressee, Danny Crabb, a coin dealer in Van Nuys, to come and pick them up. I had dealt with Danny Crabb on several other occasions and had found him to be cooperative. By 3 a.m., no one had come to pick up the coins, so we called it a night, making sure that the coins were hidden until the morning, at which time we would continue our stakeout.

The following day, Agent Yakura dressed up as an airline employee, so that when someone came to pick up the coins, Agent Yakura could pretend to take care of the delivery. An hour or so passed, and finally Danny's wife arrived to pick up the shipment. Agent Yakura loaded the trunk into Mrs. Crabb's vehicle, and then we arrested her. We seized her coins and her vehicle, and placed her under arrest. We took her to the office for interrogation, where she pleaded ignorance as to the contents of the trunk.

I telephoned Danny Crabb and told him that we had just arrested his wife and that we had seized the shipment. Was he upset! I suggested that he might want to come down to our office to discuss the matter. Sure enough, he was there in a blink of an eye! He made it in record time from Van Nuys to the Federal Building in Los Angeles. I never had a person cooperate so quickly in my entire career. He, of course, was fighting primarily for his wife's freedom.

We went through ninety-two pounds of $20 U.S. gold coins, many of which were counterfeit and/or restrikes. Restrikes are gold coins dated in one year, generally long ago, and then remade in the present year with the older date on them. Danny helped us to determine which ones were which. Danny professed not to have any financial interest in the coins. He said that the coins had come from a former American now living in Canada by the name of Robinson. Robinson had been a big coin dealer in the U.S., but he apparently got tired of the restrictions laid down by the U.S. Treasury in relation to gold coins and moved to Canada where the restrictions were not as stringent. The following Monday, the U.S. Attorney's Office declined to prosecute Mr. and Mrs. Crabb.

I don't know how Robinson heard of the seizure—probably through Danny Crabb—but it wasn't long until we began to receive letters from Robinson's attorney demanding the return of all of the coins seized. I answered each one of the letters, always inviting Robinson to our office promising that the coins would be returned to him—of course, Robinson would have been arrested immediately if he had come, not only for the counterfeit coins, but for the smuggling of them over the border. U.S. Customs was always waiting in the wings. But, Robinson never came in, and eventually his attorney stopped writing. They must have known what would happen. Sometime later, I took those coins back to Washington. Have you ever tried to carry ninety-two pounds of gold coins? It was like carrying a sack of cement. But somehow, I did it. I slept on the plane with both of my feet resting on the package of coins. I was glad to see Jack Holtzhauer of the Counterfeit Division waiting for me when I arrived at Dulles Airport, so at least I had some help carrying the coins. That was one of the biggest seizures of gold coins that we had ever made, and the U.S. Treasury Department actually made quite a profit on it.

This trip was made in conjunction with a trip to which I had been assigned: Nixon's first trip to Europe since his election in November 1968. I left Washington on February 12 en route to London and Cologne, Germany. My assignment was the Cologne Airport for the arrival of President Nixon. A great crowd was expected, but the day of the arrival it rained very hard so they put him into his limo and took off as quickly as possible.

The president spent his days in Cologne, Bonn, and Bad Godesburg. We happened to be in Germany at the time of the Fasching Celebration, a combination of Halloween and Mardi Gras. Of course, we had to join in on some of the fun. They have a strange custom of cutting off men's ties and collecting them. Some fun when you only have a limited wardrobe. We all did pretty well though, and I don't believe the Germans got too many American ties.

After Mr. Nixon left Germany, I caught a chopper down to Heidelberg, where I visited the Pepperdine campus. I was there for three days, and I spoke to the student body one night at dinner. That was a delightful experience. On March 2, I took the train from Heidelberg to Frankfurt and caught a Pan Am flight to LAX, via London. It was nice to get home. I took one day off and got back into the office on March 4.

On March 21, I pulled my first assignment for Mr. Nixon at his residence in San Clemente. The only excitement was about 2 a.m. at the San Clemente Police Station there. A California Highway Patrol officer brought in six illegal Mexicans that he had spotted in a stalled vehicle on the freeway. They had been secreted in the trunk of the car, and the officer had noted how far down the back of the car was in relation to the front.

On March 29, former president Eisenhower passed away in Washington, D.C. Headquarters notified all offices that all agents who had been assigned to his detail should report to Abilene, Kansas, for a burial assignment. I would have been honored to go, but just prior to that request, Agent Kazuo Yakura and I had been assigned to Sydney, Australia, to do advance work for Secretary of Treasury David Kennedy. Secretary Kennedy was going to Sydney to represent the United States in the Asian Development Bank, scheduled for April 10 to 12. There were about thirty-three countries that were sending representatives to this meeting. I had a big decision to make, but ultimately I opted to go to Australia. Agent Yakura and I were very good friends and always worked well together.

On April 2, as we loaded the plane for Australia, there was a bomb scare. Our plane was pulled out to a very far corner of LAX where bomb squads went through the plane and the luggage. No bombs were found and we were finally free to take off—some three hours later.

By the time we got to Sydney, we were bushed. It was the worse case of jet lag I ever had. We arrived in Sydney at 11 a.m. on April 3 and were met by U.S. State Department officials and members of the New South Wales Police Department. Fred Longbottom who was in charge of their division regarding foreign visitors, took us under his wing and led us through the pitfalls. We also worked with Joseph Smith and his wife, Kathy, both of whom were police officers.

Yakura and I met Gordon Parks, our communications expert from Washington. Gordon knew communications like no one else. He set up our command post and radio equipment, and without him we would have been lost. While Yakura, Longbottom, and I were out doing advances and running routes, Gordon remained in the command post and took care of our telephone calls as well as the radios. Often, after our long days of work, Parks, Yakura, and I were entertained by some members of the consulate or the police department, and we always had great fun as Sydney was a wonderful city.

The secretary arrived on the 8th, and for several days thereafter, we took him and his wife around sightseeing and on shopping sprees. The conference started on April 10, but it wasn't all business. There were lunches and dinners and other side meetings we had to plan on. Everything seemed to go off pretty well, and finally on April 13, the secretary and his entourage departed Sydney. After the secretary left, a friend of the consulate offered to take us on a tour of Sydney Harbor. They put together a great buffet for us and drinks that wouldn't stop. We were able to get some of the police officials and their wives aboard for the affair as well.

On Monday, Yakua and I said so long to a host of fine Australian police officials and boarded a flight for Auckland, New Zealand. Upon our arrival there, Yakura met a police officer at the airport who called the detective bureau downtown. A detective named Dick Tracy came out and very generously offered to show us the high points of Auckland. He also took us to the top floor of their headquarters building downtown, which, as is typical of most police buildings in the United Kingdom, was an officers' liquor bar. It's a custom that goes all around the world.

Tracy got us back to the airport in time to catch our midnight flight back to Los Angeles. We arrived at LAX at 5 p.m. on the 14th, and after flipping around the International Date Line and changing days, I was really confused. For a week or so I was getting up at 2 a.m. and fixing a sandwich and a glass of milk. Shirley Ann couldn't figure out what was going on. I went back to work in the office on April 16, after completing a most enjoyable assignment, despite working 107 hours of overtime. Yakura and I would work together on some more protection assignments that will be outlined later. He was an excellent partner and an excellent advance man.

June began with one of the most important counterfeit coin cases that we ever had at the LAFO in my experience. The case consisted of 2,300 pennies that had been counterfeited, and while they were in the process of making their dies, they twisted the die several degrees, making the coin a double-die, error coin. If they had been made at the U.S. Mint, they would have been worth a great deal of money. These sold for about $40 a piece, which meant that the entire case would amount to about $92,000.

A coin dealer in Anaheim scooped up every one of them for the price of $92,000. When he received them, however, he suspected something was wrong and sent two coins to a coin paper who concurred that something was definitely wrong. The coins were immediately sent to the U.S. Mint with a request that they be authenticated. The mint proclaimed that the coins were counterfeit and sent the coins to the LAFO for investigation.

Gary Miller, one of our fine young agents in the Special Investigations Squad, was assigned the case. His life would never be the same. He quickly went out to Anaheim late that afternoon and interviewed the coin dealer. Miller told the dealer that the U.S. Mint determined that the coins were in fact counterfeit. The dealer said he had put the rest of the coins in a safety deposit box at a Bank of America in Anaheim, which at this point was closed for the day. So, the following morning, SA Miller made arrangements to meet the dealer and accompany him to the bank. To forestall any problems, Miller asked me if I could go to the bank early and make sure that no one got into the safety box until he and the dealer arrived.

The next morning, I met the bank manager and explained to him what our problem was. He was very cooperative and we awaited the arrival of whoever might have an interest in the coins other than Gary Miller and the dealer—no one did show up however. A little after 9 a.m., Agent Miller arrived with the dealer and went right to the safety deposit box where the coins were retrieved.

From that point, we made several telephone calls to Roy Earl Gray, a nineteen-year-old guy who had originally supplied the coins to the dealer. Gray had been helped greatly by a well-known numismatist named Mort Goodman. In a tape recorded phone conversation between Gray and a caller, Gray made arrangement to hire someone to plant a bomb at a business, not only to obliterate the business, but to kill the occupants inside as well. Arrangements were made for Gray to meet the hit man at a bank in North Hollywood, where he would pay him $5,000 to secure the hit.

This was outside of our jurisdiction, so we called LAPD. They sent over several detectives who listened to the tapes and agreed to do the meet. When Gray showed up at the bank to pay the hit man—who was really an undercover police officer—he was immediately arrested. Gray had been involved with coins since a very early age and was certainly considered one of the experts in the field. He had never learned to drive a vehicle, but he knew his coins. His mother was his chauffeur, at least for this day. We also took her into custody, as she had driven him to the meet. When we found her parked close to the bank, she was in the back seat of a VW Bug reading a comic book. I'm not certain if she knew what was going on or not. She was subsequently released from custody by the LAPD, but her son was a keeper. The LAPD had first rights to Gray as theirs was the more important charge, and we could wait our turn on the counterfeiting accusation.

Gary Miller obtained a search warrant for the Gray home in Pasadena. Several agents went out and met Mr. Gray, Roy's father, and told him about the arrests of Roy and Mrs. Gray. It was truly a home of numismatists. Coins were everywhere—in bags, loose, in rolls, on the floor, hidden among clothing, in barrels, on the kitchen table, and in the basement. We also found some gold bars that Ray had bought in Europe and had brought into the U.S. illegally. We seized them. We also seized a ton of copper strips and ingots that we suspected were the source of the counterfeit copper coins. After sending the paraphernalia to U.S. Mint in Philadelphia, our suspicions were proven true—the Mint lab technicians were able to say with certainty that all of the material seized was related to the coins that were produced.

From there, we thought the case was pretty much over, but that turned out not to be the case. In fact, it was only beginning. We soon discovered that the coins had been made by a process started in Switzerland called the Electro-Discharge Machine (EDM), where a coin is used for a pattern and the EDM replicates the pattern exactly.

Roy Earl Gray's mentor, Mort Goodman, had been known as the guru of numismatics throughout the United States. So when we were able to prove the connection between him and Roy, we arrested him as well. Miller and I took a lot of heat from Goodman's friends, who were convinced that we had made a gross error in arresting Goodman—that such a coin-collecting icon could never be involved in a crime of this nature. But we knew we were not mistaken. Gray and Goodman would later say that 1969 was a down year in coins, and they thought that if they could introduce an error coin, it would give collectors a jump-start in getting coins rolling again—a great idea, if it had actually worked.

As a result of Gray's arrest, we seized a very large coin display board that Gray had put together from error coins—not counterfeit ones, but the real thing. We assessed that these coins had to have been made at the U.S. Mint. There were coins that were so badly struck as to make it almost an impossibility for it to be an error. We concluded that it had to be planned. The U.S. Mint sent in Morris Boley, an expert in coins. Some heads rolled at the Mint as a result of his investigation that confirmed that some employees on the midnight shift were indeed taking orders for error coins from numismatists throughout the country.

SA Miller and Assistant U.S. Attorney Allan Friedman, became a very efficient team, both of them becoming experts in coins and traveling to various parts of the United States preparing for the trial of Gray and Goodman. Agent Miller received approval from headquarters to use an EDM in order to make dies to be used in the court preparation. He also made a number of counterfeit coins in order to show the court that it didn't take a master counterfeiter to make them. All in all, Gary Miller did an outstanding job, as did Allan Friedman. Both defendants were found guilty and sentenced to serve time for the counterfeiting of the coins.

The Roy Earl Gray case became a well-known case throughout the Secret Service, and it followed Gary Miller around for the rest of his career because he had done such a great job. In 1995, some twenty-six years after the fact, I was at a retirement party where I overheard some folks talking about Miller and the Roy Earl Gray case! In retrospect, I believe that I made a huge error by not nominating Gary for a special award for all of the great work he had done. He certainly deserved it.

In September 1969, SAIC Guy Spaman retired after forty years in the Secret Service. ASAIC Stu Knight stepped in as acting SAIC until about January 1970, at which time he was transferred back to Washington to be groomed as the next director of the Secret Service, following James Rowley anticipated retirement.

1970

CHAPTER 27

Los Angeles Field Office 1970

The year began with replacing both the SAIC and ASAIC in the LAFO. Bob Powis from headquarters came out as the SAIC and Frank Leyva who was the SAIC in San Diego came up as the ASAIC. This was a dynamite duo. Robert Powis pushed for an immediate change in the LAFO work habits, adding a large amount of undercover assignments where agents were allowed to "dress down" in anticipation of working undercover. Planning became a reality with him at the helm. We increased the number of our personnel; agents were changed around to various squads for further experience; and physical training became very important.

Frank Leyva and I had worked as young agents together in Los Angeles. He spoke Spanish and had been sent to offices like San Juan, San Antonio, and San Diego as the SAIC because of his facility with languages. Frank was later chosen to go to Paris as the SAIC, but first he had to go to language school in Monterey to learn French. While Frank was in Monterey, Bob Powis asked me to fill in as the ASAIC. That was a nice temporary advancement, though as I still had responsibilities as the ATSAIC for the Special Investigation Squad, I asked Agent Roy Anderson, to cover for me on a temporary basis. Roy and I were good friends, and he had been my assistant in that squad. He did an excellent job running the squad, and as result, Roy received a promotion.

Frank Leyva stayed in Monterey until 1971 and then went to Paris. I was selected as ASAIC on a permanent basis in June 1971—thank you Bob Powis. I very much enjoyed working for him. When he took over, there was a decided difference in attitude in Los Angeles. Guys (and soon after, women as well) were working like they had never worked before. Bob was able to secure the transfer of other special personnel to Los Angeles, as he had the "ear" of Washington. There wasn't much that he wanted that he didn't get. Under him, Los Angeles earned the title, "Washington West," and we enjoyed that distinction very much. I often marveled at what some of our group of younger agents accomplished. With Bob giving them some real room to work, we had some of the brightest young agents in the Secret Service. Many of them went on to very high levels in the administrative sector.

But, I suppose I'm getting a little ahead of myself. Let's go back to the year 1970 and see what happened.

On Friday January 2, President Nixon went to Walter Annenberg's residence in Rancho Mirage. He left the next day, so we actually had some of our weekend left—it's amazing how many weekends we worked.

On Sunday, July 26, President Nixon attended a baseball game at Anaheim Stadium— the Angels vs. the Washington Senators. As it turned out, there wasn't much of a crowd, which helped us tremendously. With Nixon now at his home in San Clemente, we were spending a great deal of time there, particularly on the weekends.

Saturday, August 1, I made advance arrangements at the president's birth home in Yorba Linda, the Beverly Hilton Hotel, the Bel Aire Hotel, Chaisin's Restaurant, and then on to the Santa Monica Airport, where the president's chopper was waiting to take him back to San Clemente. It was quite a day. We pulled into San Clemente after midnight and I didn't make it home until 2 a.m.

August 20, Vice President Agnew arrived in Los Angeles for a function at the Beverly Hilton Hotel. The following day, he had an appointment with Peter Malatessa, a relative of Bob Hope, who became good friends' with the Agnews and was ultimately chosen for a position in Washington.

The summer continued on at a blistering pace of presidential detail and advance work. Between Nixon's travels back and forth from San Clemente, and Agnew's frequent visits to California, we stayed very busy working long hours and losing many weekends.

On October 8, I received my first assignment at the United Nations in New York City. Originally, I was going to be in charge of the Norwegian detail, but ended up with Prime Minister Mitja Ribicic of Yugoslavia. He was also the president of the Federal Executive Council. As this was the first experience that the Secret Service had working a United Nations function, we had a lot to learn. On my detail was Kazuo Yakura, from Los Angeles, Don Stebbins from Detroit, Norman Taylor from Indianapolis, and five other Treasury agents from Customs, Intelligence, Inspection and ATF. They all worked out very well, and our little group quickly became a strong team.

Prime Minister Ribicic was due in New York on October 13, so we had a lot of work to do rather quickly. When I received my package of instructions from headquarters, I was told that our group would have one of the most difficult of assignments because the Yugoslavs would be very suspicious. They probably were not going to let us ride in Ribicic's limo, allow us in the Mission House, or share information with us.

However, I didn't find much of that to be true. In our pre-arrival conference at the Yugoslav Mission, the people were very cordial and cooperative.

On October 13, Mr. Ribicic arrived at JFK. I met him at the top of the ramp and introduced myself as his chief of security while he was in the United States. I asked to meet his one and only security agent, Mr. Georgijevski. We met and talked. I told him that I would appreciate if he would stick close to me as much as possible, and that he would always have the front-middle seat of our limo whenever we traveled. He was extremely cooperative and I could tell right away that we would work very well together.

There were many functions to attend, both formal United Nations gatherings and social events. At one point, Mr. Ribicic was asked to speak to the entire United Nations. I wished him good luck, which I think he found somewhat reassuring. The second day of the visit, we were due at the United Nations for the normal meetings. Several minutes before our departure in the motorcade, Mr. Georgijevski came over to me and said, "Mr. Horn, he is all yours today. I am going shopping." I think from that point on, we knew they trusted us.

One function that many members of the United Nations attended was an evening at the Metropolitan Opera. Mr. Ribicic opted to attend, so Agent Yakura advanced it for us. About half way through the performance, I received a radio message in code from Yakura advising that there had been a bomb threat at the Metropolitan Opera. Yakura advised that we should depart immediately. That's all I needed. I made my way down the aisle to Mr. Ribicic and said, "Lets go now." Amazingly, he didn't balk or question—he simply got up and followed me down the aisle. When he did this, each member of his entourage immediately got up and followed us out. Agent Yakura had our cars waiting. As we headed back to his residence, I told him about the bomb threat. Bomb scares come and go, but I feel that you always have to go with it. There wasn't any bomb found at the Metropolitan that night, but my protectee was home safe, and that was all that really mattered in the long run.

One day, Mr. Ribicic wanted to go to Philadelphia for lunch at Bookbinders Restaurant. Thanks to Yakura, we had the New Jersey State Police escorting us all the way through the turnpike. We had a great lunch at Bookbinders, which at that time was one of the fine restaurants in America. I ordered lobster, which I enjoyed very much.

A side note: some people will wonder who pays for the agents' meals when they are on assignments like that one. Sometimes the protectees did, but that wasn't really recommended—the agency always preferred if the agents paid for themselves, so we didn't owe anyone anything. Sometimes the restaurant would foot the bill for the agents, but, again, that didn't occur very often.

After New Jersey, we headed for Washington, where Mr. Ribicic had a talk and a photo opportunity with President Nixon, followed by a day of sightseeing. Yakura did all of our advances, and at times, he would roll in just ahead of us in the motorcade, jump out and run to see if he could find someone from the site who could assist us. He never failed to acquire someone in time for us to stroll up and be met by Yakura and our newly found guide. It was fun to watch Yakura operate.

We left Washington on October 25, and returned to New York to prepare for Mr. Ribicic's departure that night. Upon our arrival at JFK that evening, our intelligence team advised me that a check of the manifest revealed that Abie Hoffman, the political activist, was also on our flight as far as Paris and then he would be going on to Libya. I spoke to several of the Air France administrators, explaining our concern for Mr. Ribicic being on the same flight as Hoffman. They didn't think it would be a problem and declined to remove Hoffman from the flight. The ball was now in our court, so I told the Air France authorities that we weren't going to allow Mr. Ribicic on that flight. They advised there would be another flight to Paris in two hours. They changed our flight and put us up in their first class lounge awaiting departure, where they took very good care of us from that point on.

After Mr. Ribicic and his party left, the Yugoslavian mission chief asked me to come back to the Mission with all of our personnel. I accepted the invitation, not really knowing what to expect. When we arrived, they must have had fifty or more Yugoslavs waiting for us. They had gifts for all of our people, a great dinner, and many kind words. What a pleasant surprise that was. What was originally said to be a most difficult assignment turned out to be a very enjoyable experience— a real piece of cake.

The next day our detail disbanded and we all went home, bringing the month of October—a month in which I worked 176 hours of overtime—almost to a close.

I arrived back at the office on Monday, October 26 and quickly tried to catch up on my administrative duties before I was swooped up for another time-consuming project. And sure enough, on October 30, President Nixon attended a large political rally at the Anaheim Convention Center. The following day we were at El Toro Marine Corps Air Station making arrangements for the president to depart. Later that same day, Vice President Agnew arrived and we took him to the Newporter Inn, where he remained overnight. Agnew remained until Monday, November 2, and that took care of that weekend.

November 10, I was invited to speak to the Orange County Numismatic Error Club. My topic was supposed to be "error coins," but so many of these people were friends of Mort Goodman, who was now a co-defendant with Roy Earl Gray in the very big coin counterfeiting case, that I should have expected a set up. When I arrived, Mort Goodman was sitting in the front row. Upon seeing him, I quickly changed my topic to "Ethics in Numismatics," and really dwelled upon the fact that ethics is not a sometime experience, but it is now and tomorrow and again and again and forever. I think that Mort Goodman and his friends got the message. They tried to goad me into talking about the Roy Earl Gray case, but because it was an on going case, I wasn't at liberty. I did advise them that when the case was finalized judicially, I would be glad to come back. Goodman eventually got six years in prison, and not surprisingly, I never received an invitation to return to speak. That group truly believed that the U.S. Secret Service had overstepped their bounds, and most definitely, Mort Goodman was not guilty as charged. They couldn't have been more wrong.

As 1970 came to a close, I should tell about an incident that occurred. I don't recall the exact day, but here is what happened: So often in counterfeiting cases, people become very paranoid. They begin to look over their shoulder; they check their rear view mirrors frequently; they think their friends or colleagues in the venture are beginning to cooperate with the Secret Service (which does happen on occasion); they think about their survival; and generally become very nervous.

There happened to be a group in the South Bay that had conspired to make counterfeit notes. We didn't have a clue about the group, but regardless, several in the group thought the Secret Service was near and breathing down their neck, which of course we weren't. But they became so nervous that they decided to close up the operation and get rid of everything. They put everything—notes, negatives, plates and other items including envelopes with addresses—in a burlap bag, put several rocks in it, and tossed it from the Vincent Thomas Bridge in San Pedro into the water below. They sped off thinking that all of the evidence was sinking to the bottom of San Pedro Channel where it would be lost forever. They thought wrong! The bag instead fell and twirled, and finally landed on the old Grumman Goose landing site an area where passengers used to board the planes for Catalina Island. The bag fell with a giant thud, and when several perplexed employees felt there would be no more pennies from heaven, they approached the bag, opened it, and found the counterfeiting plant inside. They called the LAPD who in turn called us.

Going through the bag, agents found a number of business envelopes with addresses that led them to the plant. As usual, most of the defendants desire to help themselves and, generally will cooperate in some manner. Such was this case.

1971

CHAPTER 28

Los Angeles Field Office 1971

January 1, 1971 saw Vice President Agnew at the Hearst home in Palm Springs. Several of us were out there to help, as Agnew was going to play tennis at the Tennis Club and golf at the Thunderbird Golf Course. Agnew was a better tennis player than he was a golfer. He had a tendency to hit people while teeing off his first hole, especially if there were a lot of people watching. After, he did pretty well but still had a monstrous slice that appeared every now and then.

On February 23, sadly our former ASAIC, Victor D. Carli, passed away. I was sent to San Francisco as the LAFO representative. I was pleased to meet Vic's family and to be with them for a short while. Vic was the epitome of a Secret Service agent as he could do it all. As I previously mentioned, I patterned my supervisory demeanor after Vic Carli and Mr. George Walker, my former SAIC in Phoenix. Both were fine role models.

During the month of June, I received a call from Assistant Director Burrill Peterson, advising that I had been chosen as permanent assistant special agent in charge of the Los Angeles Field Office. I know that Bob Powis, our SAIC, had much to do with that decision. I have always been grateful to Bob for his wonderful assistance in my career. Also around this same time, I was selected for the "Personalities of the West and Midwest Society." It was a very nice honor and probably a direct result of my association with Pepperdine College.

On June 15 and 16, we had President Senghor of Senegal in Los Angeles. He stayed at the Century Plaza Hotel and attended a function at UCLA. Los Angeles was one of the busiest offices for foreign visitors. If we weren't preparing for a visit from the president or vice president, we were preparing for some foreign VIP, and so very many of them would come two and three times each. There were times when we would have several in at the same time, and we would have to leapfrog and juggle our personnel in order to have everything covered. Occasionally, we even had to call Washington and request agent assistance from other offices throughout the United States.

August 20, President Nixon went to Loma Linda Hospital to give a speech. Later he attended the wedding of Robert Finch's daughter at the Presbyterian Church of La Canada.

I believe that at about this time, during this stay of the president at San Clemente, the following incident occurred: I was at the office when my telephone rang. It was Agent Arthur Godfrey of Nixon's detail. He said that the president wanted to go to Catalina. It just happened that Shirley Ann and I had been over there about a week before and I knew Catalina pretty well. I told Godfrey that it was too late in the day to get an agent over there, but I could have several there in the morning. He said, "No Dar, you don't understand. He wants to go over there as soon as possible, today." I told Arthur to stand by and I would get back to him.

I fished out the card of the Los Angeles County deputy sheriff who was stationed in Avalon and called his office. A secretary answered and I told her who I was and that I would like to speak to Deputy Schulz. She advised me that he was out on a call and could not be reached at this time. I then told her why I was calling him. I asked if the mayor was available. He was and picked up the line. Upon explaining my dilemma, he became excited. We agreed that Pebbly Beach would be the best place to land the chopper, and then we proceeded to make all of the arrangements. When we hung up, he had about forty minutes until arrival time. How is that for putting pressure on people?

I called Godfrey in San Clemente. I told him what I had done, who the mayor was, and that he promised he would have three cars available on the president's arrival at Pebbly Beach. I also told him about Deputy Schulz being unavailable, but the chances were that he might be available by the time the entourage arrived. We were certainly hoping that was the case as Schulz was the only deputy assigned to Catalina.

Later that night, I called Godfrey at his hotel room and asked how things went. "Splendidly," he said. Apparently, they drove all over Avalon and up into the hills, out by the Casino, and downtown. I wonder how many other presidents have ever visited Catalina. That had to be a great day for the mayor and his city

On September 25, Abba Eban, the prime minister of Israel, arrived in Los Angeles. He was a very active foreign diplomat who visited Los Angeles often and invariably stayed at the Century Plaza Hotel. Eban was a linguist. I recall going to press conferences with him where he would speak in Israeli, English, and Spanish. He was a very bright person and loved to visit the Los Angeles area as well as the many wealthy, successful Jewish people in the area. He was big in the Israel Bond sales and was responsible for millions of dollars being pledged for the support of Israel. I can tell you at times there was much pressure placed on the Jewish community to contribute as much as they could.

During the time that Eban was at the Century Plaza, we also had Vice President Agnew arriving in Anaheim where the International Association of Chiefs of Police (IACP) was having its convention and where Mr. Agnew would be the prime speaker. I was a member of the IACP so I attended the convention, and in addition, I also had to assist with the Agnew visit. By the time the IACP convention was over, Eban and Agnew had both departed, so we got back to our normal routine in the LAFO. That routine in one word was hectic, but did we enjoy it!

President Tito of Yugoslavia was due to arrive in Los Angeles during the latter part of October. For over a week, we advanced such places as the Century Plaza, Douglas Aircraft in Long Beach, the residence of Leonard Firestone, and the Palm Canyon and Riviera Hotels in Palm Springs. The Tito group traveled a great deal in Southern California, and thus our office was stripped of personnel doing advances and standing posts. It was a relief when they left our district in the beginning of November.

October 29, I attended the funeral of my old friend Ralph Bradford. Brad had retired from the Long Beach Police Department, but was still doing work for us when he got very ill. Bradford thought that he had cancer, as it ran in his family, but he didn't go to the doctor until it was much too late. However, it was determined later that he didn't have cancer, he actually died of pneumonia. What a loss for law enforcement, and what a loss I suffered. He was one of my best friends.

On November 11, I spoke to four classes at our daughter Diane's school, Miraleste High School, in relation to their "Idea Forum," which the school held each year. I spoke to classes periodically at the request of Diane and I always enjoyed myself. Both of our children graduated from Miraleste High School.

First thing in the morning on Saturday, November 27, I headed to San Clemente. As soon as I arrived, a number of us took off for Palm Springs, where President Nixon was to be involved at the Eisenhower Medical Complex. After that, we went to the El Dorado Golf Course where the president played a round of golf before returning to San Clemente.

The next day, I was back in San Clemente, and then at El Toro Marine Corps Air Station for the president's departure to Washington. I wasn't home until 5:30 p.m. Wouldn't you know our weekend was completely blown. That happened so often.

1972

CHAPTER 29

Los Angeles Field Office 1972

The year 1972 started out much too busy. January 8 and 9, we had Prime Minister Sato of Japan visiting at the same time we had President Nixon in San Clemente. On the 8th, I worked with Prime Minister Sato at the Reef Restaurant in Long Beach. Then I went to El Toro to assist in the departure of President Nixon. Later I returned to the Century Plaza to assist with Mr. Sato. The following day, Mr. Sato departed. We only worked three hours that day, but our weekend was shot already.

February 8 and 9, we had Defense Minister Moshe Dayan of Israel in Los Angeles. He stayed at the Century Plaza Hotel where he spoke to about seven hundred people, and after which, he attended a private dinner at the residence of Max Firestein in Beverly Hills. We returned him to the Century Plaza and discontinued at midnight.

March 14, I went to Sacramento to run the office until March 29. Sacramento was a very good office, and it almost ran itself. During my time there, we had Hubert Humphrey visiting us, who was running for the presidency, again.

On March 29, Jim Griffith from the LAFO was sent up to relieve me. I was glad to get home. It was good experience for both Jim and me to get some experience in running an office. We couldn't have gone to a better office than Sacramento for the learning experience.

April 15, Senator George McGovern, who was running for the presidency, arrived in Los Angeles. We took him to the Forum in Inglewood and then to the International Hotel where he remained overnight. The next morning we took him back to LAX for his departure. Again, there went our weekend.

On April 18, I went to the KXLA TV Station in Los Angeles, where I spoke on the business channel regarding counterfeiting activities in the Los Angeles area. On April 24, I was asked to appear on Channel 34 TV, again in regards to counterfeiting.

As this was an election year, the next several months would be extremely busy! We were to provide security for all parties in the running, and as such, we were kept breathless between details of each of the contenders. And as it turned out, this election year would be like no other.

April 30, several of us went to the Los Angeles Convention Center to do an advance for Julie Nixon Eisenhower, for a presentation she was to make for her father on May 3. As the daughter of the president, she was given physical protection by the Secret Service.

On May 17, Congresswoman Shirley Chisholm, the first black woman to run for the presidency, arrived at LAX. We took her to Long Beach State University, where she spoke to the student body. The following day, Mr. Humphrey arrived and I worked him for the rest of the day. May 19, I was back with Shirley Chisholm, advancing a site in Watts where she would be speaking.

On May 20, we escorted Senator Henry "Scoop" Jackson from the airport to the Beverly Hilton. Later that night, we accompanied Senator George McGovern to the Wilshire Hyatt House. I was finally relieved of duty at 1 a.m.

Bright and early the next morning, we went to work assisting Mr. Humphrey at the Beverly Hilton. We escorted him by way of motorcade to a recreational area in Monterey Park and then to a speech site in East Los Angeles. After that we took him to LAX for his departure.

My days, nights, and weekends continued at this pace, and really allowed for no other work, especially counterfeit investigation, which is what I really loved to do. We leapfrogged between visits from McGovern and Humphrey, escorting them everywhere from political rallies, to TV appearances, to special dinners,

Then, on June 19, we had President Echeverri of Mexico in Los Angeles. He spent most of his time at the Century Plaza Hotel attending receptions, luncheons and dinners. One such luncheon was for the World Affairs Council,, with about 850 people in attendance. President Echeverria departed on June 21, after a very busy three days for a majority of our agents, as well as a number of agents from San Diego.

June 25, Thomas Eagleton, Senator McGovern's vice presidential designee, came to Los Angeles, making appearances at KNBC-TV Studio, the Hollywood Palace, and the Century Plaza. But all hell broke loose when the media broke the news that Senator Eagleton had been treated for mental disabilities. He was devastated and very quickly resigned from his position. Sargent Shriver stepped in as his replacement, but I don't know if anyone could have helped the McGovern campaign at that point.

August came, and the pace didn't slow. We continued to have numerous visits from Nixon, his wife, Mr. Agnew, Mr. McGovern, Mr. Shriver, and a number of foreign dignitaries.

On October 16, I was assigned the detail of Prince Hassan of Jordan (the brother of King Hussein, who was staying at the Newporter Inn in Newport Beach. The detail had already been working for some time, but I took over as soon as I arrived. I have worked many foreign dignitary details, but I believe my time with Hassan was about the best I ever had. Ever after, whenever Hassan would come to the United States, I was assigned to him as the person in charge.

We stayed in Newport Beach until the 18th, and then flew to Washington where we stayed until the 26th, when Hassan and his wife returned to Amman, Jordan. Before the detail disbanded, Hassan wanted to see Secret Service headquarters and to meet the director, James Rowley. After that, it was out to Dulles Airport from where the Hassan entourage departed.

It was nice to get home after several weeks on the road, living out of a suitcase. But, it was out of the frying pan and into the fire when I got back to the LAFO. The last week of October and the first week of November, we had visits from Ted Kennedy, Sargent Shriver, Mr. Agnew, President and Mrs. Nixon, and Senator McGovern. We were exceedingly busy.

Finally, on November 7, the election came and went, and we were able to get back to our normal functions. I was grateful to get away from the protection field for a while. It was also nice to have our weekends off again.

But the politicians didn't stay away very long. On November 25, Vice President Agnew returned to Palm Springs, where he proceeded to go to the Eisenhower Hospital for unknown reasons before heading to Frank Sinatra's home, where he was staying. Sinatra always treated us very well. He had a magnificent cook who made the greatest breakfasts for the agents. I spent just that one day in Palm Springs, and returned home late on Saturday in order to have Sunday off. What a privilege!

December 4, I attended the funeral of Agent Dick Cameron's father in Long Beach, where I learned that Dick's dad had been involved in Secret Service work as a young man. Dick was always one of my favorite people. I had done his background investigation and that always makes an agent special. Dick and I have remained friends through the years, and it was very satisfying to see him develop into a very fine agent.

The remaining part of December and the year 1972 slipped away very quickly. It had been a very busy and interesting year. With each new election year, the campaign for the presidency became longer and more drawn out. With all the visits by the American politicians, plus the increasing amount of visits by the foreign dignitaries, the Secret Service began its change from a law enforcement agency to a protective agency. It was very difficult for agents to maintain their criminal investigations while taking part in their protective assignments.

Before 1972 slips away entirely, I wanted to tell a story about a counterfeiting case that we had much difficulty with because of the shortage of personnel. There appeared in the Los Angeles area a pretty good counterfeit note in which we had very little success in combating, although the main players were pretty well identified.

One day I suggested to Bob Powis that we could try our ace informant, Lord Jim, to see if he might be able to help us—if anyone could, Lord Jim could. We called Lord Jim in and told him what we had. He took it all down, went home, and in about an hour, he called to advise us that he had already contacted the bad guys. He said that he had proposed a gigantic deal with them for the next day and that they had bought him hook, line and sinker. That was nothing new with Lord Jim. He was one of the best informants of all time. The following day, Lord Jim met the main players, talked a lot about money and made arrangements for a big buy. We were astonished as to how quickly this all occurred, after we had worked on it for several months without any success.

The next day, all of us agents got together to determine where our guys would be placed to best assist Lord Jim for the big buy. The office cleaned out to go cover the buy. Lord Jim went to the meeting place, and within a half hour, he had what he wanted. The signal was given and guys swooped in and made the arrests—case closed, as simple as that. Just goes to show you how important informants are in the field of law enforcement: Lord Jim only needed a few minutes during a two-day period to put an end to a very perplexing investigation. Lord Jim was truly worth his weight in gold.

At Jefferson Barracks, Missouri, 1917
left to right: Victor, Steve, Herman, Ernest, Bill Kattner, Grandfather Horn, May Kattner

At Jefferson Barracks, Missouri, 1917
left to right: Victor, Bill Kattner, Steve, May Kattner, Ernest, Grandfather Horn, Herman

circa 1885
Maternal Grandmother, Luella Wright

Horn boys, circa 1905
back row: Herman, Ernest
front row: Stephen, Victor

circa 1907
Grandmother (Wilhelmina) Horn with Uncle (Thomas) Horn

1928
Dar at age two and a half

Mother, Myrtle Horn

December, 1936
Venice, California
Ernest, Mother, Father, Dar

Steve Horn
St. Louis Police Department

Mrs. Domer, sixth grade teacher and Dar

Venice, California, 1937
Mrs. Domer's sixth grade class, Nightingale School
top row, 4th from left: Louis Corso; 2nd row, 5th and 6th from left: Fraser Giles, Dar

October, 1937
Dar, Nancy Ann, Fraser Giles, Ernest Jr.

Inglewood, California, 1939
Ernest and Dar

Inglewood, California, 1937
Ernest, Nancy Ann, Father, Dar, Mother, Arline

Inglewood, California, 1939
Dar and Ernest with Ernie's 1922 Chevy

Inglewood High School baseball team, 1943
back row: Voss, Wettack, Peterson, Coons, Crampton, Peterson, Unk, Winslow

middle row: Horn, Kirkland, Hyduke, Bishop, Hastings, Gates, Walker
front row: Unk, Truhill, Green, Duitsman, Bell, Butler

USNTS vs. Redlands University

USNTS game uniform

Over the top at Cal Poly, San Luis Obispo

Coach Bo Molenda and Wally Huefner
USNTS, San Diego, 1943

U.S. Navy, 1944
Engine room crew: Moore, Webb, Willis, Penland, Smith, Horn

U.S. Navy, 1943

U.S.S. SERENE (AM300)
c/o Fleet Post Office
San Francisco, Calif.

PLAN OF THE DAY - APRIL 7, 1945

0330 Call the watch.
0350 Relieve the watch
0500 Call ship's cooks and mess cooks.
0600 Call mess attendants.
0630 Reveille for all hands.
0645 Breakfast.
0730 Muster on Fantail. Burial at Sea.
0750 Relieve the watch.
0800 Muster on stations. Turn to.
1115 Knock off. Clean sweep down.
1130 Early chow.
1150 Relieve the watch.
1200 Dinner.
1550 Relieve the watch.
1700 Supper.
1900 Make 8 o'clock reports to OOD.
1950 Relieve the watch.
2000 Make 8 o'clock reports to CO & XO.
2100 Lights out.
2330 Call the watch.
2350 Relieve the watch.

J. A. PETIT
LIEUTENANT, USNR
EXECUTIVE OFFICER.

USS Serene, AM300, July, 1944

USS Serene crew reporting, July, 1944

U.S. Navy, 1944
Engine room crew: Fries, Penland, LaRoche, Moore, Brewer, Dar

E.F. Coen crew: Graham, Tippitt, Jack Coen, George

December, 1945
Homeward bound

Pepperdine Football, 1946

Hitting a home run Pepperdine, 1947

Graduation from George Pepperdine College, 1949
with Shirley McBride

Photo courtesy of "Associated Press," 1947
Dar with Emma Aston (Drager), Shirley McBride (Horn), Sherry Meester at the campus store

The best of everything
To my Little All American Fullback
Warren N. Gaer

Warren Gaer, head football coach, Pepperdine

Wedding Bells February 14, 1950
Shirley and Dar

Los Angeles Police Department, 1951

1951
Dar with partners Tom Barnes, and Robert Ballou

1951
Dar with partner Tom Barnes

1953
Cousin Fred Krauss, Aunt Agnes, and Dar

Arlington, Virginia, 1957
The Horn family

With President Eisenhower, 1954

With Ike in Carmel, California

With Ike in Burbank, California

Black-tie function at The White House, 1956
from left to right: McCown, Dixon, Weisheit, Horn, Roberts, Burke, Roth, Marass

Russell and Ralph Bradford from the Long Beach Police Department at a counterfeiting plant

Photo courtesy of The Register, Orange County, California
Daughter Diane meets Vice President Agnew

Newcomb Counterfeit Plant
Agents Sheridan, Weaver, More, Bradford, Horn

Agents Horn, Larson, Boggs, Leyva, Henne, Polenz

Chowtime, 1966
Agents Wunderlich, Horn, Leyva, Boggs

Phoenix, Arizona
Winifred and Bill Hammonds

Photo courtesy of Jim Rayle
Teaching bankers about counterfeiting, 1971

Photo courtesy of "Long Beach Press Telegram"
Cal State University, Long Beach, 1972
On assignment with Congresswoman Shirley Chisholm

American football in Paris, 1978

Saying "so long" to Paris crew
Horn, Le Den Mat, Bell, Connally

More "goodbyes"
Shirley Ann, Le Den Mat, Provencher, Horn

On Airforce Two, 1981
President Ford, Horn, Brown, Hoskins, President Carter

Crown Prince Hassan of Jordan at S.S. Headquarters
Boggs, Barton, Prince Hassan, Hill, Rundle, Director Rowley, Horn

At the Glendale Rotary Club

Mr. Toastmaster

On the golf course with President Ford, 1981

Running marathons was fun

At the Warsaw Ghetto monument

Paris, France, 1984
President Mitterand speaks to the Simon Wiesenthal Group

With the Simon Wiesenthal Group at the Vatican

With the Simon Wiesenthal Group in Leningrad, 1985

With the Simon Wiesenthal Group in Budapest, 1984

With the Pope at the Vatican

With the Simon Wiesenthal Group at the Kremlin, 1985

Mutual Admiration Society
Horn and Powis of the Los Angeles Field Office

40 years later, 1990
Bell, Coach Gaera, Horn

Retired Agents Larson, Horn, Slocum

50 years later, 1993
Coach Bo Molenda and Dar

After 40 years with Wally Huefner

After 40 years with John Santchi

50 years later. Standing: Evans, McNeil, Wilkowski, Abernathy, Fries, Horn, Twichell, Prevatil, Bowyer. Seated: Marshall, Penland, Froeckler, Wells, Rambert

Los Angeles Field Office Christmas Party, 1991
Agents Leyva, Horn, Postal Inspector Carey, Larson, Polenz

55 years later
Gates, Kirkland, Horn, Butler, Bell, Gustavson, Hyduke, Duitsman

50 years later in front of Venice, California home

At Pepperdine with good friend, Kenneth Hahn

1973

CHAPTER 30

Los Angeles Field Office
1973

The year 1973 began with Mrs. Nixon being the guest of honor at the Rose Parade in Pasadena. She was a very shy person and didn't care much for the hullabaloo of the Rose Parade. And she didn't want agents to be seen around her car, so only the driver and her SAIC would be seated in the front seat with her during the five-mile parade route.

We however didn't think it was a very wise decision on her part, so Bob Powis had the great idea to dress a number of our agents as Rose Parade officials in ivory suits with red ties. They formed a loose phalanx around Mrs. Nixon for the entire parade route without Mrs. Nixon ever knowing she had added protection. The scheme worked and we got out of the parade in great shape. It was a nice feeling to see how well the security plan was working. Though I'm sure Mrs. Nixon would not have appreciated it if she had known how many of our agents and police officers were actually on duty along the parade route as well on the higher roof tops.

After the parade, I scooted over to Lou Corso's home in time to see most of the Rose Bowl game with him and our families. The Uno Candy Bars that Shirley Ann and I bought for Lou each year were particularly good that year. It must have been a vintage year.

On Saturday, April 14, I flew to Honolulu in preparation of the arrival of Prince Hassan. I took Shirley Ann, at our expense, because she was on Easter vacation. I'm so glad she came—we had a great time. I think that must have been her first time in Hawaii. We made a point to see a great amount of Oahu, ate out most of the time, and most of all enjoyed the Hawaiian weather.

Most of us had worked Hassan before so we knew what to expect. We did have to do some advance work at some sites but it wasn't much. It was nice working with Frank Slocum, who was still in charge of the Honolulu office. Frank had so many protection visits at Honolulu that he could probably have done most of them by telephone.

Hassan arrived on April 23, and stayed in Honolulu for three days. During one of the days, Hassan had indicated that he had wanted to go swimming at Waikiki. The Honolulu Police Department was loaded with Hawaiian swimmers, so we had a multitude of them available when the swimming party began.

On the 25th, we flew back with Hassan to the Newporter Inn. We stayed until May 6. We then accompanied him to New York City, where he attended a number of luncheons and dinners. On May 10, he went home after a very long but successful assignment. Hassan was very good to work with. He was extremely cooperative, and he once told me that the greatest ambassadors America has are the U.S. Secret Service agents. That was quite a compliment, and I believed he was sincere.

We continued to have a variety of other protective assignments. Mr. Leonid Brezhnev of Russia came over and met with President Nixon in San Clemente. President Thieu of Viet Nam came on several occasions. Mrs. Nixon made several trips up to Los Angeles for various meetings as did President Nixon. We were always expecting someone.

One Saturday that summer, I actually had the day off—or so I thought. Mr. Nixon was in San Clemente and it had been a very quiet day. I was outside doing yard work when the telephone rang at about 4:30 p.m. I was advised that Mr. Nixon was getting ready to depart San Clemente on the chopper, en route to the FBI Building landing pad in West Los Angeles. He had made arrangements to have dinner at Chaisin's Restaurant in Beverly Hills.

My job was fourfold: to get our people out to advance Chaisins; to get a team of agents to run the route and act as lead car; to get several agents to stand post prior to the arrival of the working shift; and to obtain a team of intelligence agents to accompany the motorcade. San Clemente said that their duty shift was leaving immediately with the limo and a follow up car. They would have a CHP unit escorting them, and they were going to have to hustle to make it in time to meet the chopper, as Saturday traffic on the 405 Freeway is murder.

I had to shave, shower, dress and get out to the chopper pad by 6:30 p.m. When I arrived, I found that everything had been locked tightly for the weekend. I scooted over to the main building got in touch with the chief of security. I explained the situation to him and asked him to assist me. He was very cooperative and called the fire department to send a unit and an ambulance. We went down to the pad area, unlocked the gates and set up for the president's arrival.

It was getting pretty late by this time, and the chief of security and I were the only ones there on the scene. I had been getting radio calls from the motorcade advising of their estimated time of arrival, which kept getting farther and farther away from the planned time of arrival. In addition, I kept getting calls from our advance people who were at various locations and there was no way they were going to be on time either.

At 6:55 p.m., the chief and I were still the only ones there. All of a sudden I received a call from the motorcade requesting information as to their exact off ramp. "Please get here as quickly as possible," I pleaded as the chopper was now in view and the chief and I were still alone.

As a stall tactic, I called the chopper and requested that they make one turn around the site before landing. Almost immediately after that however, the fire department units appeared on the site, followed by the lead car who had been running the route to Chaisins. Right after them came the Intelligence Unit. And we were finally in business, when very quickly thereafter, the CHP unit, followed by the limo, and the follow-up car, arrived. As those vehicles began to line up in formation, the chopper came in for landing. You could not have planned it closer.

Because the dinner wasn't going to be over until quite late, they weren't going to be able to use the chopper on their return trip. Instead they would motorcade back to San Clemente, which meant that I was free to go home. But it had been a very exciting experience.

On August 22, I went up to Ojai and spoke at an Optimist Club meeting. This I did for my old friend and former agent, Mike Mandalay".

On October 6, Prime Minister Ali Khalifa of Bahrain arrived. Bahrain was a very important ally because, at that time, it was the friendliest Persian Gulf nation toward the U.S. They were allowing us to build a huge naval facility there for our Persian Gulf Fleet. Prime Minister Khalifa was a very easy protectee. He appreciated what we did for him, and he enjoyed sitting down in the lobby of the Century Plaza to people watch. We didn't do too much with him other than to go shopping on several occasions. Khalifa left on October 15, but we'll hear more about him later. I went from Khalifa to Israel Finance Minister Sapira who stayed for several days at the Century Plaza Hotel.

Our old friend, Abba Eban, came in on November 18 but didn't stay very long. That was unusual for him because he enjoyed sitting in the Century Plaza Lobby, too.

Before the year 1973 leaves us, I should tell you of a very important occurrence. I had been jogging since 1967. I would go up to Miraleste High School and do about three miles around the track, not very fast, but it was still good exercise. When I was in Honolulu during April with Hassan of Jordan, I had taken my running gear with me and had run almost every day. It was there that I began to increase my distance each day, as it was great fun running in Hawaii. When we returned to Newport Beach with Hassan, I continued to run more and more, and found that I could run long distances pretty well. Newport Back Bay was a great place to run.

In May, one of our new agents, Bob Brown, and I were talking about running, as he was a very good runner too. He brought up the idea of running a marathon together. I thought he was crazy, if not absolutely out of his mind. There was no way that I could run twenty-six point two miles. Bob, always the optimist, said that all I had to do was to increase my daily mileage. He said that Santa Monica was having a marathon during the latter part of August and that we had plenty of time to train for it. For some crazy reason, he convinced me and I committed to running the Santa Monica Marathon with him. What a dummy! We ran more and more, and I got to the point where I would get up early, run up to Miraleste High School, run six miles, run home and then go to work. On the weekends I did more, eventually building up to nineteen miles, which I completed the week before the marathon. I figured if I could do nineteen, I could do twenty-six point two.

The day of the marathon, Bob and I went to Santa Monica early. Were we so excited! Bob was a much better runner than I, so as the race began, he took off. He finished in a very good time. I plodded around the course and finished in five hours and twenty minutes—not very fast, but at least I finished! I wouldn't have finished, however, except for the encouragement of Shirley Ann who followed me around the course and fed me cokes and chocolate bars all the way through.

Bob and I ran quite a few other marathons together—Santa Barbara, Los Angeles, Orange, Culver City, Los Alamitos, Palos Verdes, and of course, Santa Monica about five more times. All in all, I ran twenty marathons, the last being the Los Angeles Marathon in 1986. When people hear that you ran twenty-six miles, it blows their minds. Really, it is not that difficult to finish one. The difficulty comes when you try to compete time wise with good marathoners. But I never attempted that feat.

We also ran a multitude of half marathons, 5 and 10 Ks, and once, four of us from the LAFO ran a fifty-mile relay from Oxnard to Hollywood. Some fun! Bob Brown, Pete White, Terry

Torrey, and I were the runners on that relay. We really needed five runners, but one fellow had been hurt and couldn't run. Bob Brown did double duty and ran two segments.

I have some very fine memories of running marathons. It's very nice to see friendly faces cheering you on during the races—it makes all the difference in your morale. I also enjoyed many of my running partners. I was particularly pleased when Lou and Jane Corso ran a race with me. They were much better than I, but occasionally we would run across each other during the race.

Running was very important to me for many years. I ran plenty when I was in Paris and when I was out in Rancho Mirage with President Ford. Now, as I have gotten older, I don't run very often, but I do get out for a walk with Stan Moore, my old navy friend, every now and then. We still use the track at Miraleste School.

Well, its time to get into the year 1974. It was to be a very eventful year.

1974

CHAPTER 31

Los Angeles Field Office
1974

We had several foreign dignitaries in Los Angeles in January. Then on February 5, Prime Minister Ali Khalifa of Bahrain arrived in Los Angeles and stayed almost a whole month. That took a lot of manpower. Khalifa was a good protectee to work. He was very cooperative and not a difficult person with whom to get along.

In April, I received a memo assigning me as the SAIC to Henry Kissinger's detail for a trip that would begin in Washington on the 28th and last two weeks, traveling abroad through Israel and Syria. For this "Golan Heights Shuttle," as we called it, Dr. Kissinger was responsible for keeping all of the important players of the Middle East informed as to what was going on. This would mean side trips to most of the capitols of the Middle East.

On April 27, I met up with Dr. Kissinger and the detail. I had previously worked with Dr. Kissinger on many occasions, as he was a frequent visitor to San Clemente. Dr. Kissinger loved the Hollywood scene and he spent a considerable amount of time in that area when he could. Dr. Kissinger was a fun person to work. He was very witty. When he was the national security advisor, he requested Secret Service protection from President Nixon. This wasn't a bad idea because of what he knew. When he became the secretary of state under Nixon, he requested that his Secret Service detail remain intact, even though the U.S. State Department had their own security division. I don't know how state security took that, whether they were angry or not, but Kissinger got what he wanted and his detail increased dramatically.

When Dr. Kissinger's wife, Nancy, would accompany Dr. Kissinger, State Department security handled her, so we would have two details working the Kissingers together. Sometimes we would have a great many agents in close proximity to them. State Department security was a good group. I knew quite a few of them. Their problem was that they didn't have enough agents to handle all of their protective activities as well as a multitude of other responsibilities. Some of their men were as good at security as any in the world.

April 28, we escorted Dr. Kissinger from Andrews Air Force Base to Geneva, Switzerland. We arrived at 8:45 p.m. and went directly to the Intercontinental Hotel. We then took a quick trip to the Russian Mission, where Dr. Kissinger met Mr. Gromyko for a short visit. The following day,

Mr. Gromyko came to the Intercontinental Hotel for a working lunch with Dr. Kissinger. Later that afternoon, we took off for Algiers, where we stayed overnight.

The security group of Algeria put on a banquet for us. It was the typical "lamb pull," where they very ceremoniously bring in huge platters of food, one of which holds a large lamb. The others contain rice, potatoes, tomatoes, and other vegetables. The platters are placed down on tables and everyone serves themselves from the platters. There are no plates and you must use your fingers. For the lamb, you go up to the platter and start pulling shards of meat off of the carcass. It gets a little messy, but then they bring in huge urns of hot, fresh water with towels to wash your hands. It's a very festive dinner. I recall that when they were bringing in the large platter with the lamb, Jack Ready, who was the assistant agent in charge for that trip, said, "Man, I hope it's not a goat." The way it looked, it could have been a goat, but it wasn't. It was nicely done and very tasty.

The next day, we left Algiers en route to Alexandria, Egypt, where Dr. Kissinger met with Anwar Sadat After that, we left for Tel Aviv, Israel, on May 2. As we would be operating out of Jerusalem, we had to motorcade there. This took us about an hour and a half for the one-way trip. Dr. Kissinger would meet with Premier Golda Meir each time we were in Jerusalem. We made the trip into Jerusalem twenty-one times during this shuttle.

May 3, we flew to Damascus, Syria, for conferences with President Assad. Because this trip was in reference to the Golan Heights, we went to Damascus thirteen times. From Damascus on May 4, we returned to Alexandria, Egypt, and later, we left for Tel Aviv and then back to Jerusalem. We maintained our residence at the King David Hotel whether we were in Jerusalem or any countries in the Middle East.

May 5 and 6, we were in Amman, Jordan, where Dr. Kissinger conferred with King Hussein. We returned to Jerusalem late on the 6th, and then on the7th, we flew to Nicosia, Cypress, for a conference with Gromyko, again. Then a quick return flight that evening to Tel Aviv and a ride to Jerusalem. May 8, we flew back to Damascus and then return to Tel Aviv and Jerusalem.

I should relate several incidents regarding Damascus. Not very many Americans were allowed to go there as Syria was aligned strongly with the Soviet Union. Damascus is situated in a valley, and when we were flying in to Damascus, we could see hundreds of Soviet tanks dug in on the sides of the hills surrounding the city. At that time, there were serious thoughts given to the possibility that Israel was going to invade Syria and/or to bomb Damascus. It was truly a war-ridden area.

Each time we landed in Damascus, we were met by the Syrian Foreign Minister before we could travel the nineteen miles into the main part of Damascus. Along the entire route, there were soldiers stationed every fifty yards or so on each side of the road. Our route took us right through the PLO campsite, but as many times we were there, we never had one problem.

May 9, we took a quick trip to Riyadh, Saudi Arabia, for a conference with King Faisal. Then later that evening, we flew to Cairo for another conference with Anwar Sadat. May 10, we returned to Jerusalem and stayed there until May 12, at which time we flew back to Damascus. Later we returned to Jerusalem, discontinuing at midnight.

At this time, the Israeli police discovered several Russian-made rocket launchers about a half-mile from the King David Hotel. They were aimed directly at the side of the hotel where Dr. Kissinger's suite was located. That caused us much concern, and we very quickly made arrangements to learn several alternate routes in the event that we were attacked.

While in Jerusalem, I ran every day, sometimes longer runs than others, depending upon the amount of time I had. Early in the morning, I would run to the ancient walls of old town Jerusalem, and then back to the hotel. If I had time off during the day, I would go across the street to the YMCA. They had a track there, and even though it was very rough, it was adequate for my needs.

May 14, we went back to Damascus, where we stayed for only a portion of that day, returning to Jerusalem that evening and staying there until the 16th. We then returned to Damascus and remained there until after midnight before returning to Jerusalem. May 18, we returned to Damascus for the day and returned to Jerusalem late that night. This was becoming almost a daily occurrence. May 20, back to Damascus and a very late flight back to Tel Aviv and Jerusalem. With all of this travel, I noticed that some of us, including our Israeli Police colleagues were getting a little weary.

May 21, back to Damascus and then back to Jerusalem later that night. Can you see why we termed these trips a shuttle? The next two days, we had the same routine. The reason for all the back and forth was that Dr. Kissinger was in the middle of intense negotiations between the Israelis and the Syrians. He would go back and forth, each time bringing new proposals and amendments to the table. Dr. Kissinger was the big negotiator and he was very good at what he did.

May 26, we went to Damascus and remained there overnight, which wasn't our common pattern, but it did happen a handful of times. May 27 and 28, the same routine, then on May 29, Premier Golda Meir and her cabinet finally approved the final terms, and Dr. Kissinger's job was just about done.

On May 30, we flew to Cairo for one last conference with Sadat before heading back to Washington, arriving there late on May 31. I was able to get a few hours sleep before heading over to headquarters for several meetings. After that, I caught a flight home.

I was so glad to get home after spending the entire month of May in Europe, Africa and the Middle East. I worked a total of 426 hours that month, 250 of which were overtime. It was a very exhausting trip but highly interesting. I marveled at the way the Air Force, the U.S. State Department, and the Secret Service coordinated their efforts, flying personnel and equipment, including vehicles, half way around the world. The logistics were absolutely amazing and it was great to be a part of it.

Back in Los Angeles, things were just about the same. Moshe Dayan came in to Los Angeles for several days in June. On June 12, I spoke to the Inglewood 20/30 Club. Because I had lived in Inglewood, I was aware of how important that organization was to the city. The membership contained most of the very important young men of the city. I was delighted to have been asked to speak.

On Saturday, June 15, we had a very sad experience. Prime Minister Ali Khalifa of Bahrain was coming into LAX for a short layover, before heading to Stanford to pick up his son who had died while being treated at Stanford University Hospital. Many male members of his family had a genetic problem that affected among other things their ability to shed tears. Those males who were born with this genetic problem usually died before reaching adulthood. His son was about twenty years old when he passed on. Several of us who had served with Khalifa before agreed to go out to meet him and extend any assistance that we could.

He told me that he knew I had been in the Middle East with Dr. Kissinger for the whole month of May. He said that it was a big story in his country and each day there was television coverage. He said he had seen several of us whom he knew very often on the TV coverage. He said that Dr. Kissinger's trip to the Middle East was extremely important in keeping the lid on the smoking cauldron. Prime Minister Khalifa was very glad to see us and seemed to appreciate "his" agents concern for him. He was a very nice person. He didn't stay in Los Angeles much over an hour, but we had made arrangements for him to relax in the airline club during his brief layover.

July 12, we worked at the El Toro Marine Corps Air Station for the arrival of President Nixon and Vice President Ford. July 18, we did the same thing for the arrival of Dr. Kissinger.

From the 12th to the 30th of July, we were extremely busy with Nixon, Ford, and Kissinger. Then we got word that Prime Minister Mara of Fiji was coming in. If we weren't down in San Clemente working the president and/or Kissinger, we were working Mara. There was absolutely no rest for the wicked.

From September 15 to 20, I was in Washington attending a management school. On the way home, I stopped in St. Louis and stayed several days with Dar Jr, and his wife, Missy. They were both attending Washington University, Dar for his doctoral degree in anthropology and Missy for her medical degree.

On October 11, I spoke at the Rossmoor School in Los Alamitos, where Shirley Ann was the principal. It was always fun to visit her and her very fine school.

October 31, we had our first visit with our new president, Gerald Ford. He stayed and spoke at the Century Plaza. He was always good to work. There was nothing demanding about him and agents seemed to work harder for him because he was very nice.

November 11, Agents Bill Lelash, Chuck Usher, and I took off for New York City for the detail of Omar Al Saqqaf, the foreign minister of Saudi Arabia who was one of the many world leaders attending the United Nations meetings that fall.

There was much intelligence information being distributed, as this was the U.N. meeting Yasser Arafat was due to attend. We had information about Arafat being the subject of an assassination attempt. There were also a number of Israeli organizations that would be marching in protest. Of course, the Arabs had their plans as well to counteract the Israeli actions. It appeared as if World War III was going to begin in New York City. And as Minister Saqqaf was one of the top Arabs in attendance at the United Nations, it was nice to be thrown into the middle of World War III.

Some other information we received was that Minister Saqqaf was not well. He was very over weight and had a history of ulcers as well as other physical problems. We met Saqqaf at JFK during the evening of November 12. I introduced myself as his chief of security and I purposely asked him how he was feeling. He assured me that he was feeling well. We had to walk him a considerable distance to where our motorcade was parked, but he seemed to weather the walk all right. We took him directly to the Waldorf Astoria Hotel, where, eventually all of the detail would be staying. This made it very convenient for the agents.

On November 13, we took him to the United Nations, and on the 14th, he was scheduled to speak to the U.N. Forum. But Mr. Saqqaf was not feeling well that day, so he canceled his appearance there, and instead remained in bed that entire day. It was a very quiet day for our detail, something we weren't accustomed working a detail at the U.N.

About 7:30 p.m., one of the staff members came out and advised us that Doctor Eugene Beck had been summoned to check on Saqqaf. After a brief exam, the doctor determined that Saqqaf had passed away. We went back in to examine the body to make sure there were no gunshot or knife wounds and that there was no indication of poison being used. Doctor Beck advised that the foreign minister had probably expired several hours ago, as his skin was beginning to deteriorate already. He felt that Saqqaf had died of a massive cerebral thrombosis. A call was made to King Faisal in Saudi Arabia to obtain permission to remove the body and to prepare it for burial. Permission was granted. A member of the staff called the Universal Funeral Chapel on East 52nd Street, with a request that they come to the Waldorf Astoria to pick up the body.

Due to the possible explosive situation between the Arabs and the Israelis, we requested that the pick up vehicle be brought into the back service entrance. They agreed, and they very quickly arrived, picked up the body, put it into a body bag, loaded it on a gurney, and down the freight elevator we went. We had to wheel the body through the galley of the Waldorf Astoria and outside into the service entrance area. So far so good—there were very few people around and we didn't have to stop at all. We put the body into the vehicle and had a four-car motorcade escort him to the funeral home. We left some of our agents to maintain the command post and the main post at the front door of the suite, for appearances sake. Most of us went to the funeral home, where the embalming procedure began immediately.

There were some very important telephone calls to be made. I had to call the Secret Service headquarters of the United Nations. In turn, they called Washington and made arrangements for an air force jet to pick up the body when it was ready and fly the deceased back to Saudi Arabia.

The body was ready at 5 a.m., and they put it into a very large, elaborate coffin that weighed a ton, so it wasn't easy getting it into the hearse. Our lead car, a follow up car, and four staff cars escorted the hearse to JFK, where the air force jet was waiting. But due to a dysfunctional engine part, the jet wouldn't start. A quick request was made to Pan Am for assistance with the part for the jet. They replaced the part for us very quickly and the jet was up and running in no time.

We had a very difficult time getting the coffin aboard the plane. It was so large and heavy, plus Mr. Saqqaf was a very heavy person himself. There was very little room to carry it up the ramp. I don't know how, but three of us grabbed the coffin and didn't stop moving until we were at the top of the ramp. There wasn't room for any more people on the ramp, which made it a very difficult task.

The air force plane took off for Saudi Arabia at 7:30 a.m. Accompanying the body were seven Saudi Arabian staff members and Roy Atherton, deputy assistant secretary of the U.S. State Department. I can't give enough credit to our advance agents, Richard Boland of the NYFO, and Tom Brancaccio of the Training Division in Washington. They did a magnificent job for our short-lived detail. We also received much help from Lt. Walter Delaney and Officer Ralph Zalduondo of the New York City Police Department. Through them, we were able to obtain a preliminary certificate of death, a burial permit, and a letter indicating there were no unusual epidemics of communicable diseases in New York City at the time of the prime minister's death.

There wasn't much left to do. Our detail was disbanded and the agents were allowed to return to their respective field offices. It was such a sad ending to a protective detail. Agent Bill Lelash, who was the appointed driver for our detail, and I caught a flight out to Los Angeles and went directly home as we had worked enough for one day.

That just about wraps up my last assignment at the United Nations. They were always enjoyable even though we would often work eighteen-hour days. I always took pleasure in meeting up with other agents whom I knew and hadn't seen for some time. However, the United Nations is a very different place to work. They have their own police unit and are very conscious of their authority. Secret Service agents and police officers are allowed to bring their protectees into the building, but must then relinquish them to the U.N. The agents then retire to a very large holding room where coffee, doughnuts and other goodies are served continuously. There is also a very nice souvenir shop with a post office available for some quick shopping. Most of us took advantage of that. When your protectee is preparing to depart, a message is broadcast to the holding room and to the automobile holding area. They bring the cars up, you meet your protectee at the bottom of the escalator and away you go. The system always worked very well.

The rest of the year of 1974 was normal. We had our share of dignitaries coming and going. I made a number of speeches, mostly to service groups such as the Kiwanis and the Lions. I took some annual leave around Christmas time and pretty soon it was January 1, 1975. Shirley Ann and I would be at Lou Corso's home watching the Rose Bowl game as usual and enjoying some great fellowship.

1975

CHAPTER 32

Los Angeles Field Office
1975

January 23 and 24, Dr. Kissinger came out for a quick visit. He was always fun to work although you had to prepare for long days and nights. February 8, the prime minister of New Zealand arrived for a visit. He had been to Los Angeles on prior occasions and evidently found it to his liking. He stayed at the Beverly Wilshire Hotel and made a visit to the New Zealand consulate.

From April 2 to 7, I was in Palm Springs with President and Mrs. Ford. It was always nice to go to Palm Springs, as the weather is generally very good. April 9, I spoke at the Weaver School in Los Alamitos, undoubtedly arranged by my good wife Shirley Ann. School speeches are fun! The children get very excited and the time goes by very quickly. Interestingly, one of the most asked questions was pertaining to the weapon that I carried. We would generally assign school speeches to the younger agents who were just getting started in the speaking program. It was a good way to get young agents before groups.

April 24, we had the prime minister of Western Samoa in Los Angeles for several days. April 28, I attended protective operations briefing for supervisors in Washington. The way we were going in Los Angeles with our numerous VIP visits, we could have put the seminar on in Los Angeles. That briefing lasted all week, and on Friday, I left Washington for St. Louis to spend several days with Missy and Dar Jr., who were both still going to Washington University.

On May 19, Mrs. Ford was in Los Angeles, where one of her stops was Pepperdine University in Malibu. I helped out on that very special occasion. It was always great to work functions at Pepperdine. They treat you very well and it truly is a classy organization.

On June 12, we worked the King of Tonga. He came to Los Angeles quite often and always seemed to enjoy his stays. His first visit to our city makes for an interesting story: The King of Tonga was a very large person. He probably weighed around 400 pounds. His hefty weight was due to a tradition in his country. Every December, his constituency came to him with a giant scale. For every pound he weighed, he received a like amount in gold, silver, diamonds, and other metals and precious stones. I don't know if the same situation existed for the queen, but I can tell you she weighed almost as much as the king.

The first visit to Los Angeles the King made, we were not aware of how large he was. We put together a typical motorcade, using a brand new Buick for the limo. We were all set with our motorcade, and all that the King had to do was get off the plane, take the side ramp down, get in the car and we would depart. Well, he made the ramp all right, but when we tried to get him into the Buick, he wouldn't fit. He tried very hard by himself to get in the car, trying this way and that way, but he just couldn't do it. We eventually dropped the window on the back door, backed him up to the car and jack-knifed him into the rear seat. We pushed and pulled and finally got him in.

We left LAX, and due to the time of day, we elected to stay off of the freeway to avoid rush hour traffic. We took Sepulveda Blvd. north bound, en route to the Beverly Wilshire Hotel in Beverly Hills. In Culver City, the King spotted a Jack in the Box restaurant and asked if we could stop. Of course, whatever a King wants, he gets so we pulled the entire motorcade through the Jack in the Box drive-thru. The staff member who was riding in the back seat with the King ordered a dozen hamburgers, a dozen chocolate malts and a dozen French fries—all for the King!

When we arrived at the Beverly Wilshire Hotel, we were able to get him out of the Buick, putting prior knowledge to work, but not without some more pushing and pulling. The staff man had the job of getting the hamburgers, malts and fries up the King's suite. We quickly made arrangements for a larger car to be brought out so we didn't have any more problems with the King of Tonga fitting in the doorway. Ever after that, we always ordered the largest limo when the King of Tonga came to town.

I have to tell a very personal side to the above story. When my daughter, Diane, has anything to do with me making a speech or a presentation, no matter where it is, I can bet somewhere along the way she will get up and request that I tell the story about the King of Tonga. It's her favorite and I know she has heard it many, many times. There was no way that I could write a book and not put this story in, as Diane would have put it in on her own when I wasn't looking.

On September 20, President Ford spoke at Pepperdine University in Malibu, where he formally dedicated the Leonard Firestone Fieldhouse. We worked on that advance for sometime, and the event turned out extremely well. There was a crowd of about 30,000 people packed into the stands that had been erected in the Fieldhouse parking lot.

Immediately after the program, I had to hustle out to Butler Aircraft at LAX to meet the president of Paraguay. He wanted to go to Marineland. This hadn't been on our schedule so I took off before the motorcade and got there as quickly as possible to do the advance. With the motorcade going a little slower than normal, I made it in plenty of time. I think Marineland was use to it because when I found a supervisor and told him who we had coming, he wasn't the least bit flustered. He assigned a person with whom I was to work and we had the advance done in a matter of minutes. Even though we didn't spend very much time in preparing for the visit, it went off very well. The people at Marineland were very good and it became very apparent that they had done the exercise before.

September 26 was the day that SAIC Frank Slocum retired from the Honolulu office. I had requested time off to attend his retirement function, and my request was granted. Frank was one of my best friends in the Secret Service. Dick Lefler had been chosen as the new SAIC and Dick and Assistant Director Burrill Peterson met me at the airport. We went to the office, picked up Slocum, and we all went to lunch together.

At Frank's going away dinner, I was asked to speak regarding my longtime association with him. It was a sad time because Frank didn't want to retire from the Honolulu office, but headquarters wanted him back in Washington as an inspector. Frank's wife, however, had great difficulty living where the air is impure, and as a result they just could not live in Washington. So, Frank simply retired altogether from the Secret Service. That was a real loss!

I had known Dick Lefler from his first day in the Secret Service. He was brought into the LAFO after working for several years for the Los Angeles County Sheriff's Office. He had been well trained by the sheriff's office. And was a very quick learner. Soon, he became an experienced, well-balanced agent. Dick remains one of my very good friends.

October 8 was a red-letter day in the LAFO. We had Emperor Hirohito of Japan as a protectee. Given that many of us in law enforcement had fought in World War II against Japan, I'm sure some of us were thinking, "What are we doing here?" But it turned out all right. We had the emperor at a gigantic function at the Music Center in Los Angeles. After that, we took him to Disneyland, and then we deposited him for the evening at the Beverly Wilshire Hotel. That was a very long and exhausting day.

The presidential election campaign for 1976 had begun and some of us broke away from the emperor's detail and went over to Brentwood for our first presidential political meeting. It was for a politician named Jimmy Carter, a guy no one really had heard of. Mr. Carter had dinner at the residence of one of his Annapolis Naval Academy classmates. The Emperor of Japan left on October 9 without any large problems occurring. We had no incidents of former U.S. service men making any undue difficulties for the Emperor.

October 23, we had King Olav of Norway in Los Angeles. The following day, we took him to the Norwegian Church in San Pedro. There was a very large and excited crowd as San Pedro has many Norwegians who had settled there. There was quite a different feeling with King Olav in relation to the emperor of Japan for all of us in security.

November 8, we had Congressman Udall, who was running for the presidency. He spoke at the Rodger Young Auditorium.

President Ford was in and out of Los Angeles on a regular basis. Sometimes he would stay for several days. Sometimes he would be in and out on the same day.

November 30, we had Governor Reagan, who had again thrown his hat into the national political ring, at the ABC-TV Studio in Hollywood. Mr. Reagan would make a concerted effort against President Ford, but his efforts would fall short. I thought that would be his last political effort. Was I ever wrong?

Throughout the next several weeks, we had Mr. Reagan in Los Angeles on a number of occasions. We also escorted him throughout the U.S. on his political trail. He turned out to be a very active candidate. Congressman Udall returned to Los Angeles on December 4, and he left the same day. I ended up the day with Mr. Reagan at Chaisin's Restaurant in Beverly Hills.

December 8, Vice President Rockefeller was in town for political purposes. I had always thought Mr. Rockefeller would have made a good president. He had a great deal of political experience, loads of money, and he had the desire. I believe his problem was that he was just in the wrong place at the wrong time. I can recall when I was at the White House from 1954 to 1957, Mr. Rockefeller worked as a consultant for Mr. Eisenhower. Mr. Rockefeller was always very cordial and friendly, and often stopped to chat with the agents as he walked by our posts. At that time, I had the distinct feeling that he wanted to be the president of the United States. He came as close as the vice presidency, but went no higher.

The year 1975 slid past into history. I took the last days of the year off on annual leave. You had to take your annual leave when you could because there were many spans of time when there was no way you could obtain it. Some years would go by for some agents when they couldn't use their leave at all. But the good thing was that your leave time accumulated and when you retired they paid you in a lump sum for all unused leave.

1976

CHAPTER 33

Los Angeles Field Office 1976

January 1, 1976 again found the Horns' at the Lou Corso's enjoying the Rose Bowl game and some very fine company along with all of the Uno Candy Bars you could eat.

The LAFO was getting ready for a very busy year, a year that consisted of almost non-stop political activity. It would be very difficult but very exciting, and I think that our office was ready for the challenge.

The month of January was very quiet until the 20th, when Senator Birch Bayh arrived. He didn't stay very long, but immediately after, the Reagan group hit us hard. On January 30, Mr. Reagan arrived at LAX at 10:30 p.m. and we took him straight to his residence. After he was home, I returned to LAX to help out on airplane security.

February 2, Dr. Kissinger arrived and proceeded to the Los Angeles Times building for an interview, at which he was very good.

On the 3rd, Prime Minister Yitzhak Rabin of Israel arrived at the Century Plaza Hotel for an affair. We were involved with the Rabin group until 3 a.m. Later on the 4th, we took Rabin to the Los Angeles Times building for an interview. Mr. Rabin left on February 5, as did Dr. Kissinger.

From February 5 on to June 1, we worked for Governor Reagan, nine times; former president Nixon; the King of Tonga; Mrs. Ford, Jimmy Carter; Senator Frank Church, twice; President Ford twice; King Hussein of Jordan; the King of Sweden; and Vice President Rockefeller. Do you think we weren't busy?

On April 30, the LAFO was hit with one of the worse catastrophes in the twenty-two plus years in which I was there. We had a very capable agent named Fred Nagel, who was in charge of our shooting program and some other aspects of our training. Fred was an experienced agent, but had had some difficulties earlier in his career. He had been relieved from duty as the resident agent in Anchorage, Alaska, for problems that he had engendered. Fred was out of the service for several years before being reinstated as an agent. Bob Powis, our fine SAIC agreed to take him in Los Angeles, knowing that we could use him to our advantage. Fred was a very likable person could do most everything asked of him. He quickly became involved in our protection activities and handled LAX arrivals and departures extremely well. For several years, he was really an integral part of the LAFO.

Sometime in 1976, we received information that indicated that some of our ammunition was being sold at gun shows. With that information in mind, I went back to our office files to determine just how much ammunition we had received and expended in the past several years. We had received a shipment of 50,000 rounds of wad-cutter ammunition from the Nixon detail at San Clemente. They had scaled down their personnel and weren't using as much as they once had. By all rights, the 50,000 rounds should have been somewhere, either in the office safe or in our storage locker at the Seal Beach Navy Installation where we fired. We had not used wad-cutter ammunition for several years, so that ammunition should have still been in our custody. A search of our safe in the office revealed no wad-cutters.

Fred Nagel and I went down to the Seal Beach facility to run an audit on our ammunition. When we got there and opened the locker, it was empty. Nagel couldn't explain its absence. Every last round was gone and Nagel was the only agent responsible for it. He claimed that he didn't know where it was, or why it was missing.

SAIC Powis called Washington and they sent a group of inspectors out immediately for an investigation. They interviewed Nagel without any success. The investigation continued and we tried to find out who might have received ammunition from Nagel, or who might have known where it went. No success.

The U.S. Attorney's Office agreed to prosecute Fred Nagel and on May 15, Nagel was formally suspended, though he had been previously suspended by the LAFO as of April 30. I went to Fred's home in Los Alamitos to explain the details of the permanent suspension and what it meant to him. He was asked to surrender his weapon, his identification, and any other items belonging to the Secret Service. That is always a difficult task because you never know how a person is going to react. Fred relinquished it all with great emotion, but with little difficulty.

Nagel was tried in federal court and was allowed to plead guilty to the misappropriation of federal property. To my knowledge, he was sentenced only to probation and never spent any time in a federal prison. What a sad ending to a Secret Service career; what a bad experience not only for Fred, but also for his wife and children; and what a terrible experience for the Los Angeles Field Office.

A year or so later, I heard that Fred was trying to muster some political assistance in order for him to reenter the Secret Service. Apparently he had asked the same U.S. senator who had helped him on the previous occasion to intervene on his behalf once more. Nagel called me once at my home to see if I would be able to assist him, but I wasn't willing to do that. As it turned out, Nagel got off easy, penalty-wise, except for the loss of his job. That's about the end of the story of Fred Nagel. A very, very sad story.

On May 29, we flew up to a private ranch in Paso Robles for a political dinner for Governor Reagan. It was a gigantic barbecue where they had butchered beef from their own herd. What a sumptuous meal it was. It was all out doors and there were thousands of Reagan supporters there. It wasn't much of a security problem, however. We spent the most of that day there and came home very late that night.

June 3, we went up to Santa Barbara with Governor Reagan for a speech. June 5, we had Governor George Wallace, of Alabama who was wheelchair-bound in Los Angeles. We were able to take him to the Los Angeles County Fair Grounds where he made a speech in front of the racing grandstand. But there weren't too many people in attendance and it was apparent that Mr. Wallace wasn't going anywhere politically.

The following day, we had Mrs. Ford for a meeting at Mt. Sinai Hospital. June 20, we had the King of Sweden for his third or fourth visit. He liked Los Angeles and the Hollywood scene, so believe me, most of his nights were very long. He left Los Angeles after several days but returned on June 28. I got to know his agent very well. In 1977, I was in Stockholm, Sweden, at an Interpol function and saw his agent there. He very quickly gave me his card and told me to call him the next day for lunch. We had a very nice lunch in Old Town, Stockholm. After lunch, he showed me around the castle in Old Town. In particular, I was able to see the crown jewels of the Swedish ruling family. All in all, it was a very pleasant visit with a very nice security agent of Sweden.

July 6, I flew to Louisville, Kentucky, to attend the retirement party of SAIC Frank Leyva. Frank and I were young agents together in the LAFO and I followed him as the ASAIC in the LAFO. Later, I followed him as the SAIC in Paris, France.

In conjunction with the trip to Louisville, I stopped in St. Louis for several days to see Dar Jr. and Missy, who were both still plugging along steadily at Washington University. Then it was back to Los Angeles. On August 28, we had the president of Gabon. That wasn't a very big assignment, but I guess it was as important as any other.

August 31, Senator Mondale came to Los Angeles for a political rally. He would become the vice president of the United States in November, when he and Mr. Carter won the election.

On September 20, we had the president of Brazil. He stayed at the Hotel International and didn't move around very much. September 25, we worked Robert Dole, who was President Ford's vice presidential nominee. We worked him in the morning and then in the afternoon, I joined Governor Carter's group in East Los Angeles.

The following day, I again worked the Dole detail in the morning and then joined the Carter group in the afternoon for a parade in Santa Ana. We took Mr. Carter into a residence in Santa Ana so that he could put on his bullet proof vest. It had all been prearranged. Mr. Carter walked a good part of that parade route, so security-wise, it was a difficult assignment. Mr. Carter left our area about 5 p.m. from the Long Beach airport and we were glad that he left in good shape.

October 7, we had President Ford at USC for a speech. Then later, we worked Mr. Carter at the Century Plaza Hotel, where he spoke to a very large group. On October 8, we had Mrs. Ford at the Universal Sheraton Hotel for a speech. Later, we took her to the Burbank Airport for her departure. After which, we took Mr. Ford to the Glendale City Hall for a speech.

October 23, Mr. Ford returned to Los Angeles for functions at the Huntington Sheraton in Pasadena and the following day at the San Gabriel Mission, and then on to Fountain Valley for another speech. October 30, Senator Robert Dole spoke at Redlands University.

The election was fast approaching and the candidates were all over the country. Unfortunately for us, Los Angeles was a mecca, because of California's high electoral vote.

November 1, Mr. Carter held a huge rally at 6th and Broadway in Los Angeles. The rally caused the LAPD headaches with traffic, but candidates love situations like that because of the exposure. Quite the opposite is true for Secret Service agents and police because of the dangers of the exposure. After the rally, we took Carter to the Biltmore Hotel for another rally and then a departure from LAX.

November 2 was Election Day, so the candidates cleared out to get their photos taken when they voted. It was actually a very quiet day in the LAFO, catching up on a lot of our administrative work.

November 7, after Mr. Ford had lost the election, he came to Palm Springs to see his good friend Leonard Firestone and to play a round of golf at Thunderbird Golf Course. The following day, he played golf at La Quinta Golf Course. He stayed in Palm Springs until the 13th, playing golf and getting ready to turn the reins of the government over to President-Elect Jimmy Carter.

The rest of the year of 1976 was very quiet. We had an opportunity to catch up on all of our paper work and actually had our weekends and holidays off. That was a definite change for the better.

1977

CHAPTER 34

Los Angeles Field Office 1977

January 1977 continued to be slow. I even missed the inauguration of President Carter in Washington. On February 14, we had former president Ford at the Arco Building in Los Angeles. This was the second time he had come back to Los Angeles since he had been defeated for the presidency.

March 31, I attended the retirement party of Detective Gene Bell of the Inglewood Police Department. Gene and I had gone to school together in Inglewood and had worked a number of cases together throughout the years. Gene was privy to all that was going on in Inglewood and was the person to call for any Inglewood information. Gene, his brother, Jerry, and I have remained friends forever.

On May 9, Chip Carter, son of the newly elected president, visited Los Angeles for several days. He was the first of the immediate family of the president to come to Los Angeles after the inauguration.

May 17, President Carter made his first visit to Los Angeles after his inauguration. He had a speech at the convention center and departed very shortly after. June 2, Prime Minister Fairy of Grenada came to Los Angeles.

June 3, I received a telephone call from Assistant Director Burrill Peterson in Washington. Mr. Peterson had been in the Secret Service forever and knew just about everyone in it. He advised that the SAIC in Paris, France, Gene Dagg, was being transferred in August. Mr. Peterson said he had recalled many years ago that I had put Paris as one of my choices in the event I would be transferred. Mr. Peterson asked me if I would still be interested in going to Paris as the SAIC. He said that not only would I be the SAIC of the Secret Service there, but also I would be an attache at the U.S. Embassy and a U.S. representative to the Interpol Organization. That was a lot of hats to wear, and it certainly peaked my interest. But what a dilemma: I was very happy working as the ASAIC in the L.A., and I greatly enjoyed working with Bob Powis. That was as good as it could get in my mind. I told Mr. Peterson that at one time I would have gladly accepted the assignment, but I wasn't sure now. He said that there were about five other agents who had expressed a desire to go to Paris as the SAIC.

Mr. Peterson suggested that I go home and talk it over with Shirley Ann and to call him on Monday morning. I asked him if, in the event I said yes, what would happen? He said the Paris office would be mine if I wanted it.

Dar and Missy, and Barry and Diane were all visiting from their respective homes in St. Louis and San Diego. All of as a family discussed the possibility of me going to Paris. We took a vote and it came out five to one, with my vote being the only one against it. All of them including Shirley Ann kept saying that I had to go, that it would be a great experience. I kept saying I didn't have to go, and if headquarters compelled me to go I could just retire. But they all insisted so much that they finally convinced me. Shirley Ann said that she would try to get a leave of absence so she could join me.

Monday morning, I called Mr. Peterson and advised him that I would indeed accept the assignment in Paris. He said I should make arrangements to come back to Washington for a conference and then go to Paris for a week for a "look see." I was in Washington from June 19 to 22, where I had a number of meetings to attend. I was glad that Gene Dagg of the Paris office was there too. After talking to him at length, the assignment began to sound like a very exciting and interesting experience.

On Sunday, June 26, I left for Paris. Gene met me at the Charles de Gaulle Airport outside Paris and took me directly to the office where I was introduced to the staff. There was Phyllis Neftell, the office manager; Joe Le Den Mat, the French investigator; and Agent Joe Masonis. Masonis invited me to go home with him for lunch and to meet his wife, Jan. I went with Joe, met Jan, and had a typical French lunch.

I spent most of that week in Paris looking for a place to live. Driving in Paris is different and rather difficult—they drive like maniacs! We saw a number of places but nothing that Shirley Ann and I would agree on. I finally opted to live at the Embassy Apartments in Boulogne, where all the other agents lived, which was a definite advantage.

I returned to Los Angeles on July 2 and received the sad news that Shirley Ann was unable to obtain a leave of absence. It looked as if I was going to go to Paris alone, although she would be able to come over with me for about three weeks in August. We divided up our furniture. I took half with me and left half for Shirley Ann. Rumors spread that we were going through a divorce.

1977

CHAPTER 35

Paris Field Office

1977

Shirley Ann and I left LAX on July 31 and arrived in Paris the next day. We were so excited! The office had made arrangements for us to stay in a transient apartment until my furniture arrived. I took a number of days of annual leave and didn't actually take over the office on August 14. That was a Sunday and Monday the 15th was a French Holiday. One of the perks of the Paris assignment was that you got the American holidays off as well as the French ones, which sounds actually better than it was as the workload was so extensive that we rarely could afford to take all holidays off.

Besides the other employees I have mentioned, we also had Agent Peter Grant and his wife, Martha, and John Bradshaw and his wife, Ann. We very quickly became a very close-knit group. What a nice group of people they were and we had a ball working together. I made it a point to accompany each of the agents on some of their foreign travel. I also made it a point to allow Joe Le Den Mat, our French investigator, to do some traveling. That allowed him to get away from the office at times.

My first trip from Paris was to SHAPE headquarters in Belgium, to do a little shopping and to familiarize myself with SHAPE. Shirley Ann was able to go too. What a great place to shop! They had everything: food, clothing, gifts, liquor, and all at very good prices—you never went to SHAPE without a shopping list from all employees.

August 28, I left Paris for Stockholm, Sweden, for my first Interpol conference. I stayed in Stockholm until September 9, attending all of the meetings and trying to meet as many Interpol representatives as possible. One of the special guests of Interpol at this conference was Chief of Police Ed Davis of the Los Angeles Police Department.

Ed was the president of the International Association of Chiefs of Police and he was present to see how Interpol worked. I spent time with Ed during this visit as we had many mutual friends on the LAPD. Ed was a good chief of police, a no-nonsense type of person who served the LAPD very well. We had actually gone to USC together many years prior. He was working for his master's and doctorate while I worked toward my master's degree. In any event, it was nice being able to interact with a member of the LAPD even though we were in Sweden and many miles from home. After the Interpol meeting concluded, I returned to Paris.

From September 22 to 25, I went to Germany with Agent John Bradshaw and his wife, Ann. We had a formal ball to attend, as well as other meetings in Heidelberg and Stuttgart.

September 29, I left Paris to attend the IACP convention in L.A. It was fun getting home and seeing family and friends again, even though I had been gone for only two months.

October 13, my furniture finally arrived and I took the day off to move into my permanent apartment. It was a large two-bedroom residence across the street from the Seine River and about a half mile from the racetrack located in the Bois de Boulogne. The racetrack had two tracks around the outside of it, one was for runners and walkers and the other was strictly for bicyclists. Woe unto you if you endeavored to run in the bicycle track—they would run you down for invading their territory.

I ran a great deal while I was in Paris. Every day off, I would go up to the track to run. It was about two and a quarter miles around, and one day, I went around it seven times. There were also many other areas of the Bois de Boulogne in which to run. It was a heavily forested area and there were lakes and hills and small paths to follow. It was a dream for running. It was fun to try to get lost and then try to find your way out of it.

When I returned to the office on Friday, October 14, Agent Masonis was excited to tell me that he had been playing American football in the Bois on Sundays. Because of traveling, I hadn't been around much since August 14 to know what was going on. Masonis said there was a group of Americans, mostly students, who met each Sunday to play football, and he invited me out the following Sunday to play. Like a dummy, I agreed to go. Unfortunately, Joe left for a trip and wasn't home that weekend to take me with him to play football.

That Sunday I was home and I had gone up to the Bois to run. At about 2 p.m., I was running in the general area of the soccer fields and I saw some fellows throwing an American football. I jogged over to the group and saw that two fellows were apparently choosing up sides. There must have been about twelve or so Americans there, and it was apparent that they all knew each other. I went up to one of the captains and asked him if he needed another player. He looked at me and saw a 52-year-old has been. He very quickly said that the sides were even.

That had never happened to me before. Well, I very dejectedly began to walk over to the sidelines thinking I would watch for a while and then do some more running. All of a sudden, I heard some footsteps and I heard this voice behind me saying, "Hey, can you block? This other fellow has a bad knee and doesn't think he should play." I told the fellow of course I could block and he said, "Come on, you're on my side."

Well, we had a very good day. I have always enjoyed a good game of touch football and have played on some very good teams. This was a pretty tough type of game. There was blocking and block tackling and some pretty rough scenes. All in all, it was the first time my captain, George Webster, had ever beaten the other captain and throughout the game, I was his blocking back. It was strictly a passing game with virtually no running plays, so a blocking back was very important.

After one play, George was exhilarated when I was able to block two men at one time. It was a set-up play where two men were easily knocked down with one block. We had a lot of fun. We banged up quite a few of their people, but let me tell you, it was a two-way street. I was banged up and my ears were scraped raw and bleeding from blocking. I hadn't played football like that in quite a few years.

The next morning when we all met in the parking lot in order to drive to work together, Joe Masonis wondered what happened to the "old guy." I asked him where he was on Sunday after inviting me out for a little American football. Masonis said he'd get those guys who did that to me.

The next Sunday, Masonis and I both were in town and went up to the Bois to play. The one captain who had been our opponent came up to me and asked where I had played football. I told him that I had played for a little school in Los Angeles. He replied, "Yeah sure, you son of a gun, I felt you all week." It was very interesting that ever after that, I was always among the first to be chosen.

I played football for the whole two years that I was in Paris. We played against some other teams mostly consisting of American students in Paris schools. We never lost and we beat some of the other teams very badly. Interestingly, all the time I played, I can recall only one French kid coming over and wanting to play with us. Most French kids play soccer or their own brand of football, rugby, which is quite a bit different. This one French kid had a very difficult time keeping his arms in and his hands off the opponents. He couldn't quite grasp the concept.

I also played on a softball team one year. We didn't do very well, and I recall playing against the Japanese embassy team that really cleaned our clock. They were very good.

October 19 to 23, Agent Bradshaw and I took a trip to Madrid to meet Secretary of Treasury W. Michael Blumenthal, who was using Madrid as a refueling stop. After the meeting, Bradshaw had some cases the Spanish police had worked on, so we had to interact with them.

Madrid was a great place for shopping, particularly for art lovers like me, as I had become very interested in Lladros and other artwork. Madrid turned out to be one of my favorite places, especially with Bradshaw. He knew of all the great eating places that abounded in Madrid. One of our favorites was Casa Paco, where you ordered steaks by the grams. Five hundred grams, seven hundred-fifty grams, or a kilogram of red hot steak served on a red hot metal plate with the steak still sizzling. Casa Paco was just off the Plaza Mayor, which was also a great place to see, especially on the weekends when the students took over. After drinking their fill of Spanish wine, they would endeavor to scale the monument in the middle of the square. It was very funny to watch them try to get to the top—very few actually ever made it. Most of them slipped and slid down to the base, but from there, they would try again. It was evident that the fine Spanish wine had taken effect in some of the climbers.

On October 23, Bradshaw and I headed home to prepare for a trip to Germany the following day, where we were to assist the German police on an international counterfeiting case. Bradshaw did an undercover assignment in Dussseldorf that a German police officer and I covered for John. We returned to Paris on October 26.

November 2 and 3, Agent Peter Grant and I met the presidential advance group that was in Paris taking a look at some of the sites President Carter would visit on his trip during December. On November 7, we took a train out to Normandy, where the president would be visiting the American cemetery as well as the landing beaches from World War II.

On November 9, Agent Grant and I went over to London for meetings with our embassy people and some New Scotland Yard personnel. November 15, Agent Masonis and I flew to Rome, where we spoke to the Italian Interpol. After that, we took a train to Naples to confer with the Italian police for several days. On November 17, we flew to Milan for a conference with U.S. Drug Enforcement Agency (DEA) officials. November 28, Masonis and I returned to Rome and Milan to meet with the Italian police as well as the DEA people again.

We returned home on December 1, and then the following day, Masonis and I picked up Secretary of Treasury Blumenthal at Charles de Gaulle Airport and took him to the American Ambassador's residence adjacent to the embassy.

The latter part of the month, the presidential advance group arrived in preparation for the visit of President Carter. Mr. Carter was due in on January 3, 1978, and while he was in France, he would visit Normandy, Bayeaux, Versailles, and he would take a stroll down the Champs Elysees.

1978

CHAPTER 36

Paris Field Office
1978

The trip to Normandy was especially interesting. The president visited the landing beaches as well as the magnificent cemetery. This was all in conjunction with President Giscard d'Estaing of France. We flew via chopper over the beaches in order to get a magnificent view of all of the landing areas, as well as the defensive emplacements that the Germans had built, many of which are still intact. We returned to Paris on President d'Estaing's private train, which was an excellent manner in which to travel. They fed us the finest of French food and wines. It turned out to be a marvelous trip.

For extra help, we borrowed some other American law enforcement agents stationed in Paris. Noteworthy was DEA Agent Ron Provencher. Ron was a super person and he accompanied us out to Normandy. He was also on the train with us on our return to Paris. I think he enjoyed being involved as much as we enjoyed having him work with us. Eventually, we inducted Ron into the Secret Service as an honorary agent. I think that he also made Shirley Ann an honorary DEA agent.

President Carter departed Paris on January 6, and we got back to our normal business, which meant frequent traveling. Agent Masonis and I took the late Paris train to Milan, Italy, and then continued by train to Lugano, Switzerland, for a big counterfeiting case that Masonis was working on with the Italians, Swiss, and Germans. Masonis met the suspect for lunch in Lugano on the 13th. After that, we returned to Milan in order to meet an informant who was going to show us where he thought the counterfeit notes were being made. This didn't pan out, and we left Milan on the 15th for Paris.

During the middle of January, Los Angeles experienced some of the most devastating rains that it had had in many years. Our house at Number One Martingale sat on a very high hill, some of which had been excavated in order to allow the house to fit there. It rained so much in such a short time that the hill began to erode. The ground cover that was to forestall that process became so saturated that it began to roll up and slide down the hill, taking with it much of the topsoil. Before the rain was over, the hill had eroded to about one foot of the foundation of the home. Shirley Ann, being home alone, thought the house was going to fall over and go down the hill. She called me in Paris and I could tell this was a first-class emergency in which I needed to be involved.

I called Washington that night and spoke to Assistant Director Peterson. I requested permission to take annual leave in order to fly home, at my own expense, to help out in the emergency. Request denied! Did I feel helpless? My sister's son, Richard Knapp, and his wife, Linda, came out to help, as did Pat and Marlene Parker, and my sister, Nancy, and her husband, Gene Littman. Our neighbors, Mike and Marilyn Szilagyi and their boys also all pitched in to help poor Shirley Ann.

Our daughter, Diane, had a very good friend in high school, Mitzi Bowling, whose father, Dan Bowling, was a contractor in Palos Verdes. Dan became involved, bless his soul, and made a plan to save the home by counteracting the problem. His plan worked very well. He made arrangements for a builder to come out and dig thirteen caissons down to bedrock right in front of the home. He had those caissons filled with steel and cement and then tied a deck into the caissons that improved the home tremendously. He also installed a drainage system that precluded the reoccurrence of the recent debacle. And finally, he constructed a wall at the bottom of the hill that held the hill in place.

Dan Bowling not only saw to it that the work was done, but he helped Shirley Ann with her dealings with the Small Business Administration. What a friend to have. All of this went on with me six thousand miles away and unable to be of any help.

Immediately after I had talked to Shirley Ann, Agent Masonis and I left for Amsterdam to work with the Amsterdam police on a counterfeiting case. Masonis and I were going to meet the bad guys in an attempt to make a buy of counterfeit notes. On the 18th, we met with four of the group, but we couldn't make a deal with them. This was a very bad group of people. Joe Masonis and I were delighted to have the Amsterdam police close by listening to what was going on in our room where the negotiations were being made. They happened to be in the adjoining room, listening intently for the code word that if Joe or I said it, they were to come in like gangbusters. It was fun working with the Dutch police. From their command post in the hotel, we could see and hear their surveillance team following the bad guys and actually following them up to our room.

On departing Amsterdam, I took Masonis to the airport as he had to get back to Rome and Milan on another case, and I drove home to Paris alone. Along the way in the mountainous areas of northwestern France, I ran into snow—an awful lot of it. Snow and I do not get along, but I kept moving. In one small town, I got off the freeway and found the police station. I went in and introduced myself, thinking that they would invite me to stay with them for the night, maybe even offer me a cup of coffee. Let me tell you, nothing like that happened and I very dejectedly got back into my car and slipped and slid back to the freeway. I nervously continued south. Luckily however, the farther south I went, the lower the elevation became and the snow began to turn into rain. The rain continued all the way into Paris, but I was much happier driving in the rain than in the snow. I was glad to get back home in Paris.

January 24, I flew to Washington for a conference. On the 25th, I left for Los Angeles on annual leave. I was at least able to help Shirley Ann out in some of the problems that had emanated from the rainstorm the previous month. I couldn't believe all the people who had helped Shirley Ann, particularly Dan Bowling. His crew had actually put a plastic cover over the entire collapsed hill. That certainly precluded any additional slippage occurring. My vacation ended on February 8, and on the 9th, I returned to Paris.

On February 12, Masonis and I drove to Bonn, Germany, to advance the arrival of Secretary of Treasury Blumenthal. We picked him up at the Cologne Airport, took him to the Chancellery for dinner, and then returned him to the airport for departure.

Masonis and I then drove over to Utrecht, Holland, regarding a counterfeit case. We returned to Paris that night. February 21 to 23, I was in Berlin regarding a counterfeiting case of $100 notes. We supposedly had a pretty good informant, but none of his information proved to be good. You had to be careful working with informants in Europe. They have the idea that if they throw information out, true or otherwise, the very rich Americans will slip you a few American dollars. We learned to be careful to get our money's worth before we parted with any cash. We typically slipped the informant a $20, just to keep his interest up, and advised him that there would be more coming if great things happened.

February 27 to March 2, Agent Grant and I were in London, working with New Scotland Yard Detective Raymond Platt. Ray had some information regarding a possible counterfeiting case, but nothing developed from the information.

March 3, Agent Masonis and I went to Rome, where we spoke to the Interpol group. We then went to Naples to meet the police officials there. Masonis could tell this story much better than I because it was his case. I remember Masonis and the Italian police identifying over forty people in Italy who were involved in counterfeiting our $100 bills. With the information obtained, the Italian police were able to have over forty listening devices activated on each of their telephones lines. From the information they heard over the wires, they were able to get over forty warrants on people from Genoa to Sicily. What the counterfeiting group was doing was acquiring genuine American $1 bills and bleaching them out completely. After that they would reprint them as $100 bills. They made some very good notes and the group did quite well for a while. When Washington heard what Masonis and the Italian police had done, they advised me that when the arrests and searches were made, Joe and I could not be the two guys who kicked the door down. They did say that it would be all right if we went in immediately after that. That wasn't too bad, but the Italian police had all the fun on this one.

March 4 was the big day and Masonis opted for us to be at the print shop where we felt the notes had been made. At about 8 a.m., the Italian police went into the print shop like gangbusters, and Joe and I followed them. We helped in the searching of the shop, finding such things as counterfeit Italian stamps, as well as a pattern of an American note. We didn't find any plates until we asked the printer what was in a wooden barrel that was close to where he was standing handcuffed. He said that the barrel contained old type. Joe and I opened the barrel and found it to be full of the plates and negatives—some old type.

Needless to say, Masonis and the Italian police put together a gigantic case. That afternoon and evening, Joe and I were very busy making an inventory of all of the contraband seized. We worked very late, and finally after it was all counted and itemized, we left the police station and found us a very nice Italian restaurant on a square close to our hotel. Joe and I could really eat Italian food and could we drink that good Italian wine. That was one of the best cases cracked during the two years that I was in Paris. It was also a fun case, and Masonis did a great part of it.

On March 5, we took the train to Rome for conferences with Interpol. They were instrumental in the success of the above case, and we thanked them profusely. That evening, Joe and I took off for Paris. It was always nice to catch the late plane out of Rome for Paris because whoever the pilot was must have had a French girlfriend in Paris. He was always ahead of time, and he always seemed to be in a hurry to get to Paris.

March 9 and 10, I was in Luxembourg for conferences with the American ambassador, as well as the Luxembourg Interpol agents. I drove back to Paris that afternoon, but this time took a different route through Verdun, the area that the Germans had held during World War I. That area still remains a blighted area, devoid of trees and shrubbery, and not too many homes. It was much different than the area south and east of Verdun that had been held by the Allies.

I should tell a short story about a village south and east of Verdun, on the main road into the city. During World War I when the Germans had Verdun under siege, all male members of families living in this little village were called to arms in order to forestall the Germans. But during the long battle of Verdun, every single male member of the village was killed. To pay homage to the brave men who were killed in action, the name of their village was changed to Regret. The village today continues to use the name so aptly placed upon it.

Having a little time left that day, I decided to go over to St. Mihiel, which was about thirty miles east of Verdun. During World War I, my father was at Verdun as well as St. Mihiel, and I felt that I should go see where he had been as a young man in the army. I found the little village and went into a store to buy some food for a quick picnic lunch. Outside of town, I found a French army cemetery and looked around. All of the graves were from the World War I era. France lost many men during that war, so many in fact, that the nation suffered from a lack of male members for several generations. In any event, it was very nostalgic for me to be in St. Mihiel, a place where my dad had been some sixty years prior.

March 15, Agent Bradshaw and I drove to Wiesbaden for conferences with their Interpol group. Generally, those conferences meant a very good, extended German dinner. We came back to Paris that night after a long drive. March 21, Agent Bradshaw and I flew to Vienna for more conferences with Interpol, DEA, and other U.S. Embassy officials. What fun. We came back to Paris on the 23rd.

March 28, Agent Peter Grant and I left for Lagos, Nigeria, in regards to the visit of President Carter. When we arrived, we helped with some of the advance arrangements for Mrs. Carter. She was to visit a small village in the north of Nigeria on the river that borders Benin. It was a very interesting assignment. We had to advance the local chief's palace, which was a small building with a tin roof and a throne in the need of repair.

When Mrs. Carter came for her visit, it rained and was very hot and humid. Her visit went off all right, but the weather made it a bit uncomfortable. The village was composed of typical African huts, except for the post office, which was somewhat of a modern building. The village had a central well where the inhabitants had to come with their pails to obtain water. The well had one common cup for the people to drink, and I noticed that when a person was through drinking his water, the cup was generally placed down upon the ground, awaiting the next person who might be thirsty. This was a very primitive village, and it was what Mrs. Carter wanted to see.

A note of interest was one young boy, probably about thirteen years of age. He was with a group of other youngsters, maybe fifteen or so of them. The group was running around the main part of the village very quickly. The one youth in particular ran on all fours, like a monkey. He apparently couldn't stand up straight, but he could sure move quickly on all fours. I think that he was about the fastest youngster in his group. I had never heard of anyone having a disease that affected a person like that, and I truly believe that this was his normal way to run.

The Carters departed Lagos on April 3, and Agent Grant and I went with them to Monrovia, Liberia. We stayed at the airport and worked the arrival and departure. The Carters left Monrovia about 3 p.m., but Grant and I had to wait until midnight for a flight to Brussels with a connection to Paris. Waiting at the airport was a problem as it isn't very large and the facilities are minimal. They also served warm beer. Peter and I tried some, but it wasn't very good. There weren't very many flights in or out of Monrovia, so all we could do was spend some time at a gift shop. Peter bought some souvenirs for his wife and daughter. Time went by very slowly and it was very hot. Finally about midnight, our flight departed. It was always wonderful to get back to our home in Paris.

April 8, I left Paris en route to the University of Delaware at Newark for a civil service seminar that lasted until April 21. On Saturday, April 15, I went by train to Washington, D.C., for some conferences with headquarters personnel. Our good friend Jim Griffith was in headquarters, and we had planned a great dinner with his wife, Bonnie. They picked me up, we ate, and they got me back to the station in time to catch my train back to the University of Delaware. It was a very nice visit with some great friends.

The last day of the seminar, several of us had presentations to make. I made a nineteen-minute speech wrapping up the entire conference. A year later, I had a telephone call from another agent who attended the seminar the year after I did. He asked me what kind of a speech I had made because the staff was still talking about it. Thank you Toastmasters. When we were dismissed, I caught a flight to Los Angeles, at my own expense, to spend about a week and a half at home. It was great seeing Shirley Ann, the family, and friends, and too soon my vacation was over.

May 4, I left for Johannesburg, South Africa, via Guatemala City, Panama, and Rio de Janeiro, Brazil. I had made arrangements with Agent Bradshaw to meet me at Johannesburg Airport on my arrival. We stayed in Pretoria but left there after several days for some work in Johannesburg.

On May 8, we flew to Lesotho, where Bradshaw and I set up meetings and lectures with embassy people, police officers, and ministers of the government of Lesotho. The problem in going to Lesotho is that it's too far to drive, and plane service is only on Mondays and Wednesdays. If you arrive on Monday, as we did, you had to finish your work by Wednesday, or spend a whole week there. There wasn't that much work, so we were able to complete it in the three days. We did find it surprising how much of our counterfeit money is passed in a place like Lesotho.

A funny thing occurred while in Lesotho. While I was lecturing to a class of officers, I smelled this very unusual burning odor. At the completion of my lecture, I asked one of the officers what the odor was. He invited me outside, where I saw an enormous fire being stoked by huge bales of marijuana. They must have had forty or fifty bales ready to burn. I guess even Lesotho has its problems with marijuana. Lesotho was a very interesting place. We drove around the countryside endeavoring to obtain a feeling for the country. We were able to drive far out in the country, miles from the city of Maseru, where we were staying. People were walking and running to wherever they were going, as there were no cars in Lesotho like we are accustomed to.

We left Maseru on Wednesday, May 10 to return to Johannesburg and Pretoria. On May 11, we left Johannesburg for Nairobi, Kenya, where we had more meetings with embassy officials, police, and banking officials.

One evening after our work in Nairobi, Bradshaw and I thought we'd take a walk into the park that was very close to the embassy and the main part of town. It was a very warm, pleasant evening and we sat down on a bench to talk. Very quickly, a young African came scooting up on his hands and knees right in front of us and stopped. He asked if we were Americans. Before we knew it, we were surrounded by about fifteen Africans who wanted to talk about a white American professor they had when they went to school in Uganda.

Well, Uganda was a bad word because they were having problems with many nations of Africa and the world. The group asked if we could help them financially as they had all wanted to get over to Mombassa on the Indian Ocean side of Africa. We declined their request, and got up and made our way through the group without any difficulty. What they didn't realize was that we were both armed so there could have been quite a blood bath if it had come to that, though our blood would probably have been included in the bath. It was nice to get out of there safely, and later in speaking to some police officers, they advised us not to go into the park any more. The Ugandans were giving the Kenyan police all kinds of trouble. We also learned from our embassy people that the Ugandans were a big problem to them and that Bradshaw and I were very fortunate in getting out of that park safely.

May 14, we left Nairobi en route to Lagos, Nigeria, via Entebbe, Uganda. We stopped over in Entebbe for about an hour and we recognized the scene of the great raid made by the Israeli commandos several years before. They had been able to get into the airport and to free a large group of Israelis who had been seized by the terrorists.

We stayed in Lagos for several days, and on May 16, we flew up to Dakar, Senegal, where we talked to their Interpol group, embassy personnel, and local law enforcement people. On May 17, we received a wire from our Paris office regarding a person who lived in Freetown, Sierra Leone. This person, St. Vincent, had written a letter to President Carter, threatening his life. No matter where it is in the world, this is a problem for us. We had to go back down the west coast of Africa to Sierra Leone to find the letter writer. The embassy made our travel arrangements, acquired visas for us, and we left for Freetown the following day.

Embassy officials met us at the Freetown Airport and took us directly to the police station, where we told the chief of police what our problem was. He said that he knew the person who had written the threat and indicated that the man was somewhat unbalanced. The chief said that he could have the fellow available for interview the following morning.

Bradshaw and I got a room at a hotel for the night. I went for a run so far into the hinterland that I came into a rural African settlement, grass huts and all, including about two dozen mangy looking dogs that began to yip at my feet. I thought this was no place for me, so I retraced my route quickly and got out without being bitten by any of their dogs. Can you imagine being bitten by a dog in Africa? I doubt if they even know about shots for dogs.

After breakfast the next morning, we went over to the chief's office, and he advised that he had our man ready for interrogation. We weren't ready for this next episode. The man fell on his face, spread-eagled himself on the floor, and began to crawl on his belly into the office. I think that he thought we were going to kill him. When he finally got inside, we endeavored to explain our concern for his threats toward the president, but the chief was right, this man was unbalanced. We tried to talk to him and advised him that he was never, ever to write any threats to anyone, particularly the president of the United States. He agreed wholeheartedly. We had him fill out some special forms, got some handwriting exemplars, and then released him. To my knowledge, we never had any more difficulty with him. Case closed.

We left Freeport on the 19th and headed home, where thankfully John and I had the rest of the weekend off. After a trip like that, you had to spend a lot of time in the washroom getting all of your clothes clean. I was home from May 20 to June 5, at which time Agent Grant and I headed for Edinburgh, Scotland. We met with our consulate and prepared for a seminar in counterfeiting that Grant and I would be putting on the next day for police and banking personnel, as Scotland had their problems with U.S. counterfeit currency being passed. Scotland was great to visit, and the people couldn't have been more helpful and charming. The seminar turned out very well, and we left for Paris on June 8.

I was in the office for one day before Agent Masonis and I flew to Rome and then onto Naples. On the 11th, we rented a car and drove back to Rome, where we had meetings with the Interpol group, U.S. Customs, and DEA agents. On the 14th, Director Stu Knight arrived in Rome for a meeting with us and the Italian police. On June 15, Masonis and I left for Madrid, and on the 17th, Director Knight came over again for meetings with the Spanish police and us.

Knight left Spain, and on June 20, Joseph Le Den Mat and I went to the Torrejon Air Force base outside Madrid to make a presentation to a young lady who had been instrumental in arresting a Filipino man who had been stealing U.S. Treasurer's checks in the Philippines, forging them, and raising the amounts on them to very high figures. This suspect had operated for several years cashing the checks at U.S. Air Force bases around the world.

The young lady had accepted the check from the suspect but felt there was something wrong. The suspect left the scene hurriedly, and the young lady called her supervisor who in turn called the investigators on the base. Together with the investigators, the young lady went through the base looking for the suspect and spotted him in a vehicle. The suspect was arrested and placed in a Spanish jail. Spanish jails are no picnics, and the suspect wanted out in the worst way. He would do anything if the air force would accommodate him. He spent some time in jail, and I heard he received a sentence of seven years. That was a magnificent piece of work by the young lady and the air force police at that base. For her assistance, we rewarded her with an adequate amount of U.S. Bonds. Joe Le Den Mat and I flew back to Orly Airport in Paris that evening after a very busy trip. I stayed in Paris until June 28, and then went up to SHAPE for meetings with the military.

July 4 was the big holiday for Americans overseas. The U.S. Marines put on a huge barbecue in our apartment compound. They had hot dogs, hamburgers, Cokes, and all the great things that Americans eat on Independence Day. It was an incredible day, one that I will always remember.

I should describe our apartment in Boulogne. It was a gated complex that had about four buildings, some as high as three stories. We had twenty-four hour security, plenty of parking, and laundry facilities. I think there was even a childcare center for parents to leave their children. The apartments were located across the street from the Seine River. We could see the marvelous boats going up and down. Most of the boats had French flags, but there was an abundant amount of Belgium, Dutch, and German flags showing as well. There was a lock about a half-mile north of us, and the boats often had to wait in order to pass it. As the river flowed toward the lock, it would take whatever was floating in the Seine up to it. Quite often, we would hear the ambulance stopping at the lock, and later hear that they had recovered another body. Drowning was somewhat of a preferred manner in which to commit suicide in the Paris area.

I never saw anyone swimming in the Seine, but I imagine that people do in some parts of it. Sometimes during the heavy rains, the river would come up and over the banks, and our street would become a creek. That condition never lasted very long though. People used to fish in the Seine, but to be honest, I never saw any of them ever catch anything. And even if fish were caught, I'm not so sure if the people would have eaten them.

There were several bridges close by that enabled us to cross the river and go into the town of St. Cloud, where Interpol had its headquarters. I could see their building from our compound.

The people who lived in these apartments were Americans who worked at the embassy or at other embassy facilities. Our office was located in a building about a mile away from the embassy. In our building, we had the FBI, U.S. Customs, DEA, the IRS, and the U.S. Marines. The marines were in charge of security at the embassy and the other installations.

To get to our building from our apartments, you had to go through the Bois de Boulogne and the Etoile, which is where the Arc de Triomphe is located. There are six spokes of avenues that come from the Arc and it takes a great deal of experience to learn how to navigate it. One of the spokes led directly to our building, which was about a mile from the Etoile. The very first time I was driving home alone, you guessed it—I had an accident. It didn't hurt me very much, but it mangled a very small French car that a young Algerian woman was driving. It also flattened one of her tires. She was hors de combat in the middle of the Etoile. We exchanged information, but I wasn't about to go into the middle of the Etoile and change her tire. Not to worry, though, because when several young French guys saw how attractive she was, they volunteered to change her tire.

That was a very disturbing experience. I wasn't quite sure if I was ever going to learn to drive in Paris. It was something else! Amazing how you adapt though, and it wasn't very long before I was driving like a native. Incidentally, that's nothing of which to be proud.

On July 9, Agent Grant and I drove to Bonn, Germany, to help in the advance arrangements for President Carter. We ran routes with the presidential protective group, checked some sites, and then headed to Cologne Airport when the president arrived. This was an opportunity for Shirley Ann to accompany us. We stayed with State Department Regional Security Officer Lou Schwartz. What a nice person Lou was and what a pleasant person with whom to work.

Shirley Ann attended church on the American compound that Sunday before the Carters left Germany. The Carters also attended the service, and it gave many of the Americans based in Bonn an opportunity to see and meet them. The Carters were very kind in doing that. It means a great deal for foreign-based personnel to meet other Americans from home, and when it's the president and his wife, that makes it extra special.

The Carters left on July 17, and SA Grant, Shirley Ann, and I took off for Paris the following day. We traveled through Eupin and Bastogne, Belgium. What a thrill to see Bastogne, which was in much the same condition as it was during World War II. They have an American tank parked right in their town square. They also have a very fine museum that depicts the Battle of the Bulge. We also saw the field at Malmady, where a number of American prisoners had been killed by the Germans. That entire area was ripe with World War II battle sites.

July 20, Agent Masonis and I flew down to Milan, Italy, where we met DEA Agent Costanza. We worked with him for three days on a counterfeiting matter but had very little success. We returned to Paris on Saturday the 22nd.

July 27, Shirley Ann and I drove up to the Hague, Holland, and then went over to Amsterdam. I had meetings with embassy personnel, as well as some work with Interpol there. We then went down to Luxembourg on the 29th, where we stayed for a day. We left for Paris on the 30th. There went that weekend.

August 8 Joe Le Den Mat, his wife Suzzane, Shirley Ann, and I, drove over to Geneva to check on several cases the Swiss police had been working. Geneva is one of the most beautiful cities of the world, and it was always interesting to go there. After Joe and I completed our work, we checked into a hotel across the border in France. We then returned to Geneva that evening for dinner. We ate in Old Town Geneva, and we all had a great Swiss dinner of raclette. Raclette is generally an urn full of melted cheese and served with small new potatoes that you dip into the melted cheese. The raclette, plus a nice bottle of French wine, and you have all you need for a sumptuous dinner. We left Geneva the following morning and made it back to Paris at 5:30 p.m. Shirley Ann and I particularly enjoyed seeing the beautiful French countryside.

On August 10, Pope Paul III died at the Vatican. We heard very quickly that Mrs. Carter would be America's representative to the funeral. Agent Grant, Shirley Ann and I flew down there to help make arrangements for Mrs. Carter. We stayed at the Excelsior Hotel close to the embassy. While Peter Grant and I worked, Shirley Ann visited Rome and the Vatican.

Mrs. Carter received very high-level attention from the Vatican officials. We escorted her on a very extensive tour of the Vatican, including the Sistine Chapel. Mrs. Carter was in Rome for about three days and departed on August 13. Another American representative was Ted Kennedy, who was very well known, and well thought of in Rome. I noticed that when he walked down the street, many of the Italian people recognized him.

Agent Grant, Shirley Ann, and I returned to Paris on August 15, after a very interesting and historical experience. August 21, I left Paris en route to Lusaka, Zambia, a country in the middle of Africa. Through Interpol, the Zambian police asked me to come down to testify in a case involving a man who tried to cash some copies of U.S. Confederate currency. This man had bought a large amount of these notes through a magazine advertisement from an agency in New Orleans. As I understand it, he received the notes and took them to a local bank and asked them if they could be cashed. The local police were called and they arrested the man.

When I received the request to go to Kitwe, Zambia, to testify, I wrote a very quick letter to the police authorities that Confederate money was never legal tender in America, and from what they told me, I didn't think they had a case. I figured that would be the end of the request. Not so. Several days later, I received a radiogram insisting that I fly to Lusaka. The Interpol officers met me in Lusaka, and we climbed into a very small four-passenger plane in order to get to Kitwe on the day the trial began.

When we entered the courtroom, the defendant was sitting in the box in the middle of the room. He looked every bit like the condemned man awaiting the sentence of death. I happened to be the only white person in the courtroom, and unfortunately for the prosecution, their main witness. I guess I was on the stand for about three hours or so. I told them that what the person had done was not a violation in America. I think they had a difficult time believing that the Confederate states and their currency were not legal entities of the United States. I had an idea that they felt that the copies of the currency they had seized from the defendant were genuine currency of America. But it wasn't, so they could not prove a crime had been committed.

Interestingly, the presiding judge wrote down every word of my testimony. He didn't have a short hand stenographer or a steno typist, and he stopped my testimony a number of times in order for him to catch up. The outcome of the case was that the defendant was acquitted and released. I'll bet he never dreamed of that outcome. I felt sorry for the officers who had worked so diligently on the case, but I believe justice was certainly served. I can't recall that the officers showed any animosity toward me. Afterward, we had a very nice dinner together and they took me to a real African trade warehouse where prices were certainly right. They had a great quantity of ivory art work on display—what else could you expect from that deep, deep part of Africa?

I was in Zambia until August 26. The last day, I lectured to the employees at the embassy, and later I gave two talks to the Interpol group as well as other police officials regarding the counterfeiting of American currency. Even in Zambia, they had problems with our currency being made illicitly.

I figured that while I was in Africa, I should make the most of it and go to other countries to help them in the counterfeiting field. While at the embassy in Lusaka, I called the embassy in Dar Es Salaam, Tanzania, and asked if they could get some police and banking people together for a counterfeiting lecture. It was a weekend, but they were successful in getting some people who had an interest in counterfeit American currency.

While I was at the embassy in Dar es Salaam, the Paris office called and advised that President Kenyatta of Kenya had died. Washington was going to send the president's son, Jefferson Carter, as the American representative. Washington wanted to know who from Paris would be assisting in the advance. Paris wanted to know if I would go over to Nairobi or if they should send another agent down.

I agreed to do it but it wasn't going to be easy. Kenya and Tanzania did not have civil relations with each other. Their borders were closed to traffic, including air flights. Pan Am flew out of Dar Es Salaam but not directly to Nairobi. There was very little air traffic out of Dar Es Salaam. The embassy people called the Pan Am representative and the manager agreed to meet us at the office immediately. Even though the office had not been open that day, we met him and he was extremely cooperative. The solution was to ticket me to the Seychelles Island, which are almost directly below India, and then redirect me back to Africa on another airline to Mombassa, Kenya, and then on to Nairobi.

It took me three and a half hours to fly to the Seychelles. Then I had to wait several hours for my plane in the Seychelles. What I saw of the Seychelles reminded me a great deal of Tahiti—much rain and very green. It was very warm and humid. Since then, I have read a number of articles about those islands. It is an extremely poor nation but abounds in fish and spices. In hindsight, I am deeply disappointed that I didn't leave the airport to do any sightseeing.

My flight finally came, and it took me another three hours to fly to Mombassa. I finally arrived in Nairobi at 9:30 p.m. The cab drive in from the airport in Nairobi is like no other. The people there drive their cars until they fall apart. Then they leave them where the breakdown occurred. Therefore the road into Nairobi is littered with tons of broken down vehicles. It looks like an American junkyard.

On August 27, I met Jeff Carter's advance agent. The official group arrived on the 30th. President Kenyatta was buried on August 31, which was a big "to do" in Africa. Kenya had been an English Colony and Kenyatta had been the president of Kenya forever. Prince Charles of England came down for the funeral and all the major political people of Africa were in attendance, even Idi Amin from Uganda. He received the biggest ovation of all from the people who surrounded the burial site.

The day after the burial, Jeff Carter wanted to go on a photography safari in the midlands of Kenya. The embassy made the arrangements for land rovers with sliding roofs for photographers. This allowed the people to get their shots yet still be protected from the animals. What a great experience that was. On the flight to the safari, the pilot had to buzz the landing strip four times before he could land because there were so many animals of all types on the airstrip that we could not get in to land. One time, I actually thought we were going to make it when several wildebeests ran out in front of the plane. The pilot poured the coal to the plane, and we veered up and out of the danger area.

We finally made it in without hitting one animal, and then we were off and running. We saw a million wildebeests and several prides of lions who were just finishing lunch—an unfortunate wildebeest was in the wrong place at the wrong time. The lions were all bloody and their snouts were completely covered with a million flies—they didn't look much like kings of the jungle at that moment. We saw hyenas, giraffes, hippopotamuses, and a hundred other types of animals. We all had a great time, especially the photographers. Later that night, we returned to Nairobi and still later, Jeff and his group departed Nairobi.

I left Nairobi on September 2, en route to Rome in order to assist making arrangements for Vice President Mondale, who was arriving for the coronation of the new Pope. He arrived on the 3rd, and we took him to the Excelsior Hotel, one of Rome's finest. Vice President Mondale left on September 5 and so did I.

September 14, I drove to Wiesbaden, Germany, for a conference with German police. The next day, I drove to Heidelberg in order to attend the annual Military Police Ball, a very nice affair that involved all of the American law enforcement personnel stationed in Europe.

September 17, I headed back to Paris. That evening, Agent Masonis and I caught a flight to Rome for a conference with embassy, U.S. Customs, and DEA officials. We left Rome on the 19th en route to Tel Aviv, Israel, where Masonis and I were putting on a counterfeiting seminar for the Israel police. That was the only presentation I made in my two years in Paris where I had to use an interpreter completely throughout the presentation. It made for a very long presentation.

October 2 to 4, I was in Berlin regarding an unknown person who had written a threatening letter to President Carter. I worked with investigators at the Berlin Mission, but we were unable to identify the person. It was at least a good opportunity for me to show the flag in Berlin. There were a number of conferences with mission personnel, particularly regarding counterfeiting activities. Berlin was a very interesting place. I saw many historical sites, including the Berlin Wall, Checkpoint Charlie, and the Brandenburg Gate. There were some parts of Berlin that were still showing the effects of war damage. In particular, the cathedral downtown was being maintained in that condition to show the terrible damage that war can cause.

I returned to Paris on October 4, and the next day I went to SHAPE in Belgium for my annual physical examination. That also gave me an opportunity to do some shopping I needed to do. October 12, Agent Bradshaw and I flew to Austria to do an advance for the Winter Games in Innsbruck, in the event that some of our protectees decided to attend the games. The following day, we conferred with the Interpol group, and on October 14, we returned to Paris.

October 24, Agent Grant and I flew to Copenhagen, Denmark, regarding another letter writer who had threatened President Carter. We worked with the Copenhagen police on this case. They were very good, and with their assistance, we located and interviewed the letter writer. We returned to Paris on October 26, and I didn't leave again until November 14. Meanwhile, we had an office inspection beginning November 7, which lasted for one week. I don't think we had any major problems in the office, but they always find something that needs more attention.

November 14, Agent Masonis and I left for Rome and then the following day to Tehran, Iran, to do the advance for Secretary of Treasury Blumenthal. He arrived on the 20th, so we had ample time to put together his agenda. The secretary departed Tehran on the 22nd.

Upon our departure, we left fourteen of our radios in the custody of the embassy security officials with a request that they return them via official pouch through the embassy mail when they were finished with them. That turned out to be a huge mistake. They didn't get around to shipping them back, and later when the embassy was taken over by the Iranians, the terrorists acquired them. The radios cost about $1,100 dollars a piece. There was no way we were going to get them back. I have often wondered what use the Iranians found in those radios. They needed a very special power package and I doubt the package was available in Iran. And sadly, Masonis and I found out later that a number of the police officials with whom we worked on that trip had been executed when the Shah was deposed.

Masonis and I arrived in Paris on the 22nd, just in time to start advance work for a visit from former president Nixon. Nixon arrived on the 25th, and stayed at the Ritz Hotel. I had to shake loose from that assignment on November 28 in order to pick up my visa from the Russian Embassy. Agent Bradshaw and I were going to Moscow to do some advance work for Secretary Blumenthal.

We left for Moscow on November 29. It was typical Moscow weather, very cold and snowy. I recall going through Russian customs at the airport and having the female inspector look at my class ring from Pepperdine. She asked me if it was gold and I said that it was. She advised me that I had better have the ring in my possession when I departed Russia. Was that odd? I certainly hadn't come to Russia to sell my class ring!

On the 30th, we met our counterparts from the KGB, one of whom was Vladimir Slopkin. Vladimir spoke English with a Canadian accent. He was very good and the visit went along very well. One night, Vladimir invited me to the Bolshoi Theater to see the Nutcracker Suite. We had great seats compliments of your kindly KGB agent. I'm not much for that type of entertainment, but Vladimir seemed to be proud to have me as his guest.

Secretary Blumenthal arrived on December 3, and stayed at the Lenin Hills facility, where the Russians house their political VIPs. Mr. Blumenthal had conferences at the Kremlin and one of the large banks in Moscow. Ordinary traffic was not a problem to us, but when we saw the location of the bank, we discussed our concern with Vladimir. He was very cooperative and asked us if we would like to shut the street down. That would have been impossible in America, but this was Moscow and Vladimir had the street closed down, no problem.

While the Secretary of Treasury was in Moscow, he had appointments all over the city. We had to go into the Kremlin, cross Red Square, and into several of their larger banks. One night, he was invited to the Kremlin for a state dinner. It was a magnificent experience. The KGB agents with whom we were working showed us all around, including their large ball room that contains about twenty of the most gorgeous chandeliers I have ever seen. They certainly rival the chandeliers at the White House. They also showed us the original portion of the Kremlin that had been built of wood. Much of the original wood is still in use. It has to be at least seven hundred years old.

December 7, Secretary Blumenthal departed Moscow. Bradshaw and I opted to stay one more night to have dinner at a good restaurant in Moscow. One of our Embassy counterparts suggested a restaurant and said that he would call and make a reservation for us. He also said he would have to write a letter to be shown at the restaurant when we arrived. That was a little bit odd, but after all, this was Moscow so we went along with the program.

Our reservation was for 7 p.m. It was snowing out as we approached the restaurant a few minutes before seven. There were about twenty people standing in front. We didn't know quite what to do, so we waited and watched for several minutes. Then we decided that because it was approaching 7 p.m., we should go through the crowd and check in. But the front door to the restaurant was locked. We knocked, and after a while, someone came to the door, saw that we had a letter and opened the door. He took the letter, closed the door, and left, leaving us still out in the cold.

Bradshaw and I went back to the rear of the crowd and waited for several more minutes. Finally, the same person came out into the elements. We hoped that it was us he was looking for. Sure enough, he spotted us at the rear of the group and waved us in to the restaurant. All of a sudden, the crowd parted like the Red Sea and John and I made our way to the front door amid the cheers of the waiting crowd. Strange? It certainly was! When we got inside the restaurant, we were shown into a huge room that could seat more than thirty people. However, we were the only ones in the room.

This is a bizarre story about a bizarre place. You have to go there to see how strange it is. You also have to go there to see how bad it is, and how great we have it here in America. We found the food at that restaurant to be very heavy but acceptable, and it was indeed plentiful. We particularly liked their caviar and black bread and borsch. Some of the wine that we had that evening was very good as well. I think it was from the Ukraine area. Bradshaw had been to Moscow before, so he knew if you placed a package of American cigarettes by your plate, the waiter knows it is for him. He takes it and presto your service is excellent.

It was a very interesting trip, but Bradshaw and I were glad to get back to Paris. I can tell you that November and December are not the months to visit Moscow. Ask Napoleon and Hitler! There is somewhat of a tradition I have experienced each time I have gone to Russia. No matter which flight you are on, as the plane leaves the Russian border, they make an announcement and most of the people on the plane clap wildly. That gives you an idea of what most people feel about that country. I don't know if things have changed much since the fall of communism, but I'm sure they haven't become any worse. They couldn't have.

Paris, however, is a very special place no matter what part of the year you are there. You have all heard of Paris in the spring. That's nice. Paris in the rain—that's even nicer. Paris in the winter is also exciting. It doesn't snow a great deal, but it does snow a few times each winter. When I could during the winter, I would leave the office at noon and go up to Montmartre for a stroll around the square. I would have a lunch of French onion soup in one of the many quaint restaurants in that area. You might guess that they make it very well in most French restaurants. Montmartre is the old square up by the Sacre Coeur Cathedral that over looks the city of Paris. It is well known for the artists that live and work in the immediate area. It matters not what the weather is like, any time you go there, you can find some artists busily engaged in their work. I believe that Van Gogh, among other artists, actually lived and worked there at one time.

I did quite a bit of haggling and buying at Montmartre. It's expected that you haggle. No one pays the original quoted price. It becomes a very interesting game, and I enjoyed doing it. One of the nice traditions at Montmartre is that the artists sign their name and address on the rear of the work you buy. They are very proud to do that. I believe they do it hoping that they too will become famous, and their autograph will only enhance their work.

Another area of Paris that I particularly liked was the Trocadero, overlooking the Eiffel Tower. This was one of the very few sites that Adolf Hitler visited after the fall of France in 1940. It has a magnificent view and I placed it among one of the must-see areas for all of my guests who visited me in Paris.

I also enjoyed Notre Dame and went there often on Sundays. How would you like to say that your usual church was Notre Dame? The structure is magnificent and quite overpowering. I liked going over to the Left Bank and walking among the book and art dealers. I also enjoyed going down to an area close to the American Embassy on Saturdays and Sundays where the stamp dealers congregated. I acquired many stamps during my two-year stay in Paris and many of them I purchased at this stamp flea market. That was fun and I met some French dealers whom I would seek out each time I went.

I enjoyed taking guests out on the Bateau Mouche, a boat that goes up and down the Seine River at night. It also serves as an excellent dinner facility with some of the greatest views a person will ever see. I also liked taking guests to Club Med in Neuilly, as it was the finest place in the world to eat. I hosted a number of dinners there for our staff. We always invited DEA agent Ron Provencher and his wife, Kathy. Ron served as an integral member of our group and was always doing things with us. At the Club Med, you started out with one of the greatest buffets that you've ever experienced. Then they would serve the steak course. Then the cheese cart came around, and to top it off, the desert cart came. This, plus all of the wine you could drink certainly made it a night to remember.

I often reminisce of my time in Paris. So many of my fondest memories are of that time. I miss running up and down the River Seine and running in the Bois. I also miss the weekend football games. They were fun.

On December 16, I left Charles de Gaulle Airport en route to Los Angeles for a three-week leave. I stayed until January 5, and then flew to St. Louis for several days with Missy and Dar.

1979

CHAPTER 37

Paris Field Office

1979

January 7, I flew to Washington for conferences until January 11, at which time I flew back to Paris. It was determined at these conferences that when my two years were up in August, I was to take over former president Ford's detail in Rancho Mirage, California. Incidentally, they said, Mr. Ford was taking a trip to Egypt, Israel, and the Middle East during the latter part of January, so it would be a good idea for me to join the group as quickly as possible to have a "look see" at the detail.

On January 15, Agent Bradshaw, Agent Bell, and I flew to Cairo to help in the advance arrangements. I stayed in Cairo until January 20, at which time it was determined that we needed an advance agent in Cyprus, where Mr. Ford was to make a pit stop on his way to Tel Aviv, since at that time, you could not fly directly from Egypt to Israel.

So on the 20th, I caught a flight to Athens and then another flight to Larnaca, Cyprus. On the 21st, I went back to the airport with all of my luggage to await Ford's arrival. He arrived about noon and after some perfunctory actions were taken care of, we departed for Tel Aviv. We arrived there at about 2 p.m., went via motorcade to Jerusalem's King David Hotel. It was like going home after spending so much time there with Dr. Kissinger in May 1974.

On January 23, Agent Masonis and I drove out to the historical Masada to advance it for Mr. Ford. The Masada is where the Zealots fought the Roman Army to a stand-still in Biblical times. The Romans couldn't get up to the mesa where the Zealots lived, so they filled, with rubble, the space between the mountain where they were and the mesa where the Zealots were. When it was high enough for them to simply walk over to the mesa, the Zealots all committed suicide. Some victory! Many of the foundations of the buildings are still intact. It rained very hard during our stay there, which is quite unusual as it's right on the Dead Sea, but it did and we all got soaked. I'm sure there would have been better days for Mr. Ford to have visited .this site.

From Israel, I went back to Cyprus for several days, then over to Athens, and then to Amman, Jordan, where I helped advance some of the sites. During one luncheon with Prince Hassan and Mr. Ford, I had to go through the dining area in order to leave. Prince Hassan saw me and jumped up, surprised to see me. He hadn't heard that I was with the Ford group. Hassan asked me what my plans were, and I told him that Amman would be my last stop with Mr. Ford before heading back to Paris.

Prince Hassan insisted that I stay over and have lunch with him and his family at the palace. What could I say? The lunch was a sumptuous affair with the prince, his wife, and his children. I was very pleased to be there and felt very honored to have been invited. I hadn't seen them for about four years, and it was so nice to see them again. They were very good friends.

The following morning, I took off for Rome for several meetings, and then the following day, I left for Paris, arriving on January 30. It had been a very busy month. January 31, I was at Interpol headquarters in St. Cloud for the 8th European Conference. These meetings lasted until February 2. It was always an interesting time at Interpol headquarters, especially when other Interpol representatives were in attendance. February 3 and 4, I was in Wiesbaden, Germany, for a retirement party of Colonel Martin of the OSI, U.S. Air Force.

February 7, Agent Masonis and I went back to Milan, Italy, for meetings with the consulate as well as DEA representatives. Milan was one of our favorite places because the food was so very tasty. Masonis and I always thought we had to uphold the honor of American eaters. And we did it proud.

February 14, I took a quick trip to SHAPE for my annual physical examination. On the 16th, Masonis and I made arrangements for Ambassador Hartmann to visit Interpol headquarters. I don't think he had much of an idea what Interpol was all about and I had the feeling that he would have rather just dispensed with some of the American law enforcement personnel who were assigned to Paris, including the Secret Service. It was almost as if he thought we were intruding on the sacred soil of State Department.

There was one ambassador stationed in East Africa right on the Indian Ocean who gave us a particular problem. One time, a predicament arose that was strictly our jurisdiction, but he declined to allow our agents from Paris to come down there to do the investigation. He advised Washington that the State Department would take care of the situation.

Washington didn't understand why he did not want us to come into his country, so I had to plan a trip there, not only to do some liaison work with the local authorities, but to interview the ambassador himself. When I arrived, some one from the embassy picked me up at the airport, as the ambassador was "up country" with his family taking care of some problem there. There was no secure place to stay in that city for Americans so I was asked to stay at the ambassador's residence for safety sake. I never spoke to the ambassador, but the embassy people treated me very well, though they wouldn't let me go for a run outside the compound because it wasn't safe.

February 18, our French investigator Joseph Le Den Mat and I headed to Istanbul, Turkey, for Interpol liaison work. We then went on to Ankara for several days, and then on down to Adana, Turkey, for a counterfeiting case. There was a USAF facility there, and at one time it had been a base from which the U2 spy planes had operated. The Turkish police had put together a very large counterfeiting case, and Joe and I were going down there to assist them.

From Adana we returned to Ankara and then Istanbul, and on the 23rd, we flew over to Belgrade, Yugoslavia, for Interpol meetings. On the 25th, we flew into Zagreb, Yugoslavia, and then on to Paris. As it was Sunday, we both went home and enjoyed the rest of the weekend.

February 28, Joe Le Den Mat and I drove to Berne, Switzerland, to meet Boris Wuethrich, chief of their National Crime Bureau. Later, we had a liaison dinner with the Swiss Interpol group. The following day, we left Berne to go to Zurich for another case. After working with the Zurich police, we left for Paris.

March 14, I flew to Warsaw for some meetings with embassy officials. On the 16th, I flew over to Budapest for more meetings with embassy officials. Later that day, we went out to the airport to pick up Agent Dan Connolly who had recently been transferred to our office. We were in Budapest for several days, and then on the 18th, we flew back to Paris.

March 22 and 23, I was in Madrid for a number of meetings with embassy officials, as well as with Spanish police and Interpol officials. March 29 and 30, I was in London for more meetings and a liaison dinner with the English officers from New Scotland Yard.

April 1, I went to Charles de Gaulle Airport to pick up Hal Thomas who was assigned to headquarters in Washington. It was no secret that Hal wanted to come to Paris as the next SAIC. Hal stayed with me in my apartment and spent a lot of time in the office. I didn't realize it at the time, but it must have been a done deal because Hal eventually did make it to Paris as the SAIC following my completed two-year assignment. He was a good choice and I know he did a fine job there.

April 9, I left Paris for Reykjavik, Iceland, in preparation for a visit by Vice President Mondale. For several days, we ran routes and did advance work in preparation for his arrival. Mr. Mondale arrived on the 11th and I stayed until the 13th, at which time I left for Bergen, Norway, to do some advance work there. Due to the Easter holiday, Bergen was mostly closed down. It was difficult even to find a good place to eat. After Mondale's arrival at Bergen on the 16th, several of us took a great train ride to Oslo, to do some more advance work there. Mr. Mondale didn't stay very long in Oslo, and on the 18th, we headed for Copenhagen, Denmark. On the 19th, we left for Stockholm, Sweden, where we stayed for a day. Then on the 20th, we flew over to Helsinki, Finland. On the 21st, I left the detail and flew back to Paris.

April 23, I headed to Washington in preparation for a retirement seminar. Although, this seminar was very important, it was really to get me back to the U.S. In order for me to take over Ford's detail in August, I had to go out to Rancho Mirage to make arrangements for housing.

I left Washington on the 26th, and arrived in Los Angeles that night. I took seven days off on annual leave, and Shirley Ann and I went out to Palm Desert to look for a place to buy. We found one at Condolane on Highway 74 about a half mile south of Highway 111. It was a very comfortable residence and served our purposes well. May 8, I headed back to Paris.

May 20, I went to Bucharest, Romania, for talks with embassy personnel and Romanian police officials. On the 22nd, I gave a presentation at the Romanian National Bank. May 30, I flew to Rome and then on to Athens for a liaison dinner. May 31, we had Secret Service work in Athens, and then we had a meeting with the Interpol personnel. That night we had another liaison dinner, this time with embassy personnel. On June 1, we returned to Paris.

June 11, Joe Le Den Mat and I were invited to the Paris Air Show. What a magnificent experience that was. Most airplane production nations of the world participate in this show. All of the latest planes are displayed at this show and many of them are flown for the spectators. You might imagine that the food is unending and great French wines flow like there's no tomorrow.

I was especially interested in spending some time at the Northrop facility. They had their latest models on show, and I spoke to several of the people representing Northrop. I was disappointed though that they didn't know my brother, Ernest, who had been employed at Northrop since the latter part of the 1940s.

After the excitement of the air show, we picked up advance agents from Orly Airport for Mrs. Mondale's visit. The following day, I flew to Vienna to join the advance team of President Carter and his family, who were arriving on June 14 for the signing of the SALT II Treaty with Mr. Brezhnev of Russia. Much of my time was spent with Amy, the daughter of the president. During the signing of the treaty, I was assigned to Mrs. Carter.

June 25, Agent Bradshaw completed his four-year assignment in Paris and departed for Dallas, his next duty office. That happened to be the same day that Shirley Ann was arriving in Paris. So after I picked her up at Charles de Gaulle, we went down to Orly Airport to see the Bradshaws off. The Bradshaws had mixed emotions about leaving Paris. Some of their children were crying because they had enjoyed Paris so much. They had all made many friends and were reluctant to leave them. The same can be said for John. He was such a likable person and a wonderful partner. I was very sad to see him go, but I knew that four years was about the maximum the Secret Service would allow for assignment in Paris. It was a good thing that I was going to be leaving Paris soon as well. I couldn't imagine running the Paris office without John Bradshaw there. We had a very nice going away party for John at the office. Many of John's friends, French as well as American, came to wish Big John good luck at his stateside assignment.

After four years of unique working conditions in the Paris office, I'm not sure that John was ready for Dallas. It wasn't long after he arrived in Dallas that he resigned from the Secret Service. What tremendous talent John had. He could do anything and everything, and what a loss our service took when John left. John went into private business in Amarillo, Texas, and I call him every now and then just to keep in touch. He now calls Amarillo home.

July 14 was Bastille Day in France. Phyllis Neftell, our office manager, Shirley Ann, and I celebrated together. Bastille Day is like New Years, Valentines Day, St. Patrick's Day, Independence Day, and Halloween all rolled into one. We visited a number of neighborhood sites and really became involved in the French celebration. It was like nothing we had ever experienced. Those people really know how to celebrate. In one of the neighborhoods we visited, we were told that the Communist Party of France sponsored the celebration. Well, we ate their hot dogs and corn on the cob and drank their Cokes anyway. No one tried to recruit us and we had a very enjoyable time.

July 19, Shirley Ann and I left Paris for Shannon, Ireland. The vice president was coming through for a refueling stop and we needed someone on the ground in the event he wanted to get out and look around. He came in on the 21st and left very quickly thereafter. Shirley Ann and I had an opportunity to see a little of Ireland and its people. This was particularly of interest to Shirley Ann as her forebears were from Ireland. Ireland was fun but their food was bad. It rained a lot too. We left the same day Mondale did, and we flew back to Paris via London.

July 31, Shirley Ann and I flew to London for some meetings at the embassy as well as with some people from the New Scotland Yard. They knew that my time was coming to an end in Paris, and they really took care of us, particularly Shirley Ann. Their wives took her on a shopping spree in London. The group took us on a boat ride up and down the Thames River on their police boat. Shirley Ann and I rode the big red buses and saw several Broadway type plays. We rode in the typical black London cabs and had Guinness in a pub with the Scotland Yard guys. They were a great group with which to work. I have kept in touch with several of the Scotland Yard detectives throughout the years and some years ago, two of them, Ray Platt and John Harris, were in Los Angeles on business. They called me and we had dinner together.

Shirley Ann and I returned to Paris on August 2, and on the 6th, Joe Le Den Mat, Shirley Ann, and I drove down to Bordeaux on business at the consulate. We then worked our way back along the coast returning to Paris on August 7.

August 9, I went to SHAPE for my last physical examination and some last minute shopping. Because SHAPE is a multinational organization, you never knew what nationality your doctor and nurse would be. All nations contribute personnel to the hospital, so it's similar to the United Nations.

August 13, the office threw a going away party for Shirley Ann and me. Phyllis Neftell was in charge and she had invited some of our colleagues, both American and French. They had a barrel of French wine and cheeses, but it was a very bittersweet function, saying good-bye to some very fine friends. One good friend said to me that he would drink my wine, but today it will be sour. What a quaint way of saying "so long."

Paris was a very interesting and active assignment. I missed the personnel greatly after I had gone. I have kept in touch with most of them throughout the years, as they were a very special group. I miss other things too. I miss being able to call a French language teacher and having her come up to the office for an hour of intense study, one-on-one. I miss being able to show guests what a great city Paris is.

Our last guests were my brother, Ernest, his wife, Betty, and their children, John and Marilyn. Did we have a ball! We went up to Montmartre the first night, and the second night, we had dinner at Club Med. Did the Club Med lose on that night! After dinner, we went down to an old boat on the Seine, just north of our apartment, and had coffee. What a great time we had. We also went on the Bateau Mouche, the boat that goes up and down the Seine.

August 16, we spent packing. August 17, after our apartment was all cleaned out with the help of movers, Shirley Ann and I went down to the office to say a final farewell to our office personnel. Phyllis took us to Charles de Gaulle Airport, and we left on a 3 p.m. TWA flight, en route to St. Louis via New York. We spent several days with Missy and Dar, and then took off for California on August 20. That happened to be my birthday, and upon arriving in L.A., we went immediately to my parents' home in Hawthorne for a home coming party. That was fun! I think most of the family was there, as Mom's apartment was packed. It made me realize how much I had missed family gatherings during my two years in Paris.

CHAPTER 38

President Ford Detail
Rancho Mirage, California
August 1979

Shirley Ann and I went out to Palm Desert on August 23 to take possession of our new home there. I began to make preparations to take over President Ford's detail on August 26. The Fords were still in Vail, Colorado, at that time so there wasn't much to be done at the office until they returned.

I was really excited to be working on Ford's detail. I had worked Mr. and Mrs. Ford when he was the vice president, and also when he took over as president in August 1974. They had always been very nice people with whom to work. You can generally tell what type of people the protectees are by how their agents feel about them. Ford's agents always spoke well of them, and that proved to be true for the twenty-eight months in which I was involved with them as their SAIC as well.

The Fords returned from Vail the last week in August. Jack Merchant, the SAIC whom I was replacing, brought them into the Palm Springs Airport and I took over at that point, and Jack was reassigned to another post of duty. He left me a very smoothly running detail. He had some very good personnel, including my good friend, Bob Kollar. Bob had been an agent in Los Angeles and then he was the resident agent in Riverside for a number of years. When they formed the former president's details, they made Bob the number two man, making him my first assistant. I also had another assistant, Warner Brown, a very experienced supervisor who was a delightful person with whom to work. Warner was the number three man on the detail. I also had two other Los Angeles agents on the detail: David Behler and Jim Davidson. Both of these agents, however, left the detail shortly after I arrived.

When I took over the detail, we had twenty-seven agents, two assistants to the SAIC, ten uniformed police, and one stenographer, Kathy Davis. I don't know how Kathy managed all of the work that we generated, but she did. We had eight-man shifts, one shift on duty at all times, around the clock, with one designated shift leader for each shift. When you counted all of our personnel, it came to thirty-eight people. Our budget was over five million dollars per year. That's a great amount of money, but as Mr. Nixon had previously declined protection, Mr. Ford was the only former president to have Secret Service protection at that time.

Mr. Ford was on a number of boards throughout the country in addition to being on the speaking circuit. He also played in a few Pro-Am golf tournaments throughout the year. All of this meant that I was in for a great deal of travel in this new assignment.

During my two-year assignment in Paris, I kept track of all of my trips. They amounted to sixty-two total. During my two years and four months with Mr. Ford, I took eighty-seven trips. We went all over the United States and the world, but I never became tired of the travel. It was almost always first class and mostly via small private jets, although we did take our share of red eye flights, mostly to New York City from LAX.

The first full month I was on the Ford detail, we took six trips. Keep in mind that one trip could entail multiple stops. For instance in September, we flew to Atlanta; Orlando; Las Vegas; Vancouver, B.C.; Chicago; Tulsa; Richland; Washington; Los Angeles; Napa, California; Denver; Cleveland; Carlisle and York, Pennsylvania; Washington, D.C.; Pittsburgh; and Nashville, Tennessee. Quite a month, but we were just getting started.

Some of the above trips stand out in my memory like the trip to the War College at Carlisle Barracks in Pennsylvania, and the trip to Tulsa where Mr. Ford played in a Pro-Am golf tournament. I had called Jack and Shirley Kirkland, my good friends from Inglewood and advised them that we would be at that tournament. Jack, being an avid golfer, made arrangements to meet us at the golf course. I was able to walk most of the eighteen holes with Jack and Shirley, while Bob Kollar stuck close to Ford. After the golf game, the Kirklands and I had dinner together, which was quite a perk. I was beginning to like and appreciate my new assignment.

I should expound somewhat on Jack Kirkland. Jack and I went to Inglewood High School together and we played football and baseball together for a number of years. In our senior years at Inglewood in 1943, we both played first string backfield and played on one of the finest baseball teams Inglewood High School ever had. Jack was a standout athlete in both sports. When it came time to go into the service, I went into the navy and Jack went into the marines. After the war, Jack and Shirley got married and asked me to be their best man. I was delighted with such an honor.

Jack was a very good softball pitcher and after the war, he hooked up with the North American Aircraft Company, working during the days and playing ball for them at night. He parlayed that great ability into an excellent career at North American Aircraft, and later at Rockwell, when they took over North American. Jack Kirkland is a great story all by himself, and I am pleased to be a part of Jack's story. We continue to be great friends.

October saw us going to San Francisco; Williamsburg and Charlottesville, Virginia; Washington, D.C.; New Orleans; Ashland and Lexington, Kentucky; South Bend, Indiana; Chicago; and Durango, Colorado. In November, we only took two trips—Honolulu and New York City. That was probably the month that I traveled the least in all of the time that I spent on this detail.

1980

CHAPTER 39

President Ford Detail
1980

December was a quiet month, but January made up for it. We went on four trips, ending up in Monterey, California, on January 30, where Mr. Ford played in the Pebble Beach tournament there. That was a fun trip even though it rained much of the time. This was the trip where Mr. Ford let loose a long approach shot to a green. It went a little past the green and bonked a person in the head. It wasn't really Mr. Ford's fault—the man should have been more aware of the dangers in standing close to the green when a Pro-Am is in progress. In any event, the man was bald and the ball hit him right on top of the head. It broke his skin and he dropped to the ground, out cold. He bled profusely and was carted away by an ambulance. People blamed Mr. Ford for what happened, but that's not really fair. Even though Mr. Ford was a very good golfer, amateurs get a little nervous when people are out watching them. You might notice that when the amateurs tee off with all of the people around, they occasionally don't do well and consequently will hit some spectators. If you had followed Mr. Ford around, you would have seen that he was quite a good golfer.

Mr. Ford often had appointments with President Carter at the White House. It was nice being back in Washington. Once, I recall waiting for Mr. Ford in the outer office, adjacent to the Oval Office. When Mr. Ford came out, he was talking to several people. I kept reading a magazine, as I knew Mr. Ford would spend some time chatting. Without looking up, however, I noticed that someone had come up and was standing right in front of me. I looked up to see President Carter looking down at me with his hand out stretched for a handshake. That was a very nice gesture and quite unusual of most presidents. The Carters were very pleasant, accommodating people.

We took a number of trips to Ann Arbor and Grand Rapids, Michigan. This was during the time that the Ford Library was being built on the campus at the University of Michigan. Mr. Ford's museum was also being built at that time in Grand Rapids. We didn't get there that frequently, but we were always amazed as to how quickly they were being erected.

During the fall when we were in the area of the university, we choppered right onto the University of Michigan football practice field. Prior arrangements had been made, of course, and Coach Bo Schembechler met the chopper. He had the team come over and chat with Mr. Ford.

Being one of their great alumni as well as one of their great football players, Mr. Ford was well received by the players and I know that he enjoyed the experience too. Go Big Blue!

On May 17, we headed for Kansas City and Chicago. The following afternoon, we were due in Worcester, Massachusetts, for a dinner honoring the deceased Hubert Humphrey. The Humphreys and the Fords were good friends. As we were flying into Massachusetts in a small, private jet, the weather began to close in at our primary airport, which was about forty miles north of Worcester. We were advised to abort the primary site and use an alternate airport, about forty miles south of Worcester. There was no way the advance team could get the motorcade down to the new location in time.

So, after we landed, we walked over to the fire station and asked the firemen if we could spend some time with them while we waited for the motorcade to arrive. Were they surprised and pleased to have Mr. Ford as their guest. There was coffee all around and quite a few autographs. We spent a very enjoyable hour with some very accommodating firemen. The motorcade finally arrived to take us into Worcester. Actually, we had to go beyond Worcester some distance first to our over night site. By this time, the cars were running on air and guts, as the agents did not have time to stop and refuel.

On our way through Worcester, we passed the auditorium where the scheduled dinner had already started, which did make Mr. Ford nervous. He said, "OK Darwin, how much longer until we get there?" I didn't know so I asked the driver who said about fifteen minutes. Well, he wasn't very happy with that answer as he was a very punctual person and hated being late. Every five minutes or so, he would again ask how much longer.

When we were about five minutes out, the driver tapped me on the arm and pointed to the gas gauge. It was below empty. We were really running on fumes and I wasn't sure we were going to make it. Finally, the driver said that our destination was just around the next curve in the road. We would be there in about two minutes. I said "Two minutes, Mr. Ford." He was very upset about being late and said that when we arrived, he was going to do a quick change and leave immediately back to Worcester.

Unbeknownst to Mr. Ford, our car literally ran out of gas as we pulled into the driveway of the hotel. A hostess met us and took us to Mr. Ford's room, where he indeed did a very quick change and was ready to head back for the dinner—except we weren't. The limo was out of gas and there were no gas facilities for miles. The manager saved our lives—particularly mine—by giving us the gas they had stored for their lawn mowers. It was just enough to get us back to Worcester. The guys dropped us off at the auditorium and then got the tanks filled. I'm not sure that Mr. Ford ever knew how close we had come to running out of a gas. On a protective assignment, that situation is inexcusable. I have never come that close before or after, but I have stopped on a number of occasions to gas up while the protectee was still with us. I hope that people don't think I'm chastising the agents who were driving the motorcade cars. Not so—they did their very best under some trying circumstances.

The next night we were in Columbus, Ohio, and one of our hosts was Woody Hayes, the Ohio State football coach. Hayes was a very good friend of Mr. Ford.

I have a daily schedule for Mr. Ford dated June 4, 1980, that reads: "9:25 a.m. – motorcade departs office en route to Jack's Barber Shop. Driving time – five minutes arriving at 9:30 a.m.

At 9:55 a.m. haircut concludes. Motorcade departs en route to office. Driving time – five minutes. President Ford arrives office at 10 a.m. and proceeds inside. At noon – President and Mrs. Ford meet with Darwin Horn in Ford's office. 12:45 p.m. – meeting concludes. Darwin departs office."

That could have been a real chewing out, but the Fords weren't like that. It's no secret that there are problems that occur on protective details. Ours was no exception. I can't recall what the subject was in that meeting. It could have been a problem, but whatever it was, we would have taken care of it immediately. Mr. and Mrs. Ford were an easy couple with whom to work.

I remember one problem that we had with Mrs. Ford. She had a stopover in Dallas, but there weren't any Dallas agents around at all. So the agents with her had to scramble to get some help, which they did and they finally ended up in the first class waiting salon. But that shouldn't have happened at all and Mrs. Ford was somewhat disappointed in us. I couldn't blame her. Here is why it happened: We always sent a teletype to all offices involved, advising our travel plans, dates, times, and locations. Dallas received the teletype, but because it was only a layover, their agents chose not to respond to the airport. But we weren't aware of it because we didn't follow up our teletype with a telephone call requesting the name of their agent who would be in charge of our layover. After that debacle, we instituted a policy where our duty agent would call each office in order to determine who the agent would be and who would handle our group. It was also required that some request of them would be made in order to make sure they would show up. Pretty sneaky.

On June 29, we transferred our base of operations from Rancho Mirage to Vail, Colorado. The Fords retreated to Vail every summer, as summers in Palm Springs are extremely hot. That was my first summer with the Fords in Vail. The Secret Service allowed each agent on the detail to rent an apartment or condo in Vail for the summer. Most of the agents took their families up for the summer. It turned out to be a fun vacation. The Secret Service picked up the rental tabs and then paid us an additional $24 per day per diem. Shirley Ann and I rented an apartment right on Vail Creek, close to our command post, and of course very close to the main part of Vail Village.

Vail was a charming place with much to do. It was a great place for running too, even though it was 8,000 feet above sea level. I ran in several races there. One was up to the Eisenhower Tunnel, which was thirteen miles straight up to 11,000 feet. The other was from downtown Vail, up the fire trails to the ski lift station. It was a difficult run on rough terrain.

A cute story about that last run: I had been in Vail for about two days and decided that I would run the race to the ski lift station. The morning of the race we all lined up. The gun sounded and we all took off. There were some rabbits in the group, so I knew that all I was going to be able to do was to make it to the finish line—I didn't care about my time. Very quickly though, I was the last runner in the entire group. The only thing behind me was the ambulance. They came up on me several times and told me to get in, as they could see that I was really hurting. I declined their offer over and over until I finally made it to the first ski lift station. No doubt I was really beat, but I made it. I also received a trophy, as I was the only person running in my age group. I received a letter in the mail several days later from the Vail Recreation Association congratulating me on my finish. It said, "Congratulations, out of the seventy-eight runners who competed in the Vail Ski Run, you came in number seventy-nine." Someone had a real sense of humor.

Though Vail was supposed to be a summer vacation site for the Fords, they did still travel some. It wasn't easy or quick, however, to fly out of Vail. We could leave from the airport at

Eagle if we were traveling in a small jet, or we would have to go into Denver for larger plane service. It was a two-hour drive to Denver, so it was to our advantage if we could leave from Eagle, which was much closer.

When we weren't traveling, Mr. Ford played golf at the Vail Golf Course, a very nice scenic course nestled between the mountains and Vail Creek. I don't know how difficult that course was, as I never played it, but I know that in 1980, they had a tournament and many of the top-notch players from the circuit showed up to play. I wouldn't doubt that many of them came because of Mr. Ford. He was friends with many of the top golfers in the United States and an integral part of that fraternity.

For me, the Vail Golf Course was a great place to run. There usually weren't many golfers around so I never worried about getting in their way. At the end of the golf course, there was a giant beaver dam, but in all my runs through the course, strangely I never saw any beavers.

By late August, it began to cool off considerably, and we started to see snow in the upper elevations. For the Fords, that meant it was approaching the time to return to Rancho Mirage.

August 27, we drove to Denver, caught a flight to LAX, and then caught a Japanese Airline flight to Tokyo. We stayed in Tokyo for three days and then returned to the Denver, via San Francisco. That was the first time I had been to Tokyo. I did a little sightseeing, visiting some World War II sites I had heard about—it was quite exciting that I was actually there in person after hearing so much about it.

Mr. Ford spent much of September campaigning for Ronald Reagan, who was running for the presidency. September 2, we left Vail and caught a private jet to New York City, where Mr. Ford had a speech. The next day, we went to Providence, Rhode Island, and then returned to New York City that afternoon. On the 4th, we left New York City for LAX, and then drove to Palm Springs, where we remained for over two weeks without any travel.

Then on the 22nd, we flew by private jet to Pittsburgh, Charleston, and Philadelphia. From there, we headed for Monmouth, New Jersey. On the 25th, we departed Monmouth, en route to Willmer, Minnesota. Willmer was close to Stockholm, South Dakota, where my sister, Arline Berg, and her husband, Stan, lived. They came over to meet us at the airport and were able to meet and spend some time with Mr. Ford while he was politicking. After Willmer, we took off for Boise, Idaho, where there was a big Reagan blowout. Later that night, we ended up back in Palm Springs after a very busy day.

October was a very busy month. We were in the following cities, some of them twice: New York City, Detroit, Ann Arbor, Chicago, St. Louis, Los Angeles, San Francisco, Medford, Yakima, Portland, Seattle, Grand Rapids, Santa Rosa, Battle Creek, Saginaw, Pontiac, Bridgeport, Washington, D.C., Cincinnati, Peoria, and Kansas City. That was a great deal of travel and it was mostly campaigning for Mr. Reagan.

November was a bit slower. After Election Day, we didn't do too much. On November 15, I took time off to attend the first annual Hall of Fame Dinner at Pepperdine University. I was thrilled to have been chosen in the first group of athletes for the honor. Also included in that group was my old friend from football and baseball, Terry Bell. Along with Terry and me, a number of other Pepperdine athletes were chosen: Nick Buzolich, Pete Fogo, Gene Vollnogle, Bob Morris, and Gail Hopkins. Several fine coaches were also inducted: tennis coach Hubert Derrick; basketball coaches Robert "Duck" Dowell and Al Duer; and baseball coach John Scolinos, for whom I played for three years. These were all excellent athletes and coaches who had been fine representatives of Pepperdine for many years.

The rest of November and December remained rather quiet. The Fords went to Vail to ski during the latter part of December and the first part of January. Bob Kollar liked to ski, so he took the detail to Vail and skied every day. Therefore, I was freed up for several weeks of vacation. With my regular days off, the Christmas holidays, and annual leave, I was off for twenty-three straight days. That was unheard of in my Secret Service career. It was wonderful bringing in the New Year on vacation with my family.

1981

CHAPTER 40

President Ford Detail
Rancho Mirage, California
1981

My last year in the Secret Service was 1981.

The month of March was a very important month for the detail. We were involved in a trip that took us around the world. The planning was a very difficult assignment, but Bruce Bales, one of our shift leaders, volunteered to put the entire trip together if he could stay home and direct the trip from Rancho Mirage. I took that deal! And Bruce did a magnificent job. He had to know Mr. Ford's itinerary; he had to get our advance agents out in plenty of time; and he had to leapfrog those advance agents to make sure we were always covered from stop to stop.

Our detail didn't have enough personnel to do all the work, so we asked for help from headquarters. We were fortunate to obtain some excellent agents who not only did advance work, but also filled in on shifts as needed in the various stops. My old friend from Paris, Peter Grant, joined the detail because he had a great deal of experience in foreign advances. We also leapfrogged some of the agents and the trip went very well. Bruce Bales really did a superlative job.

We took off from Newark, New Jersey, on March 5. The main party flew in a BAC 111, a jet that held about twenty people. I was always on that plane with the working shift. We flew across the Atlantic to Shannon, Ireland, where we stayed over night in a genuine castle. Our time in Ireland, however, was not very pleasant. The castle was old, the showers didn't work, and it rained and rained. One night, several of us went into a little village to visit an Irish Pub, where we hoped to have a nice Guinness and relax. But the fireplace wasn't working very well, it was very crowded, and the smoke was so thick we had to leave.

We were originally slated to leave Ireland on March 7 en route to Paris, but Darius Keeton, the owner of the BAC 111, invited us to his vacation home on the Island of Jersey in the English Channel. Mr. Ford accepted his invitation, so we made a very quick advance arrangement call to the local police on the island. They were very cooperative and upon our arrival, they had transportation ready and waiting for us. We spent several enjoyable hours in an area that felt like a bygone era. It was like going back in America for a generation or more.

After several hours in Jersey, we flew into Paris for a three-day visit. Meeting us at Le Bourget Airfield were several of the agents who had been with me when I was in Paris. Ron Provencher, the DEA agent, was also a part of that arrival group. He had wanted to be involved and I was delighted to see him. Ron has always been one of my most cherished friends outside the Secret Service. Every New Year's Eve, I call Ron to wish him a happy New Year. He is now retired from the DEA and lives in Texas, where he works in the wine industry. There was never a better-suited person for that DEA job than Ron Provencher.

It was fabulous to be back in Paris enjoying the wonderful French food, which is really the best in the world. I visited my old office and saw quite a few of the friends who worked for other agencies there. I also had time for a dinner at the Club Med in Neuilly, which was among my favorite restaurants in Paris. It was also good to see some of the French security agents with whom I had worked so often.

On the 13th, we left Paris for Bonn, Germany, but we didn't stay very long there. We then took off for the Persian Gulf area, landing in Muscat, Oman, where it was very hot and humid. We operated out of Muscat for several days, taking trips to Qatar and Abu Dhabi. We saw firsthand what our dollars spent on gasoline and oil are doing there. The wealth of the Emirates is extremely evident. Oil has made them a very significant part of the world.

We left Muscat on the 16th and flew directly to Singapore where we spent three days. I met a police officer who showed me around, though it was extremely hot and humid. I saw the causeway where the Japanese came into Singapore from the north at the beginning of World War II. I saw the old Ford Plant where the British were forced to sign for the surrender of the city. I also managed to get out for a quick run. I always packed my running gear for trips because I knew that on most days, I could get away for at least an hour or so to get my run in.

On the 18th, we flew to Jakarta, Indonesia, for a two-day stay, where it was still hot and humid. Jakarta was teeming with people. I happened to be outside our hotel at about 5 p.m. one afternoon just as the workers were going home. I have never seen so many people in all my life coming out of the woodwork. They depended greatly upon bus transportation, so the busses were totally full—so full in fact that people were hanging on to the outside since there was no room left inside.

The countryside outside Jakarta was lush and green. They get a large amount of rainfall and the jungle is not too far away from the city. On the way in from the airport, we went through a number of villages where chickens, goats, dogs, and a number of other animals ran freely through the village streets.

From Jakarta, we flew to Hong Kong—a great place for shopping and business! The Fords and I were guests for dinner one night at a very sumptuous hotel dining room. It was a dinner for the economic elite of Hong Kong in honor of Mr. Ford. There must have been about twenty-five of us in attendance. Generally, I wouldn't have been invited to a dinner like that, but for some reason in Hong Kong, I was. It was one of the best dinners that I've ever had. It was truly elegant. They had a divine dessert made of white chocolate—I had never seen a dessert like it.

We made our way around the Hong Kong area pretty well, going one night to a dinner on the far side of the island, the area where the Japanese had landed during World War II in order to take Hong Kong.

On March 22, we left Hong Kong en route to Beijing. Mr. Ford was very well received in Beijing. We attended a banquet one evening at the Great Hall of China. Some of the food wasn't very appetizing to look at. How do you like your chicken feet prepared? Their rice was always good though, and I did eat a lot of it. Beijing is a very interesting city, unlike any other in the world. There are, of course, millions of people, but the city itself is somewhat blah and I have never seen so many people on bicycles.

On the 24th, we left Beijing and flew to Chungking. We were apparently the first Americans in Chungking since the end of World War II. The Chinese people there constantly stared at us, making the visit a rather uncomfortable one. Chungking had what they called the hard currency store, a five-story building where only foreigners are allowed to shop using any currency other than Chinese. The shopping was very good.

As we were shopping, I noticed two Australian men whispering. They suspected that something unusual was going on with all of us agents lingering around the Fords. I wasn't sure what they were after, so I watched them carefully. One of them came up on an aisle in order to get a better look. When he did, I could see the lights and bells go off in his mind, and he rushed back to his friend. I slid over to where they were and I heard the one fellow tell the other, "It's President Nixon." Well, not quite buddy. I never told Mr. Ford about that incident.

Upon leaving the hard currency store, we had a motorcade of about four vehicles waiting for us. Swarms of Chinese appeared from nowhere, lining up on both sides of the street. I don't know how the word got out, or who put it out. The crowd, fortunately though, was very quiet and complacent and we had no difficulties.

We had gone to Chungking in order to take a Yangtze River boat through some of the gorges of that great river. We were on the boat for a part of two days and saw some awesome scenery. The gorges were magnificent. We stopped the first night at some town and tied up for the night. Bob Kollar and I went into the town and looked around. We bought some linen handkerchiefs for about three-cents each. There wasn't really too much else to buy because it must have been about 11 p.m. and most of the shops were closed. The next day, we left the town and continued down the river. At about 2:30 p.m., we got off the boat at Doy Shan Tuo, where our bus was waiting to drive us to the airport at Dangyang. We then flew back to Beijing, arriving that evening.

The following day, March 27, we left Beijing for Osaka, Japan, where Mr. Ford had a golf engagement. I recall vividly how brown the golf course was. Of course, they were just getting out of the winter, but I thought with all of the interest they have in golf in Japan, that they would take better care of their golf courses.

After Osaka, we flew to Tokyo on the 29th. It was there that we first heard about the assassination attempt on President Reagan,. There was a great cry for information regarding the protection of the president from the Japanese press. I declined all requests for interviews from the press, mainly because I was not fully aware of what happened in Washington. The Japanese security forces wanted to increase their protection of Mr. Ford, providing a number of additional personnel, but I also declined that. When a foreign VIP comes to your country, the indigenous security force has the responsibility of protection. So in Tokyo, the Japanese security had the say so. In those instances where emergencies arise, a conference is held and each side has its say. I told them that we had enough protection as it was, and so the level remained at what it had been. It worked out satisfactorily.

We stayed there until the 31st, and then left for Anchorage, Alaska. On the way, we crossed the International Date Line gaining hours, so we arrived in Anchorage on the 31st. It was great to get back to America. My arrival in Alaska completed a very significant goal in my life. Entering Anchorage meant that I had finally traveled through all fifty states. Ever since I was a youngster, I knew that I had wanted to do that—well it only took me fifty-five years to reach that goal!

The round-the-world trip with the Fords was a great adventure. It was the only truly around the entire world trip that I ever made. It capped off my career in a very nice manner. I don't suppose that a person could have traveled in a better way or with a nicer group of people.

In April, we resumed our domestic travel. We hit such cities as New York City; Philadelphia; Austin, Texas; Grand Rapids, Michigan; Searcy, Arkansas; Nashville; Abilene and El Paso, Texas; Columbus, Ohio; Louisville; and Charlotte, North Carolina.

We were in New York City on three different occasions, and generally stayed at the Waldorf Astoria Hotel, which is one of the finest hotels in the world. I also recall that on our trip to Nashville, we went to the Grand Ole Opry. After the show, the Fords were invited backstage which turned out to be a very interesting experience.

On April 29, we left Palm Springs and didn't get back until May 7. We were in such cities as Dallas, Nashville, Columbus, Charlotte, New York City, and Los Angeles. When we arrived in Los Angeles, I took off for five days and went home. Bob Kollar had come to Los Angeles from Rancho Mirage with the cars and took over so I could get some time off. Later in May, we went to Oklahoma City; Detroit; Columbus; and Vancouver and Edmonton, Canada.

June saw us traveling to New York City again. From there, we left for Rio de Janeiro, Brazil. We spent four great days in Rio and a day in Sao Paulo. Brazil was a very interesting country and Rio is a magnificent city. I ran a great deal on their boardwalk, as the weather was fantastic. I particularly enjoyed going to their barbecue restaurants where you go in, sit down, and they come to your table with skewers of barbecued meat. You stay as long as you want and eat as much as you can. You had your choice of about eight different types of meat, plus an unending supply of salad and bread.

On June 11, we flew to Miami and then caught a private jet back to Palm Springs. June 28, Shirley Ann and I took off for Vail, as the Fords were ready to head to their summer retreat again.

July was a busy month operating out of Vail. On July 17, we caught a plane to San Francisco. Mr. Ford spent several days at the Bohemian Grove, a privately owned organization located north of San Francisco, near Santa Rosa. That was quite an experience. Some of the most important and wealthiest men in America attended the festivities, but there were absolutely no women allowed, not even to cook. Throughout the years, outside organizations have attacked Bohemian Grove for various reasons. The meeting, which lasts for a number of days, allows the VIPs of America to have an opportunity to let their hair down, and believe me they do. They really get down to the very basics. It doesn't matter who you are or what you have done, at Bohemian Grove, you're just another member. They write their own rules and do they have fun!

July 29, we went up to Durango, Colorado, on the old train that surprisingly still services Durango. The train ride begins and ends in Pueblo, Colorado. It was a most enjoyable time. We spent the night there and returned to Vail the following day.

August 5 and 6, we were in Washington. On the 6th, Mr. Ford had a board meeting outside New York City. Our plan was to go to New York City for the meeting, then catch a late flight to Denver and motorcade back to Vail, hopefully arriving near midnight. This was important because I was starting my vacation on the 7th, and we wanted to get a good start. Shirley Ann and I had a trip planned up to Stockholm, South Dakota, to see Arline and Stan. After that, we had planned on going over to St. Louis to see Missy and Dar and then get home in time for Shirley Ann to prepare for her new school year.

Well, while Mr. Ford was in conferences, I had been speaking to one of the administrators about our vacation agenda. He said that the company had a private jet that wasn't being used, so our detail could use it to get Mr. Ford back to Vail. With that small plane, we could land at Vail/Eagle and really save a great amount of time. Was I thrilled? We flew into Eagle and landed at 7 p.m., putting me four hours ahead of schedule! When I arrived at our condo, Shirley Ann had everything already packed and ready to go. She had even paid all of the bills. We left Vail early the next morning and arrived in Stockholm, South Dakota, at about 11:30 p.m. that night.

We were very late in Stockholm because when we were driving through Nebraska, we saw a road sign to O'Neill, Nebraska. That was the town where Shirley Ann's father, Edward McBride, was reared. So we took a little side trip. We made a few stops, talked to a few people, even went out to the cemetery. We were able to find where Shirley's sister, Florence, had stayed when she was an orphan, but all in all, we didn't learn too much about the McBrides. We left O'Neill and ended up late in Stockholm. We had a delightful time with Arline and Stan for several days, and then we left for St. Louis.

It was nice seeing Missy and Dar. They certainly enjoyed the time they lived in St. Louis. We spent several days with them, and then took off for Palm Springs, making it back in three days. It was nice to get back to Rancho Mirage. I had several more days off before I reported back to work on August 25.

September was an interesting month. On the 21st, we flew to London for the English Bob Hope Classic. We spent our nights going to a number of the Broadway plays that are always playing there. We had a delightful five days in London. I had a number of opportunities to run in Hyde Park and took advantage of each one of them.

On the 28th, we flew over to Stockholm, Sweden, for a day and then to Copenhagen, Denmark, with a return trip to Stockholm that same day. On the 30th, we returned to London and caught a Pan Am flight to New York City. That was a huge amount of flying in a short time, but we enjoyed it.

On October 7, Anwar Sadat of Egypt was assassinated in Cairo. President Reagan invited former presidents Nixon, Ford, and Carter to attend the funeral. He also invited former secretary of state Henry Kissinger. Each of them had worked with Mr. Sadat in some form or another over the years, so their presence at the funeral was appreciated. Everyone agreed to meet in Washington on October 8 for a planning meeting and then we all departed for Cairo on a U.S. Air Force plane.

Just prior to landing, all of us agents put on bulletproof vests, as the word was out that the Egyptian security forces didn't know for sure if the insurrection was over. Even though we knew it was going to be very hot in Cairo, the peace of mind that the bulletproof vests brought were worth a little extra heat under the collar. After I put mine on, I grabbed one for Mr. Ford, but it was apparent that he didn't want to put it on. He asked me what the other fellows were doing. By "fellows," he meant Nixon, Carter, and Kissinger. Quite a fraternity! I told him I didn't care what the others were doing; I wanted him to wear it anyway. As it turned out, I don't think any of the fraternity brothers wore bulletproof vests that day.

That night in Cairo, the fraternity attended a wake held in honor of President Sadat. One by one, they each relayed many of the great experiences they had had with Sadat. Mr. Hosni Mubarak, who later took over as president, was present at this function as well. It turned out to be a very emotional experience especially because Mrs. Sadat was also in attendance.

The next morning, we were all anticipating a very hot, long, and dangerous day. Several of us were standing in front of Mr. Ford's suite when all of a sudden the door opened. There was Mr. Ford standing there with his bulletproof vest in his hand. He said, "Darwin, come in here and show me how to put this darn thing on." It was cumbersome and uncomfortably hot, but if your life is on the line, you suck it up and wear it. We all looked like line backers for the Green Bay Packers—or perhaps more accurately, we looked like over weight, shoddy Americans.

When we got out to the burial grounds, we learned that it was adjacent to the assassination site, which was rather eerie. After the service, we lost no time in getting into our motorcades and out to the awaiting plane, thankful that everybody was safe and sound.

Nixon and Kissinger had other business in the Middle East, so they left the party in Cairo. Ford and Carter traveled together, where they enjoyed sharing with each other about the museums and libraries that each of them were in the process of building. Carter was just beginning to put his together, and Ford's was just about finished. Ford and Carter became good friends during that trip, and afterwards they telephoned each other often.

On the way back to America, the official photographer took some photos of Ford and Carter with all of the Secret Service personnel. It is one of my prize photos and proudly hangs up on the wall in my home. After the agents received their photos, I had a rash of requests from them to have Ford autograph the photos. He was always very nice about doing that though it was a bit of a chore. There were also several photos taken of all four presidents together before we departed for Cairo on October 8. Many of the agents had gotten each of the presidents to sign their name on the photo. Unfortunately, I never got one of those pictures. I wonder what a photograph with all four signatures would be worth today.

We arrived back in Washington late in the evening on October 10. The U.S. Air Force supplied us with a small jet to fly Mr. Ford and some of our detail back to Palm Springs. The following day, we flew to Phoenix and returned the same day. That type of trip was not unusual—back and forth in the same day. On the 14th, we left Palm Springs very early in the morning, flew to LAX, and caught an early flight to Chicago, where Mr. Ford spoke to some group. We left Chicago at that same night, arriving in Palm Springs at 10:50 p.m.—another day of a lot of flying.

On the 19th, we flew to Houston. The next day, we flew to Midland, Texas, and then later that night, we departed Midland, en route to Chicago. After Chicago, we flew to Grand Rapids, Michigan, and then back to Palm Springs, arriving on the 23rd at midnight. On the 25th, we flew to Honolulu and then on to Maui, where Mr. Ford played golf for several days.

On the 28th, we flew back to Honolulu, before heading for Sydney, Australia. After crossing the International Date Line, we arrived in Sydney at 9:10 a.m. on the 29th. We stayed in Sydney for a day, and then flew down to Canberra, where we stayed for about four hours. Canberra, the capital of Australia, is a beautiful city. From Canberra, we flew all the way across Australia to Perth, where we remained overnight. Perth is on the Indian Ocean and it was quite warm and humid. The following morning, we flew up to Mount Newman via a private plane.

Mount Newman is the site of one of the largest open pit iron mines in the world. We stayed at the mine for about three hours, where we were taken on a great tour. It was extremely hot, humid, and dusty, but very interesting just the same. We learned that an Australian who had a great interest in going out on weekends and plinking for metal deposits found Mt. Newman and its great iron deposits. It so happened that one weekend, the man was in the Mt. Newman area looking around and he found some ore deposits that looked promising. They assayed out very high and began mining, which resulted in him finding one of the richest iron deposits in the world. Needless to say, he became a very wealthy person.

After our tour of the mine, we flew back to Sydney in the private plane. We didn't have much free time during this trip but I enjoyed being back in Australia. It's nice going to a foreign country where they like Americans. Much of that feeling emanates from World War II experiences. So many Australians thanked us for the magnificent work the American GIs did for Australia during that war. But it was a two-way street—the Australian soldiers and sailors (called ANZACS, along with New Zealanders) fought in many decisive battles and held their own with the enemies.

Crossing the International Date Line on October 31 made that day an extra long day. After all was said and done, we arrived in Honolulu at 9:50 a.m. on the 31st, and went right back to Maui, where Mr. Ford got in another round of golf. The following day, we left Maui, flew to LAX via Honolulu, and then headed home to Palm Springs.

November wasn't a bad month for travel. I recall one of the last trips of the month was up to Reno, Nevada, for a visit to the University of Nevada (UNR). They had sent a plane down to pick us up in the afternoon of the 13th. We flew up the crest of the Sierras and it was a very rough ride. The plane was somewhat underpowered, which made for a very long and slow trip. When we arrived in Reno, it was raining very hard and we all got soaked because they didn't have a limo waiting to pick us up planeside. We had to run about a hundred yards in the rain to get to a building where a part of the festivities were to occur.

I was able to meet my old friend from my Pepperdine College football days, Dick Dankworth. Dick had been a coach at UNR and later went into the administrative group working his way up the ladder after obtaining his doctorate. It was nice to see him and his wife, Carla, after too many years.

On our way back to Palm Springs on that same miserably underpowered plane, we ran into a gigantic storm. It rained and snowed something horrible. It was a great relief to arrive safe and sound in sunny Palm Springs again.

The month of December—my last month in the Secret Service—began with us in New York City. We arrived there on November 30, and departed on December 4, stopping in Des Moines, Salt Lake City, and San Francisco before arriving back in Palm Springs. On the 12th, we took a quick day trip to San Diego.

My last trip with Mr. Ford began on December 14, when we left Palm Springs at 9 p.m., flying to Des Moines, where we stayed until 3 a.m., and then continued on to Louisville, Kentucky, arriving there at 5:05 a.m. We left Louisville at 10:35 p.m., and returned to Palm Springs at midnight.

For the rest of the month, I worked in the office in Rancho Mirage getting ready for retirement. There were quite a number of forms to execute and a whole lot of goodbyes to say to my numerous Secret Service employees. On December 30, I was pleased to turn in my weapon, handcuffs, radio, and identification book. When I handed over my gun, I was delighted to say that I had never had to use it in an extreme manner. Sure, like most agents, I had pulled my weapon on a number of occasions, for effect mostly, but never actually fired it at a suspect. I had carried a weapon for two years on the LAPD and over thirty years in the Secret Service and promised myself that I would never carry a weapon again, at all, and forever.

Before I left Rancho Mirage, I had an opportunity to talk to Mr. Ford. I told him that the two years and four months I had spent with him and Mrs. Ford, were some of the highlights of my career and I sincerely meant it.

I knew that I would dearly miss being involved with the Secret Service—after thirty-plus years of service, it was all I knew. I was also going to miss traveling with Mr. Ford and the detail. We had taken some wonderful trips, going to practically every major city in the United States as well as many of the main cities throughout the world. All in all, I took a total of eighty-seven trips with Mr. and Mrs. Ford. Most lasted three or four days; some were there and back in one day; but the longest, of course, was our month-long around-the-world trip in March 1981.

I knew I would miss the hullabaloo of travel days and working with some very fine agents in the process. I would miss going to the political conventions and being involved in the campaigns. I would miss seeing many of the excellent agents from the field offices who were assigned to us on our trips. Many of those agents were guys that I had done background investigations on and I was pleased to see them working their way up the Secret Service ladder.

You can't spend over thirty years on one job without being heavily attached to it. That was certainly true of the Secret Service. Some of the factors about the time that I spent in the Secret Service are still embedded in my mind: the amount of overtime the agents worked; the many weekends and holidays that we worked; the amount of speeches that I made; the thousands of protection assignments that we had, not only for the American political people but for the foreign dignitaries as well; the many times that we worked past midnight and then reported to work at 9 a.m. Looking back on it all, I wonder how we did it. So many assignments were given out in the L.A. office, and amazingly there were very few glitches. That certainly was due to SAIC Bob Powis and his great leadership skills.

The amount of speeches I delivered was a direct result of the fact that from 1970 to 1977, I was in charge of assigning speeches in the LAFO. Bob Powis and I did many ourselves, but we had a program where all agents took their turn. Many of the agents had some experience in public speaking already, so they generally went out more than other agents. Those who didn't have any experience went out with senior agents several times to observe, and when it came time to do one on their own, we gave them one that wasn't very demanding. We did this to help the agents, knowing that in their careers, they would be called upon many times to express themselves before a group .Our program was established to help those agents when that opportunity arose.

The Fords left for skiing in Vail several days prior to my final departure. I never liked to go there in the wintertime, but Bob Kollar and Warner Brown, my two assistants, both skied and enjoyed it tremendously. How would you like to go to work on the ski slope and get paid very well for being there? And they never even had wait in lines for the chair lifts!

My last day of work was December 30. Shirley Ann and I packed the car and headed back to our Rancho Palos Verdes residence just in time for the New Year.

1982-2000

CHAPTER 41

Retirement
1982-2000

I began running heavily again and training for marathons. The telephone began ringing more, as my old friends knew I was home for good now. In June 1982, wanting to give some time back to our community, I volunteered to serve as a traffic commissioner in Rancho Palos Verdes. Two local papers, the Peninsula News and the Daily Breeze, set up interviews and both articles came out very well. Pepperdine University also sent a crew out for an interview and photos.

I also rejoined Toastmasters, this time the San Pedro chapter. I knew that I was going to be doing quite a bit of speaking, so I wanted to sharpen up my speaking skills. The San Pedro chapter was a very old and distinguished group. I had competed against them on a number of occasions when I had previously belonged to the Rolling Hills chapter, and some of those San Pedro members were still there. Joe Marino and Terry Croskrey were two members whom I recalled very well. Later, Ed Ralls joined, and he and I became very good friends. Ed had played football at Occidental College at about the same time that I was playing at Pepperdine so we had a lot in common.

I stayed with the San Pedro Toastmasters for six months, which gave me a total of five years in the Toastmaster organization. At the end of six months, I started the South Bay Professional Speakers Bureau. I was the only person involved so I elected myself as the president. I had cards printed and for a while, business was pretty good. The problem that I found in professional public speaking, however, was that it was very difficult to charge members of my family for speech appearances. How could I charge my wife, daughter, brother or grandchildren who wanted me to speak to their classes? I made it a point not ever to charge them, nor would I ever charge Pepperdine University for any appearances there.

November 1982, I received a telephone call from Northrop Corporation in Hawthorne, requesting that I interview for the chief of security at their Pico Rivera plant. This plant had previously been the Ford Motor Car plant and was one of the largest plants in the world. At this time, it was being renovated for Northrop's use. I went to Northrop and interviewed with a number of their executives and was ultimately chosen for the position.

But it turned out to be a nightmare. They placed me in a very uncomfortable position, electing to keep the outgoing chief of security as my assistant. He was a very talented person, but the arrangement was not conducive to good relations throughout the division. Northrop has been one of the leading defense organizations in the United States for decades and they have had some magnificent accomplishments, but I did not feel right in my assignment, so after seven weeks, I resigned.

After Northrop, I was able to hook up with a number of groups that were traveling to Europe. I acted as their advance agent as well as their security agent. The first group was the Simon Wiesenthal Organization in West Los Angeles. They asked me to accompany them in 1983, 1984, and 1985 to Europe for their Trips of Remembrance. On each trip, we visited different concentration camps, beginning in 1983 with Auschwitz, Poland. We ultimately visited death camps in Russia, Czechoslovakia, and Germany. In 1984, we went to Budapest to pay homage to Raoul Wallenberg, the Swedish diplomat who helped save many Jewish people during the German occupation. One year, we went to Bergen-Belsen to view the camp where Anne Frank had been incarcerated and ultimately put to death. We also visited Wannsee in Berlin, which was where the final solution of the Jewish problem was initiated. Interestingly, the site at the time of our visit was a pre-school for young German children.

I enjoyed my association with the Wiesenthal group. They were a very serious group, but when it came time to unwind, they knew how to do it. I have to thank Ira Lipman, owner of Guardsmark Corporation in Memphis, Tennessee, for my association with this group. He was a very good friend of Stu Knight, former director of the Secret Service, who told Ira about me and my experience in Europe. That experience in Europe did me very well while I was involved with the Wiesenthal group.

With this group, I was able to visit many of the capitals of Europe as well as many other interesting sites. We went to Rome on one of our trips and had an audience with the Pope, which was a very special experience. We visited East Berlin and came through Check Point Charlie on our way back to West Berlin. We visited Warsaw and paid homage to the brave Jewish people who fought the Germans at the Warsaw Ghetto. Of course, the ghetto had been torn down and there is a very large grassy mall now where the ghetto used to be. There is also a very nice memorial near where the entrance to the ghetto was. We had a meeting with President Mitterand of France on one of our trips to Paris, the trip in which Simon Wiesenthal joined our group for several days. On one trip, we ended up in Nice, France, for a few days of rest and relaxation. This was after our Russian trip, which was a very difficult trip. On another trip, we spent some extra time in Paris where I was able to see some of my old friends.

I also accompanied other groups to Europe as a result of my Wiesenthal experience. In 1986 and 1987, I escorted the executives of Nynex Corporation to England, Holland, and Switzerland. They were a very fine group and always treated me very well.

Also in 1986, I accompanied the top people of Pepsi Cola to Moscow and Copenhagen. It was my third trip to Moscow. Depending upon what group you represent, the treatment you receive from Russian Customs varies tremendously. For instance, the Wiesenthal Group had a very difficult time. Much of the kosher food they brought with them was seized and some of the people were even taken out of line for interrogation. One member of our group received word the night before we were to take off for Moscow that he would not be allowed into Russia. His visa was withdrawn and he remained in Berlin while we went on to Moscow. Later, I learned that as a young man he had been to Russia and caused some difficulty fighting for Jewish rights there. Pepsi Cola, however, was a very successful company in Russia and when we arrived in Moscow, there was no problem and very little interest shown to us by Russian Customs. I have always said that the two most difficult cities to go through customs are Moscow and New York City. Los Angeles would be a very close third. It's no fun and I wish I had a dollar for every hour I have spent doing the customs shuffle. Kick your bag up a few feet and wait. Kick it up some more and wait. That's the customs shuffle.

July 1984, I began working for the U.S. State Department in Los Angeles, doing some of their background investigations. I worked for them for nine years in California, Arizona, New Mexico, and Hawaii. I suppose that of all of the groups for which I worked after retirement, I probably did more work for the State Department than any other organization though I did work for a number of other investigative groups. When you become involved in background investigations, there are so many groups that are involved in that activity that your name gets passed around a lot. It got to the point that I was working almost every day, which was far too much for me, considering I was supposed to be retired!

On January 31, 1987, my brother, Ernest, retired from Northrop. We immediately began to play golf every Thursday. We experimented at most of the courses in the area and finally settled on the Victoria Golf Course in Carson as the course of our best liking. Initially we invited Dean Gibbs, Ernie's brother in law to join us. Then we had such good friends as Keith Sharpe, Dewey Parke, Harry Nelson, Vic Riley, Dave Uritz, Ed Plank, and Ed Hyduke to join us. Ernie and I must have played for about eight years and then we both gave it up. Golf is such a frustrating game. If you've gotten along thus far with out it, I recommend that you don't take it up now. Who needs all of that frustration?

In 1987, I took and passed the California examination for private investigator. I started my own business called "Darwin Horn, Private Investigations." I used my PI card quite a lot, but I never pushed my business. I had enough to do without looking for more work. Having the PI card was a distinct advantage though. Sometimes I used it for identification instead of showing my State Department or other identification that I had.

Shirley Ann retired in June 1987 as the principal at Los Alamitos Elementary School. She had been involved in education since 1948 and had been a principal for twenty-one years. She had a great career. We always knew that everything extra we had obtained was a direct result of what she had done.

Several months before she retired, she had started a " before and after" school child care program at her school. When she retired as principal, the district rehired her as the director of that program. The program very quickly went to all of the elementary schools as well as the intermediate school. It was very aptly named Kids Korner. It was a very quick, huge success. Shirley Ann did that for about five years for the Los Alamitos District. Then the Long Beach School District contacted her with a request that she do the same for that district. She ultimately opened up Kids Korners at twelve schools in Long Beach and worked for them for several years. For a while, she was working for both the Los Alamitos and Long Beach Districts at the same time. She did very well financially. Later on Shirley Ann was hired by the Palos Verdes School District to do much the same for that district. She became the great guru of childcare and certainly a real expert in the field.

In September 1987, Pepperdine University celebrated its fiftieth anniversary. To celebrate, the school chose twelve of their most outstanding alumni. I was fortunate to have been chosen along with such great people as Helen Young, Kenneth Hahn, Mike Scott and Dennis Johnson. It was indeed a great honor.

In October 1987, we moved from Number One Martingale in Rancho Palos Verdes, to 38 Chuckwagon Road, in Rolling Hills. Most people when they retire move into a smaller residence. We did the opposite, however, buying a more expensive and larger home on a much larger piece of property. We did it primarily for the grandchildren. The new home has a very fine pool with a barn, corral, and pasture for horses. We have run the gamut with animals from horses, ponies, goat, sheep, pig, chickens, rabbits, and raccoons. It's been pretty interesting, but the grandchildren's interest has waned, and where at one time the horses were ridden a lot, now they do not get ridden very often. Most of the animals have departed in one way or the other and currently all we have left are a horse, a sheep, and a pig.

The people in our area are very nice but all seem to be very busy. We have made some very nice friends but none with whom we socialize. We have met David and Margo Canas. David has done some work for us and is a very accomplished worker. David and Margo are from El Salvador and both work for our next-door neighbors. These two people are very hard working people who are trying to get into the American way of life. They have a daughter Adriana, who is now five years old. With their great work ethic, David and Margo are going to do well in America.

My father passed away on January 1, 1986, after a very difficult year. He had broken his hip in December 1984, thus 1985 was a very difficult year for him and our family. My mother, passed away on February 5, 1988. She hadn't been excessively ill, so we didn't realize she was having problems. She refused to go to a doctor for years, but finally made an appointment on February 5. She passed away, however, before my brother could get her to the doctor's office that day. It seems like more and more of our family and friends have begun to pass away. It's a very sad but inevitable process. Sometimes it seems impossible that friends and relatives are not here any more.

Shirley Ann and I have maintained our interest in Pepperdine University throughout the years. We have also kept up our interest in that very fine football team on which I played from 1946 to 1948. Almost every year, that team gets together for some type of event. In 1990, we all went back to Atlantic, Iowa, where Coach Warren Gaer and his wife, Martha, had retired. We had a great time and many people could not believe that an entire team would go that far to honor their college coach. Well, we did and that's what makes that football team a very special group of people.

Some of the very dedicated people at Pepperdine with whom we have worked throughout the years have been: Dave Gorrie, Chris Sangster, Nancy Strouse, John Katch, Ed Hyduke, Harry Nelson, Claudia Arnold, Tim Wilhelm, Wayne Wright, Mike Welch, Dewey Parke, Dr. Oly Tegner, and a host of others. It's always nice to be able to work with dedicated people and Pepperdine University is loaded with those types of people.

I believe that this is the time and the place to mention some of my forebears, as much as I know. Several individuals in our family have done some genealogy work. Our son, Dar did quite a lot of work on my mother's family when he was living in St. Louis. I don't know how much he did on my father's side, but my brother's daughter, Marilyn Horn Fahey, has been involved recently. I'm not sure how far she has gotten.

Very basically here is what I know of my family: My paternal grandmother was Wilhelmina Neu Krauss Horn, born September 13, 1862 or 1863 in Neustadt, Germany. She passed away in St.

Louis in 1911. When she came to America as a young lady, she lived in New Haven, Connecticut. She apparently married Anton Krauss in New Haven. Mr. Krauss passed away after giving her two sons, Lou and Fred, and a daughter, May. After sometime, Grandmother married Charles Edward Horn. He was born on September 15, 1847 or 1848, in Cologne, Germany. As a result of that union, they had children Stephen, Ernest, Herman, Victor, and Margaret. Margaret died at a very early age.

The Horns moved to St. Louis sometime prior to 1895, which was the year that Stephen was born. Ernest was born in 1897, Herman in 1900, and Victor in 1903. I'm not sure when Margaret was born but probably about 1906. Grandfather Horn passed away on April 15, 1920. Uncle Steve, who was a police officer in St. Louis, passed away in 1930 as a result of a traffic accident. Dad passed away January 1, 1986. Uncle Herman passed away in 1955, and Uncle Victor passed away about six years ago.

When I was in Paris, I asked the German Interpol representative if he would check records at the city of Neustadt, close to Frieberg and the Swiss border. We have always thought that that was the Neustadt where grandmother was born because she told someone that they lived near the mountains, which was interpreted as the Black Forest area. The Interpol agent, however, could find no record of her in that area.

Unfortunately, there are about six Neustadts in Germany and we aren't certain which one is the proper one. Some time before Uncle Victor passed away, he told me that he thought his mother was born in the Neustadt that was about forty miles south of Frankfurt, Germany. He also said that our grandfather had worked on the Great Cathedral in Cologne before he joined the German Merchant Marines. I understand that after a trip to Brazil, Grandfather sailed to New Haven and jumped ship there and stayed.

My maternal grandmother was Luella De Roy Wright. She was born in Kentucky around 1863, probably on a boat on the Mississippi River. Her husband was killed, supposedly in a race riot either in Memphis or Nantchez sometime around 1907. He had been living on a houseboat on the Mississippi with my Uncle Peter Wright. Peter was sent home alone when the trouble was brewing, and that's the last any member of the family saw our grandfather. Grandmother received a trunk that had belonged to Grandfather, but she never received any information about his death.

Dar, was able to acquire some additional information on the De Roy family. They were longtime residents of St. Louis and St. Charles, Missouri, even prior to 1800. There have been some thoughts that a member of the De Roy family had accompanied the Lewis and Clark Expedition all the way to the Pacific Ocean in 1804. In any event, there are quite a few grave sites in St. Charles bearing the name of De Roy.

Perhaps sometime I will become involved in genealogy. What I'm afraid of is that once I become involved, it's all I will do and I just can't afford to spend a lot of time in that sector at this time.

I suppose that all books must come to an end. I began this book thinking that I would write only for the benefit of my immediate family and particularly for the children, grandchildren, and others who will follow in our family. It has been a most enjoyable task just as my great friend Dan Bowling professed it would be. For a fact, Dan was right and I am glad that he continued to inveigle me to sit down and start writing. This book would not have been without that insistence.

Thanks, Dan. I owe you.

Index